Covering the Plague: AIDS and the American Media

Covering the Plague: AIDS and the American Media

James Kinsella

Rutgers University Press
New Brunswick and London

To Robert and Dolores Kinsella
and Richard Hess

"The voice of the intelligence is soft and weak. It is drowned out by
the roar of fear. It is ignored by the voice of desire. It is
contradicted by the voice of shame. It is hissed away by hate, and
extinguished by anger. Most of all, it is silenced by anger."

C. G. Jung, 1955

Library of Congress Cataloging-in-Publication Data

Kinsella, James, 1959–
    Covering the plague: AIDS and the American media /
by James Kinsella.
        p.   cm.
    Includes index.
    ISBN 0-8135-1481-9
    1. AIDS (Disease)—Social aspects—United States.   2. Mass media—
United States.   I. Title.
RA644.A25K56   1989
362.1'9697'9200973—dc20   89-35221
                                                                CIP

British Cataloging-in-Publication information available

Contents

Acknowledgments

Any list I compile of people who deserve some credit for this book will necessarily be incomplete, because hundreds of thousands have contributed by being a part of the story of the AIDS epidemic. I am indebted to those with AIDS, their friends, lovers, and families. I hope I do their lives some small justice.

Among those I can name, none is more important than Robin Nagle, who worked as my research assistant during my ten-month sabbatical at Columbia University's Gannett Center, and as a contributor and reader afterward. (She is the author of Chapter 11.) Her insight, sense of humor, and, most of all, dedication to this project saw me through the worst and the best of the work.

Richard Hess offered a keen editing eye and loving support, even from six thousand miles away. Mike Werb not only corrected flaws in my prose, but also taught me a good deal about narrative style in the process. My colleague and compatriot David Kirp, as always, challenged and provoked me. Our conversations in the early years of the epidemic spurred me to write this book.

My brother, Dr. John Kinsella, was essential in my effort to understand better the medical and research worlds. Any of this book's errors in those territories are most likely due to my not listening to his good sense.

My fellow fellows at the Gannett Center deserve acknowledgment as well, especially Paul Perry, Jane Brown, and Victoria Fung. Everett Dennis, director of the Center, has my sincere gratitude for believing in this project and encouraging it all along the way. I also am indebted to John McCabe, the chief operating executive of the *Los Angeles Herald Examiner,* who granted me the sabbatical, and to Sheena Paterson-Berwick, a friend and media wiseperson who recognized the importance of this chore from the very beginning.

Of course, this book would have not gotten done if it weren't for the incredible access my fellow journalists gave me. I am particularly thankful for the lengthy interviews provided by the *New York Native*'s Chuck Ortleb; Dr. Lawrence Mass; the *New York Times*'s Dr. Lawrence Altman; Vincent Coppola, formerly of *Newsweek;* Randy Shilts of the

viii   *San Francisco Chronicle;* Jim Bunn, formerly of KPIX-TV; *Newsday*'s
Laurie Garrett, formerly of National Public Radio; and playwright
Larry Kramer. To the hundreds of other jouranlists who spent time
with me, you were not taken for granted.

    Finally, I must not forget my staff at the *Herald Examiner.* Their
hard work and dependability in getting out our daily section during
the final six months of this project, as well as their incessant opinion-
making on everything but especially on media agenda-setting, was of
extraordinary assistance. Thank you, Cheryl Heuton, Joel Bellman,
Kathy Buttrey, Gary Spiecker, William Bramhall, and Timothy Lange.

Covering the Plague: AIDS and the American Media

Introduction
When does death become news?

For the past decade, the AIDS story has challenged the ground rules of American journalism. It has forced reporters to acknowledge that their treatment of the news, far from being objective, is often shaped by their personal prejudices and their assumptions about their audience. Such biases are often elusive, but in AIDS reporting, they have taken on exceptional importance, and they cut both ways. AIDS was discussed most promptly, vigorously, and forthrightly where journalists had direct personal experience with people suffering from the disease: Vince Coppola at *Newsweek,* for example, whose brother was gay and had AIDS, or Chuck Ortleb, the publisher of the gay-oriented newspaper, *New York Native,* whose friends were dying by the scores. Conversely, almost no one who worked for the networks' nightly news broadcasts admitted to knowing a single person with the disease—and the television coverage reflected that lack of individual knowledge and concern. No modern news story has been shaped more by such personal connections, and disconnections, than this epidemic.

AIDS has by now become a staple item of the news and a part of American consciousness, and much of the credit lies with the journalists who dared to use their own experience and outrage as the lead into a major story. At the same time, at least some of the blame for the ravages of AIDS in America must lie with members of the media who refused to believe that the deaths of gay men and drug addicts were worth reporting.

Where It All Began

In 1979 a physician began recognizing a pattern of disease in New York City. Young, otherwise healthy gay men were dying of rare infections that usually struck only the elderly and the severely infirm. It would take another six years and twelve thousand deaths before

2 most of America's mainstream media—general-audience newspapers, magazines, network and local television—started aggressively covering the epidemic. Why did it take so long?

Why did, for instance, the cyanide-laced Tylenol tragedy, which claimed seven lives in 1982, and the outbreak of Legionnaire's disease in 1976, which initially affected twenty-nine, get front-page, top-of-the-news coverage across the country?

Science and medicine have been the stepchildren of news organizations, often covered by poorly trained, poorly educated reporters. In large part because of that lack of expertise, outbreaks of disease are treated haphazardly by the media. Some journalists coming to their own defense have claimed that AIDS was covered like any other disease. Initial stories identified the outbreak, and subsequent reports detailed the scientific breakthroughs. If only journalists were so predictable. In fact, the rise and fall of media interest in AIDS had little to do with the degree of crisis or with scientific advances.

Contaminated Tylenol seemed to be a threat to every American—that is, every reader or viewer. Legionnaire's disease struck white, middle-aged and elderly men, whom many newsmakers focus on when producing the news. On the other hand, in the beginning AIDS affected social outcasts: gays. Editors who gave reasons for not covering the AIDS story most often stated that news about homosexuals would not interest the great majority of "family newspaper" readers. The later discovery that the disease was found among junkies, yet another group of social undesirables, was hardly likely to boost media appeal.

Even when a concerned and science-savvy reporter tried to cover AIDS, the technical side of the story raised special obstacles. By the rules of etiquette of scientific research, many medical journals refuse to publish results that have already been announced to the press. As a result, AIDS researchers often declined to talk to the media about their latest findings for fear that professional journals would blackball their work. For reporters and their editors, that lack of fresh, accurate information from the experts on the epidemic meant they had no story to report—and so the public remained in the dark.

The Joke around the White House

The government also has to take some blame for the press's failings. The United States has the most sophisticated scientific and medical establishment in the world, much of it paid for by taxpayer dollars. Yet the politics of the conservative Reagan era served to undercut the poorly funded programs that were pursuing answers to the epidemic. Government action and spending help set the news agenda. Until 1983, AIDS was not an item on that list. *(for spending help)*

3

Even as late as 1986, the epidemic was not given much serious attention by the Reagan administration. Nothing sums up that attitude better than a joke reportedly told at a meeting of the president and some of his key advisers in 1986. The White House was considering further action against Moamar Gadhafi's Libya, which the United States had bombed that spring in retaliation for terrorist attacks against American servicemen abroad. The Libyan leader was rumored to be a transvestite, so at the meeting Reagan asked, "Why not invite Gadhafi to San Francisco; he likes to dress up so much." To which Secretary of State George Shultz allegedly replied, "Why don't we give him AIDS?" In the private confines of the Reagan administration, the disease was a laughing matter. In public, the president had uttered the word "AIDS" only once. *← through 1986.*

Without the government taking AIDS seriously, and without individual journalists being seized by the seriousness of the epidemic, the disease became a kind of curio. That is how the Associated Press covered the crisis. The wire service is often the first major news source to a story and one of the most important guidelines for journalists throughout the country to determine how significantly a piece of news should be played. AP's consistent but perfunctory coverage helped set the tone for much of the media.

The *New York Times,* an even more powerful agenda-setter for major national news, took the same tack, but for very different reasons, many of which can be traced to the newspaper's executive office.

major papers refused to discuss AIDS

If the *New York Times* did not think the story was worth highlighting, then the network broadcasters, who often take their cues from the *Times,* were not about to focus on AIDS. When they did, their reports were studded with errors of omission and wrongheaded emphasis. Many of those blunders were due to the networks' prudery. To explain AIDS transmission, words like "semen" and "penis" and "vagina" were absolutely essential. Unfortunately, in the first years of the epidemic they were strictly avoided.

Ironically, during the 1980s the network censor's role in broadcast television diminished, as a result of budget cuts at the networks and competition from cable TV, which offered far more risqué programming. In 1988, this weakening of "Standards and Practices," as the

4 watchdog is called, was parodied on NBC's "Saturday Night Live." Six naked men, their groins hidden by a bamboo shield, chatted about the fact that they were now free to say "penis" on the air (like naughty schoolboys, they repeated the word no fewer than fifty times). The skit ran only weeks before the networks reaffirmed their refusal to run ads for condoms, a basic prevention against AIDS transmission.

Not everyone shied away from the AIDS story in the early years, but almost all of those who covered the plague from the beginning had one thing in common: they were touched by it in some personal way. Surgeon General C. Everett Koop and the Public Health Service understood the importance of that personal connection, and they tried to play off it. To increase interest in the disease, they encouraged the notion that AIDS was a threat to every American, including the white, heterosexual, middle-class couple featured in the PHS national ads. However, that group was and remains at the very lowest risk for transmission.

Every surge of AIDS coverage at almost every newspaper, magazine, or TV and radio station came when the disease seemed to move closer to individual newsmakers or to the people journalists perceive as their audience. The three peaks of AIDS reportage, in fact, correlate to events that suggest such a movement, or a way to contain it. In 1983, fear of widespread and rampant infection was triggered by rumors that AIDS could be spread by simple household contact. In 1985, actor Rock Hudson's death spurred a wave of interest because it appeared as though the disease was affecting even all-American types. And in early 1987, the discussion around containing the threat with widespread testing for the AIDS virus caused another explosion in news coverage. These highly personal concerns gave rise to intimate involvement in reporting on the epidemic.

Telling the Story behind the Story

This book is about AIDS, certainly. But even more important, it is about how news gets made in America.

□ Why were the nation's top doctors so inept at sending out the word about this epidemic?

□ Why weren't the initial stories put out by the Associated Press, a major source of breaking news for the mainstream media, picked up by newspaper and TV journalists?

□ How did an iconoclastic gay publisher come to have such influence that the director of the Centers for Disease Control would fly cross-country to visit with him and offer the publisher one of the most important scoops of the epidemic?

5

□ Why did the editor of America's paper of record, the *New York Times,* virtually shut news about AIDS or gays out of the paper for the first years of the crisis?

□ How did a reporter for the *San Francisco Chronicle,* who was actively involved in the gay community, use the news to encourage City Hall to close down the bathhouses?

□ What are the pressures in small-town journalism that forced a weekly newspaper editor to hide behind the shield of objectivity to avoid offending the locals who wanted to keep AIDS children out of school?

□ How did the revered science journals use their clout to control the news, and sometimes even distort it?

The answers are disturbing. So is the analysis of how the TV networks covered, and failed to cover, the AIDS crisis, and how local broadcasters, who are gaining more influence, are trying to emulate those foolish patterns.

This work offers the most comprehensive look at media coverage of AIDS to date. Thousands of newspaper and magazine articles, hundreds of hours of local and network news programming were reviewed to understand how the American media handled the story. The score of media outlets this book focuses on were selected for two reasons: either they serve as agenda-setters in the United States (the *New York Times,* Associated Press, the networks, science journals, and, to a lesser extent, *Newsweek*), or they help describe the diversity of the nation's journalism (*New York Native, Kokomo Tribune, DeSoto County Times,* KPIX-TV). That research was followed up with interviews with hundreds of reporters, editors, writers, correspondents, and those people they covered, including doctors, scientists, public officials, and people with AIDS.

The chapters are arranged chronologically, focusing in turn on particular institutions as they came to play a major role in the development of the AIDS story. The twelve profiles necessarily overlap. As a whole, they describe the diversity that is American journalism.

This book is largely critical of American journalism's handling of the AIDS crisis. And it is pessimistic about the prospects of the nation facing up to the next wave of AIDS, striking heterosexual minorities, as well as the next major health crisis, which is already brewing in

6 large American cities. There are some bright lights, however. The dramatic change in how the *New York Times* covers AIDS has encouraged media throughout the United States to rethink health and science coverage. Laurie Garrett's extraordinary reporting on AIDS in America's own Third World serves as a model of how a journalist can be touched by a story, yet maintain enough distance to be able to tell it. The performance of KPIX-TV in San Francisco, led by former general manager Art Kern and reporter Jim Bunn, offers some real hope for the increasingly powerful and persistently inept local TV stations. The book ends on a positive, prescriptive note.

Why This Tale Was Told

The story of the AIDS epidemic includes gays and sex and drugs and death and hysteria. But mostly it is about change in America, about how the nation's conventional wisdom in all these areas, and many more, has been set on its head. Understanding the experience journalists went through in coming to grips with that change, and with AIDS, is to understand how a nation faced up to a modern-day horror. Making sense of where we have been is crucial to our meeting the present challenge: controlling AIDS and even deadlier, more subtle, threats to people and communities that have no voice in the mainstream.

Chapter 1
Whispers in the whirlwind

"Sex in the Age of AIDS," *Newsweek*'s March 14, 1988 cover shouted. As if the headline alone was not seductive enough, it was laid atop rumpled bed sheets. The virus had invaded "the broader population and is continuing, even now, to make its silent inroads of infection," the article contended. What is more, "infection with the AIDS virus does *not* require intimate sexual contact or sharing of intravenous needles: transmission can, and does, occur as a result of person-to-person contact in which blood or other body fluids from a person who is harboring the virus are splashed onto or rubbed against someone else." That meant AIDS could be spread by something as innocent as a kiss. Writing elsewhere in the article, the authors asserted it could even be passed on a toilet seat.

All this flew in the face of what was understood about the disease by experts at the Centers for Disease Control (CDC), considered command central in the effort to track the epidemic. Nearly every respected epidemiologist who was studying the disease said that AIDS was not spread by such contact. The fragile virus, in fact, was difficult to get. There were no reported cases of health-care workers becoming infected through routine contact with patients. No one had gotten the disease through saliva. Even after repeated sexual contact with carriers, many people remained uninfected. So what did *Newsweek* base its story on?

The source was a soon-to-be-released book, *Crisis: Heterosexual Behavior in the Age of AIDS,* by the well-known sexologists Dr. William H. Masters and his collaborator-wife Virginia E. Johnson along with Dr. Robert C. Kolodny. They purported to have done their own study of the epidemic, using eight hundred sexually active adults, all of whom claimed to be heterosexual and most of whom could be described as promiscuous. To get a representative sampling of Americans, they chose their subjects from two cities with large AIDS case loads—Los Angeles and New York—and two cities with small numbers of AIDS cases—St. Louis and Atlanta. Generally well regarded as sex therapists, the Masters and Johnson team seemed less adept at mathemat-

8 ics. After testing all participants, they concluded that 7 percent of the women and 5 percent of the men were infected. These were remarkably high rates, similar to those in some besieged areas of Central East Africa. The authors were claiming their figures proved the AIDS virus was far more widespread than ever suspected. But the CDC estimated less than 1 percent of the American population had been infected. Did Masters and Johnson really do a random study? Or were the participants more likely to have come in contact with the virus, and thus more likely to want to be tested for it? And were those in the study all exclusively heterosexual? Or did some of the men also have sexual relations with other men, but were unwilling to reveal this fact to the researchers?

The government did not respond to the *Newsweek* cover story by challenging Masters, Johnson, and Kolodny. "We can't spend all our time responding to garbage in the media," explained one highly placed CDC official. He had his reasons. By this point in the epidemic, AIDS coverage was cropping up in almost every medium: from national magazines to small-town newspapers, from the networks to the local stations. A few months earlier, *Cosmopolitan* magazine wrongly claimed, "There is almost no danger of contracting AIDS through ordinary sexual intercourse." Only days before, a Miami TV station ran an outrageous series proposing that the disease just might be syphilis erroneously diagnosed.

But didn't the CDC have some responsibility to the public to respond to media misrepresentations, like the *Newsweek* cover story, that could conceivably spur a rash of other news reports based on the same misleading information? By the spring of 1988—seven years into the AIDS epidemic—the government still had not decided what its role should be. The official confusion had undermined efforts to deal with AIDS since the first days of the crisis.

The Long Wait

In June of 1981, the CDC's Dr. James Curran wondered when the phone calls would come. A week had gone by since the Centers for Disease Control published a highly unusual article, but Curran had yet to hear from more than a couple of curious journalists. In the piece, two doctors from Los Angeles reported a bizarre outbreak of pneumonia in five otherwise healthy men. Two had already died. The only characteristic the men shared, the June 5 *Morbidity and Mortality Weekly Report* (*MMWR*) said, was that they were gay: "The fact that these patients were all homosexuals suggests an association between some aspect of a homosexual lifestyle or disease acquired through sexual contact and *Pneumocystis* pneumonia."

Every Friday, the CDC sends out forty thousand copies of the *MMWR* to doctors and local public health officials. In addition, 835 copies of the pamphlet-sized journal go to reporters. Usually about twenty pages long, the black-and-white document is unmistakably "government issued": except for an occasional map of the United States dotted with "measles cases reported," the brief descriptions of the latest diseases are broken only by the all-important lists. These rows and rows of tabulations of how many Americans have come down with which diseases, and how many have died, are the medical profession's version of the Top 40: the most active "morbidity," the most widespread "mortality." Those statistics are the first thing journalists glance at when they get their copies.

The *MMWR* is an important tool for doctors and others on the frontline fighting new epidemics, because it helps get out the word. That is the first step in figuring out how a new disease is spreading and how to stop it. The report on *Pneumocystis carinii* pneumonia was expected to generate some interest among science and medicine reporters at many major papers. After all, the disease usually appeared only in elderly patients or people with severely taxed immune systems. The five Southern Californians infected were apparently otherwise healthy men between the ages of twenty-nine and thirty-six. And it was obviously deadly.

The Associated Press wire service ran a small story right after the report was released, as did the *Los Angeles Times* and the *San Francisco Chronicle*. Otherwise, the media were uninterested. As head of the CDC's venereal disease prevention services, Curran was used to being ignored by journalists. He had spoken at countless conferences to generate interest in the fact that diseases like syphilis and gonorrhea were skyrocketing. Rarely did he get anyone's attention. For decades, Americans had assumed that because these conditions could be cured, usually with just one shot of penicillin, they were under control. But there was no cure for this fatal new outbreak. Earlier that spring,

10   Curran had been named to direct a task force that was investigating the new malady. Getting the word out, it seemed, was going to be even tougher with a disease that seemed to be affecting only gay men.

Curran, then in his thirties, was a traditional family man, with a wife and two children and a house in a comfortable Atlanta suburb. His training and work in the CDC's Epidemiological Intelligence Service had brought him into close contact with gays, who had been prime targets of sexually transmitted diseases since the early 1970s. There were others at the CDC with similar experiences. During a fellowship in Chicago a year earlier, chief epidemiologist Dr. Harold Jaffe had spent time diagnosing sexually transmitted diseases in gay men at a local clinic. And Dr. Donald Francis, head of the CDC's laboratory effort during the early years of the AIDS epidemic, had worked closely with Phoenix gays in the campaign to develop a hepatitis B vaccine. All three men knew how fast diseases could rage through the gay community. If this new malady could be transmitted sexually, or somehow in gay venues like bars or bathhouses, it had the potential to devastate.

A month after the first *Pneumocystis* article appeared in the *MMWR,* CDC Director Dr. William Foege approved the publication of another submission on the pneumonia and on another, related illness: Kaposi's sarcoma. This rare form of cancer had struck twenty-six gay men, most of them living in New York City, Los Angeles, or San Francisco. Fifteen cases of *Pneumocystis* also had been diagnosed. Some of the men were infected with both diseases.

"Kaposi's Sarcoma and *Pneumocystis* Pneumonia among Homosexual Men—New York City and California" was the title of the July 3 report. "It is not clear if or how the clustering of Kaposi's sarcoma, *Pneumocystis* and other serious diseases in homosexual men is related," said the study. "What is known is that the patients with *Pneumocystis* pneumonia . . . showed evidence of impaired cellular immunity." Kaposi's, *Pneumocystis,* even cytomegalovirus, a childhood disease usually harmless to adults, were showing up with alarming frequency, and they all seemed to be taking advantage of an immune system somehow made ineffective.

This time the *MMWR* drew a little more interest. The Associated Press was on top of the story immediately. And so were two broadcast outlets, National Public Radio and the Cable News Network. The *New York Times* ran a column-length story buried in the back of the paper's national section.

At the CDC, Curran believed that these outbreaks looked like the start of a major crisis, and the *MMWR* reflected that concern. That 11 two lengthy articles on the same malady appeared in the *MMWR* in less than a month was a rarity and warranted attention. But beyond that, neither the CDC nor its parent agency, the Public Health Service, nor even the Department of Health and Human Services did much to try to interest the media or to educate Americans directly. The government did not work like that.

The Surgeon General's Army

At the core of the CDC are doctors and scientists, but there is a military aspect to the enterprise. The Public Health Service (PHS), which includes staff at both the CDC and the National Institutes of Health (NIH), is designed not unlike the Navy, the Army, the Marines. Many of the doctors and investigators are commissioned; they hold rank. And, though they report to the secretary of health and human services, their commander is the surgeon general. There is even a uniform that goes with the service, complete with epaulets.

Few in the PHS are fond of the military metaphor for their branch. Most of those at the CDC would feel more comfortable being associated with the Peace Corps, where a good many of them have spent time, than with the Marine Corps. Many of those who signed on at the agency during the sixties and seventies did so to avoid the Vietnam war. Because of such prevailing attitudes, by 1981 the uniform had vanished from the CDC. (By 1988, however, Surgeon General C. Everett Koop, in an effort to generate more esprit de corps, made it mandatory to wear a uniform on Wednesdays.) True to its military-like mission, the institution has an in-the-trenches feel about it, more so than the headquarters of the real military in Washington, D.C. Even the CDC's location, outside Atlanta, makes it seem less a part of the official government complex. The labs and spartan offices are housed in dull brick buildings that together look more like an overgrown high school campus than the Pentagon of disease prevention. Some facilities are little more than old Army barracks. One of the best ways to describe the CDC is to compare it with its older cousin in the U.S. Public Health Service: the National Institutes of Health.

The CDC was established in 1942 as an afterthought. First called

12 the Malaria Control in War Areas, it was given the mandate to find ways to protect American soldiers from that troublesome tropical disease. The NIH had begun in an equally inauspicious way. When it was founded in 1887, it was housed in a one-room Laboratory of Hygiene. But by the time the CDC was created, the NIH had grown into one of the most important biomedical research centers in the world.

The National Institutes of Health, located just outside Washington in Bethesda, Maryland, on more than three hundred acres of green hills, could easily be mistaken for the campus of a prestigious and well-endowed university. Colonial-style buildings and sleek new high rises are ringed with trees. Doctors dressed in casual slacks and sweaters roam the "quads." Inside the buildings, men and women are engaged in serious lab research. (Interestingly, when Surgeon General Koop introduced the mandatory uniform day, those in the Public Health Service Corps at NIH were exempted after the Institutes' director complained, according to sources close to the surgeon general.)

The CDC Approach

The field of epidemiology, the basis of the CDC's work, can be traced to London of the 1830s. There Dr. John Snow pursued an epidemic of cholera to one source: a city water pump. The outbreak was ended when the pump's handle was removed, thus shutting off that contaminated water supply. Spotting outbreaks of infectious disease, uncovering their sources, and controlling them has been the CDC's approach since its inception, and the key to its successes in battling a wide range of once deadly scourges. That is how the agency dealt with the mysterious disease that was killing middle-aged men who had gathered in July 1976 for an American Legion Convention in a Philadelphia hotel.

Within days, the CDC was combing the hotel grounds, studying microscopic samples from the rooms, restaurant, convention halls. Just as quickly came the reporters, tipped off by local public health reports. They swarmed the Atlanta facility in search of elusive details, data, anecdotes, anything to build a story on. For journalists not covering the presidential campaign, or who hadn't been assigned the Bicentennial beat that year, word of a disease running rampant through a hotel in Philadelphia—which was hosting millions of tourists from throughout the world—was major news. For six weeks reporters fought over the eight phone lines of the center's office of public affairs. According to Don Berreth, the CDC's chief information officer and the conduit between the media and the medical staff, that was the busiest period in his thirteen-year history with the agency. It was the only time Berreth has ever called a press conference, a media device he avoids using because he believes it too often ends up "like a circus." He made the exception in the case of Legionnaire's disease because the crush of journalists at the CDC was so demanding.

By New Year's of 1977, the microbe culprit that had infected 221 people and left 34 dead was found. Despite the "circus" atmosphere, the media's intense interest had spurred researchers on and encouraged government officials to redouble their early efforts against the scourge. It was a researcher working late into the night during the Christmas holiday who had discovered the cause of the deadly outbreak.

In the same year the CDC was wrestling with the Legionnaire's outbreak, another disease erupted and threatened—or so some of the agency's experts believed—to grow into an epidemic. It started at Fort Dix, New Jersey. A young private in basic training had been complaining of high fevers and nausea for days. It sounded like a classic winter flu, his sergeant thought, nothing that should keep a good soldier down. So when the rest of the troops set out on a grueling march through the cold night, the ailing recruit joined them. He never finished the trek.

Private David Lewis died on February 4, 1976, a victim of swine flu, a strain of virus usually found only in pigs. He wasn't the sole Fort Dix recruit to come down with the illness. Many of the several thousand men who crowded into the barracks that winter had been griping about coughs and aches. Some even had been hospitalized, and four were found to be infected with the swine flu virus. A rampant illness most epidemiologists thought had all but disappeared from the U.S. population drew crowds of journalists again. For years, public health officials had been fearing a flu epidemic like the influenza outbreak of 1918–19, which had claimed the lives of more than a million Americans. Swine flu could be that virus, thought David Sencer, CDC's director at the time.

Pressure from the media, and from an embattled Gerald Ford struggling to hold on to the presidency, pushed the issue into Congress. An unprecedented bill was quickly passed to encourage drug

14 companies to develop a vaccine by relieving them of liability. By the fall, less than nine months after the Fort Dix recruit died, Washington kicked off a national inoculation program.

Swine flu got national media attention, but the CDC, as usual, made no special effort to deal with the press. Most journalists accepted Sencer's claims that this huge expenditure made sense. Those few reporters who were more critical could get little information out of the CDC. Don Berreth admits that during an emergency the agency tends "to pull in the horns" and to avoid comment. In the end, the vaccination program rushed through the government approval process turned out to be more deadly than the epidemic itself. Instead of guaranteeing President Ford's election, it further weakened his administration.

Unfortunately, the CDC did not learn much about how to deal with the press from either the Legionnaire's episode or the experience with swine flu. In the AIDS epidemic of the 1980s, the agency held no press conferences, neither to put out information nor to attract attention to the crisis. It took no coordinated approach to educating Americans about the epidemic or ways to avoid infection. On other vital issues like inadequate funding, the agency once again pulled in its horns.

Discovering an Epidemic

Most important, the press was not as interested in "gay cancer," so called by the *New York Native,* the popular gay-oriented weekly newspaper, as it had been in Legionnaire's disease or swine flu. Unlike both those diseases, which first erupted in single, contained places—a Philadelphia hotel, New Jersey Army barracks—Kaposi's and *Pneumocystis* were occurring in small numbers from New York to San Francisco and Los Angeles. Even if there had been a journalist hot on the story, finding its center would have been tricky.

The CDC was the storm trooper for epidemics. It identified the enemy, isolated and then conquered it. The agency's artillery included vaccinations and cures. But against this new problem, Curran had no vaccine and certainly no cure. He wasn't even sure what "it" was. His only hope was to gather as much information about the problem as possible and send out warnings. The media weren't cooperating in either effort. He could wait for journalists to react to the CDC's official missives. But the media didn't work like that. Journalists weren't efficient scientists, or even bureaucrats, who identified a problem and then focused on how to solve it. There are pitifully few guideposts that indicate precisely what deserves to be covered, and what doesn't. News gets covered by a reporter for a thousand and one reasons, many of them personal. And in 1981, almost no one at the major media outlets was admitting a personal connection to a disease affecting gay men.

The CDC was completely unprepared to counter such indifference. "We weren't supposed to go to them [the media]," said Dr. Don Francis. "They were supposed to come to us." The *MMWR*'s lack of influence had something to do with reporters' lack of interest in AIDS. It is prepared like a newsletter. Doctors throughout the nation contribute, but most of the information comes from public health officials affiliated with the CDC. The process of getting published in the *MMWR* is less formal than that for almost any other major medical or scientific journal. The submissions are rushed through in order to get breaking information out to people who need it. The director of the CDC signs off on each week's issue before it is sent out, but it does not have the imprimatur of the medical establishment as do the *New England Journal of Medicine* and the *Journal of the American Medical Association*.

Dr. Michael Gottlieb, one of the authors of the original *MMWR* article on *Pneumocystis*, attempted at first to get the piece published in the *New England Journal*. But because of the publication's lengthy review process, it can take as long as two years before the most worthy manuscript fights its way into print. Many doctors and scientists believe the prestige that goes with publishing in the journal is worth the frustration. Since the 1970s, when the Associated Press began covering the weekly on a regular basis, the *Journal* has become one of the most important "tip" services for medical reporters. So, by late fall of 1981, if the *New England Journal* had nothing to say on a particular medical subject, reporters were apt to ignore it as well. Although the *MMWR* had run several articles on what the CDC was calling an "epidemic of immunosuppression," it was the *New England Journal of Medicine*'s December 10, 1981, issue on the subject that prompted Dr. Curran's first invitation to appear on a national network to discuss the diseases. The "Good Morning America" spot lasted all of forty-five seconds.

At about the same time, a group of New Yorkers asked the CDC to send someone to talk to them about the new outbreaks. Curran found himself in the makeshift headquarters of the Gay Men's Health Crisis, an organization begun by gay volunteers to put out information on the diseases. Curran faced the scores of frightened men who were crowded into the small Greenwich Village apartment and detailed what he knew about the maladies: something gay men were doing, maybe too many sexual partners, perhaps too many drugs, was spreading the illnesses.

By late 1981, the number of cases of Kaposi's and/or *Pneumocystis* had doubled, to about eighty. Of those reported having these illnesses since the CDC began keeping count, 40 percent had died. The more Curran understood about the diseases, about how they were transmitted like hepatitis, and how they were killing like a brushfire of cancer, the more convinced he became that stopping them meant stopping any possibly dangerous behavior. But changing behavior, whether it be sexual practices or drug use, was an extraordinarily tough task, one that the CDC approached awkwardly or avoided altogether. The CDC's artillery against health crises generally did not include education and counseling.

Scrambling for Dollars

Not everyone in the U.S. Public Health Service was as open as Curran to pursuing what was being collectively labeled "Gay-Related Infectious Disease," or "GRID." The Reagan administration had been elected less than a year earlier on a platform that called for a return to the values of the fifties and for significant reductions in government spending. Any politic scientist understood that with such a presidential mandate, federal funds for research on this latest eruption of disease would be hard to come by. Within the NIH, some small voices shouted about the importance of doing work on the developing epidemic. But they were not having much of an effect. Basic laboratory research, the main job of the NIH, was not being implemented quickly for Kaposi's and *Pneumocystis*. Despite repeated attempts by the CDC staff to bring a small part of the NIH's vast resources to bear on this new outbreak, the Institutes remained aloof.

Even at the CDC, where there was strong interest in finding the cause of the diseases, everyone seemed to know better than to ask for more money. "They knew they wouldn't get it," according to John

Bennett, who was deputy director of the CDC's Center for Infectious Disease. The epidemiologists and other scientists struggling to make sense of the data pouring in often grumbled to each other about how resources were being stretched too thin.

Prompted by continuous complaints from inside the CDC, Assistant Secretary of Health Dr. Edward Brandt sent a confidential memo in early 1982 asking that some institutes of the NIH think about devoting part of their research funds to Kaposi's sarcoma and the other opportunistic infections. Although the NIH ignored Brandt's request for the most part, shortly afterward he told Congress no additional funds were needed. CDC staffers, for whom Brandt was responsible, followed his lead. From press officer Don Berreth to CDC Director Dr. William Foege, the word was that the agency had plenty of funds to do its job. Even Curran, probably the one person most aware of the problems caused by the shortages, said nothing. The career government physician, a good soldier in the PHS corps, seemed willing to play this one safe. "The government's official policy became not to talk to the press at all on the issue," said Dr. Donald Francis.

Francis, thirty-eight, was a good deal less subtle than his colleague Curran. He had built an international reputation as an epidemiologist and was on the team of scientists that helped eradicate smallpox. He often had a weary look, as though he were constantly in mid-battle against some enemy disease. But Francis was extremely sharp and quick-witted. Now he was losing his patience. He was overseeing the laboratory effort from poorly equipped offices in the basement of a CDC building. He and his staff were clocking working days of twelve hours and more in 1982, yet they were being slowed down by a lack of necessities: money couldn't be scraped together to put doors on makeshift offices or provide sufficient lab supplies. "I was just trying to keep alive in the government buying and spending system," said Francis. He decided to tell the truth, that progress on finding clues to this epidemic was being thwarted by a lack of resources. He began his own public information campaign, phoning up a handful of reporters at major media outlets like the *Washington Post* and the *New York Times,* reporters who had interviewed him for other stories. Once the news broke, he was certain, the Reagan administration would have to react by providing the badly needed funds. But no reporters bit. "They told me it wasn't a news story," said Francis.

When the *MMWR* or the *New England Journal* was detailing the crisis, the Associated Press dutifully reported the developments. The Cable News Network, located in Atlanta, followed in AP's footsteps,

18 and a few gay publications were taking special interest in the story. In mid-1982, the most intensive reporting on AIDS was being done by the *New York Native*'s Dr. Larry Mass, and his concern was finding out how to stop gays from getting the disease. The *Native* occasionally posed the question of funding, but it was years before the newspaper had any real impact on the mainstream press. No one was broaching the issue of the government's responsibility.

If Francis could not interest reporters in the funding crisis, by mid-1982 some at the CDC, with the help of organizations like New York's Gay Men's Health Crisis and San Francisco's AIDS Foundation, were having success in spreading the word among gays about the dangers inherent in a sexually promiscuous life-style. But Curran was hesitant to suggest ways in which gays might change their behavior. For his and the CDC's part, pointing out the problem was the extent of their offensive. After all, encouraging behavioral change was not really the agency's role, according to CDC director Dr. William Foege. Curran believed he was politically savvy enough to know that trying to change sexual behavior among liberated gays meant facing the fury of an organized community.

A Newsworthy Victim

From mid-August 1981 to May 1982, the *MMWR* was silent on the growing epidemic, except for noting the rising number of cases of Kaposi's sarcoma, *Pneumocystis,* and the rage of opportunistic infections that signaled the disease. Curran excused this gap by saying that in the nine-month period, the CDC was busy gathering data. Not surprisingly, the few mainstream news sources—most notably, Associated Press and CNN—that had been tracking the epidemic through the pages of the CDC's weekly report carried almost no stories on the issue during the hiatus. When the *MMWR* finally included another update on May 12, 1982, "Generalized Lymphadenopathy among Homosexual Males," the article was ignored by every major news source. By the summer, hundreds of cases had been identified; it was known that not only homosexuals but intravenous drug users and even Haitians and hemophiliacs were being infected. None of those facts, all of which were dutifully announced in the *MMWR,* elicited much media interest. All those groups were out of the media's focus.

Finally, in the late fall of 1982, Dr. Jaffe saw a case of an infant with the disease. A twenty-month-old boy, born to healthy parents in San Francisco, had received a blood transfusion more than a year before. The donor, who at the time had no symptoms, was now ill with *Pneumocystis*. On December 10 the *MMWR* reported the finding, and it brought scientists one step closer to discovering how the disease was spread: "it may be caused by an infectious agent transmitted sexually or through exposure to blood or blood products." The day the CDC released the *MMWR*, Jaffe remembers, a pack of journalists and cameramen appeared in his doorway. The long wait for media attention, it seemed, was finally over. The CDC staffers always had been uncomfortable with the term "GRID," "Gay-Related Infectious Disease," which linked the epidemic solely to homosexuals. Diseases were not caused by groups, after all. "Acquired Community Immune Deficiency Syndrome" had been popularized by some scientists. And now that it was clear the malady was affecting more than gays, more than just one community, its name could be clipped to "AIDS": "Acquired Immune Deficiency Syndrome."

AIDS was suddenly a much bigger story. All the major networks featured a segment after the report on the AIDS baby, and the news appeared in *Time* and *Newsweek* as well. But AIDS still was not making it on the front page of America's major papers. The *New York Times* ignored the transfusion story altogether.

"We realized we had a disease with about a 10 percent mortality rate," said Francis. In other words, for every one hundred people who came down with AIDS, ten would die. Researchers have since upped that mortality rate significantly, with some estimating that for every one hundred people diagnosed with AIDS, one hundred will die. "This virus is incredibly dangerous," said Francis, the kind the CDC keeps down in its maximum security P-4 containment facility, protected by a shell on top of a shell and maintained by an entirely separate air-conditioning system. That is where the eradicated smallpox virus is kept. And yet, it still wasn't getting the kind of attention less deadly diseases had warranted.

A Fifties Approach to an Eighties Crisis

By early 1983, the CDC had gathered enough data to determine exactly how AIDS was being transmitted. The March 4 issue of the *MMWR* included "Prevention of Acquired Immune Deficiency Syn-

drome (AIDS)," the government's official recommendations. Those
20 individuals who belonged to groups "at increased risk for AIDS should
refrain from donating plasma and/or blood. . . . Members of high
risk groups should be aware that multiple sexual partners increase
probability of developing AIDS."

As for particularly risky sexual practices that should be avoided,
the *MMWR* wasn't going to be specific. After all, the document was
being reviewed not just by trained scientists like Dr. Brandt—conservative and fiscally cautious, but with a commitment to the AIDS problem—or by experts like Dr. James Mason, the Mormon official who in
1983 had been appointed by Reagan to replace Dr. William Foege at
the CDC, and who had made a career out of his concern for public
health. Now, according to CDC insiders, the *MMWR* was being
checked over by Reagan administration apparatchiks before it was
sent out to the public.

Mason claimed the administration did not blatantly tinker with the
MMWR. He does admit, however, that other interference from Washington made him wary of attempting to disseminate AIDS information through channels traditionally not used by the CDC, such as
press releases. Foege said AIDS should be the crisis to change the
weapons of his former agency. In the 1950s and 1960s, according to
Foege, the government used its disease-fighting tools to tackle a health
threat, but today "the scientific explosion has made individuals more
powerful in changing their own health destiny." More frequently, the
individual is able, given the right information, to prevent illness: to
take off the pump handle, as it were. But it should be the government's responsibility to teach Americans precisely how to do that, said
Mason.

As early as 1970, a decade before AIDS, a federal advisory committee that included Mason concluded that the CDC should be educating
the public in this way. As a result, the Center for Health Promotion
and Education was created in 1980. Nonetheless, when AIDS hit, said
Mason, "we weren't prepared to deal with it." The official disregard
for this disease seemed rooted in politics, which also played a part in
determining what information the CDC could publicize about the epidemic. For example, because of the conservative political current in
Washington, any explicit educational material, even basic sex education in the schools, was suspect. Some researchers who have worked
with the CDC assert that such an attitude hindered research, and
sometimes prevented possibly lifesaving data from being publicized.

For example, in 1984 a California physician named Bruce Voeller got a CDC grant, approved by Dr. Francis, to do what he thought was 21 basic research on sexual transmission of AIDS. He had proven that the virus could not seep through latex, the material used by many condom manufacturers. Now he wanted to study the effect of spermicides on the virus. What he discovered was groundbreaking: birth-control creams, particularly those that contain a potent chemical called nonoxynol 9, can kill the AIDS virus and help prevent its spread during sex.

The CDC had been promoting condom use as one device to help stem the epidemic, and nonoxynol 9 spermicides seemed to be the perfect complement. Voeller's team rushed to piece together a paper presenting the new information and sent it to the CDC. Francis signed off on the study and recommended that it immediately be sent to a medical journal. Then Curran got hold of it. He was familiar with Voeller's work. In fact, Voeller had first proposed the idea to Curran, head of the AIDS task force, who turned it down. Curran doubted the experiment would be a success. Even if it were, he feared the CDC would seem to be promoting sex in the midst of a sexually transmitted disease epidemic. But, most important, according to Voeller, Curran had told him he could anticipate strong opposition from the White House.

"The agency is a ball-playing institution," said Francis. The CDC has had to learn to play the games of politics because its funding is often cut for political reasons. In fact, the agency can be ravaged if powerful political players are against it. Voeller's paper languished in Curran's hands for months. Finally, the California researcher contacted acquaintances on Capitol Hill who were actively involved in the AIDS issue. Voeller wouldn't reveal names, but it is likely he approached Representative Henry Waxman from Los Angeles and his aide, Tim Westmoreland, who had become the two most important operators within Congress in pushing the government to do more about AIDS. Westmoreland and Bill Kraus, an aide to San Francisco's powerful Representative Phil Burton, helped reveal the inside story about the CDC's lack of resources to do fundamental work on the epidemic. Waxman had used that information in Congress to embarrass the Reagan administration and produce more money for the effort.

Shortly after Voeller approached his Capitol Hill contacts, his study was dislodged from the CDC. By mid-December, the report on the effectiveness of spermicides to thwart the AIDS virus was published in

22 the British medical journal the *Lancet*. Ironically, the article's list of authors included Dr. Curran's name. A handful of major newspapers covered the story of CDC infighting, but for the most part the incident didn't spur any reporter to take a closer look at the intergovernmental squabbling that was slowing down AIDS research.

Some of the missteps in the AIDS epidemic clearly indicated a lack of organization on the government's part. In mid-1984, shortly after announcement that the AIDS virus had been discovered, the National Cancer Institute focused a large amount of its resources on developing a blood test to monitor transfusions in the United States. At the same time, the Food and Drug Administration was denying that there was any real threat to the nation's blood supply, making such a test largely irrelevant.

There were other pressures working against getting the word out. Public health officials had to consider that excessive warnings could ignite hysteria. Often, fear of frightening the public paralyzed the CDC or forced agency officials to lie. When rumors began circulating that AIDS could be spread by mosquitoes, for instance, the CDC immediately and loudly denied it; there was no mention of the fact that the agency had not yet finished its own study of the mosquito–AIDS link. As it turns out, AIDS is not spread that way.

The most important deterrent to AIDS education was lack of money. In 1985, when more than twelve thousand people had been diagnosed with AIDS, the U.S. Department of Health and Human Services budgeted $120,000 for AIDS education: $10 for every person already ill, pennies for those estimated to be infected, and almost nothing for the millions of Americans who could be prevented from getting the disease. Not until 1985 did the federal government attempt to produce a comprehensive plan to fight AIDS. Called the Coolfont Report, it projected there would be 270,000 AIDS cases by 1991. More than 1.5 million people were thought to be infected in 1985.

In the end, pushing the federal government to publicize straightforward prevention methods fell to conservative family men like Mason. But even he admits he was wary of the politics involved in the effort. That is in part why his "Information/Education Plan to Prevent and Control AIDS in the United States" didn't make its debut until the spring of 1987. By that time, Surgeon General C. Everett Koop, another conservative Reagan appointee with an unshakable commit-

ment to public health, had taken on AIDS education as a personal
campaign. Descriptions of body parts and sexual activity that had
Reaganites scurrying were showing up in the regular addresses made
by the sixty-seven-year-old pediatrician. Koop, more than any other
player in the AIDS epidemic, was responsible for breaking down language barriers in the American media. There was still opposition from
people like presidential aide Gary Bauer, who fought any government
warnings that could be interpreted as educating homosexuals and un-
wed heterosexuals about how to have sex safely. The White House
was rife with such know-nothings. Another Reagan aide, Carlton
Turner, made a name for himself on Capitol Hill with his erroneous
claim that marijuana use caused homosexuality.

Despite those obstacles, Koop and others were able to bring in a
new progressive era in public discussions of the disease. Mason's 1987
document hardly offered startling information about how AIDS was
transmitted, but it did explain it explicitly and accurately: "Individuals in all groups need to know. The AIDS virus had been shown to be
spread from an infected person to an uninfected person by . . . sexual
contact (penis/vagina, penis/rectum, mouth/rectum, mouth/genital)."
After almost six years, and the diagnosis of thirty-two thousand AIDS
cases, this most basic of advisories was finally being sent out to the
American public.

Curran, the good soldier of the CDC, had fought his own fights on
funding issues and language barriers, but for the most part, he had
done this quietly, without overstepping the boundaries of his official
job description. Yet Curran refuses to accept the blame for the lack of
publicity about the epidemic. "I could have fallen on my sword on the
Capitol steps," but the media wouldn't have paid attention. Francis
disagrees. "If we had 'camped' on the doorsteps of public officials in
Washington," more money would have been available sooner, and the
government response would have been much better coordinated. Unfortunately, for the majority of Americans who needed explicit information about the spread of AIDS, it was necessary to rely almost
solely on the media for the first six years of the epidemic. As the following chapters detail, the media rarely are effective public health
educators.

The government simply should have taken more of a leading role
in the education process. Much of the blame has to rest with President
Ronald Reagan. In 1988 he maintained staunch opposition to basic

24 legal protections for people with AIDS, as well as common-sense approaches to education, despite the advice of his own handpicked AIDS commission. Analyzing the U.S. performance during the crisis, the commission's chairman concluded: "the federal government is ill prepared to respond effectively to future public health emergencies or epidemics."

Chapter 2
Taking it personally

It started as a rumor. In mid-May of 1981, a gay man who had visited his doctor to be treated for a venereal disease overheard the physician mention that some gays were being treated in intensive care units in New York City for a strange pneumonia. Like any good tipster, he phoned his community newspaper, the *New York Native*.

The publication for gays was a product of both the visions and whims of Chuck Ortleb, its editor and publisher. Ortleb had no experience covering the news, but he did know his readership. There also seemed to be an endless supply of energetic young men and women willing to work long hours at low or no pay to write about their burgeoning community.

The gay press was a journalistic oddity. Spawned by a political movement that itself came to life in a clash between cops and drag queens, the gay press was at once revolutionary and campy. Gay newspapers serving neighborhoods where homosexuals congregate—New York's Greenwich Village, for example, and Castro and Polk Streets in San Francisco—dished up hefty servings of sex and humor. Politics and news were often given only secondary consideration.

There were notable exceptions, such as Boston's *Gay Community News* and Washington, D.C.'s *Blade*, both of which featured politics and critique as their main course. But the biggest and most successful publications, like the *Advocate*, the first nationally distributed gay newspaper, rarely strayed from the formula. The *Native* followed suit, until young gay men began dying inexplicably in New York City. Nowhere in America were journalists more personally affected by this crisis than in the offices of Ortleb's newspaper. The *Native* reflected that. Ortleb eventually did more than publicize the story in his paper. He reached out, cajoled, and sometimes verbally assaulted mainstream journalists in attempts to get them to cover the issue more closely. Unfortunately, as the death toll among his readership rose, without any quick solution in sight, Ortleb grew frantic. His "tips" moved from the provocative to the preposterous. Still, he had a surprisingly big impact on the mainstream media. That success altered the gay papers and the way mainstream journalists view them.

26 The Pork Salesman's Son

Ortleb grew up in New Jersey and the Midwest, the son of a pork salesman and a nurse and the oldest of ten children. He attended an exclusive prep school in St. Louis and went on to the University of Kansas. It was no hotbed of sixties student activism when Ortleb was there. But like most college students in that era, he was affected by the climate of potential political upheaval. The spirit of the times encouraged Ortleb to declare his own homosexuality, at the age of twenty-two. His parents blew up at the news, which convinced him to leave the Bible Belt far behind after graduation from college in 1972.

Like generations of young men and women before him, Ortleb headed for New York. Soon after he arrived, he met Arthur Bell. The famed *Village Voice* columnist was a member of an activist alliance attempting to give a voice to the politics of gay liberation. At the time, the modern movement was an infant, having been born in the riots that erupted in 1969 when gays fought back against police harassment of patrons of the Stonewall nightclub, a drag queen hangout. Bell and others had been watching the feminist movement, only slightly more mature in its own modern incarnation, with an appreciative eye for its political tactics. *Ms.* magazine, established in 1972 to encourage women's politics, inspired Bell's group. They thought a similar publication for gays might be able to tap into a growing sentiment for change, especially strong in areas of New York like Christopher Street in Greenwich Village, where gays had carved out communities of refurbished homes, trendy shops, and bars.

Bell was a stirring writer, but a not-so-brilliant organizer, and the idea never got off the gound—until Ortleb ran with it. Ortleb had less of an interest in the politics than in the literary product of the movement. He had studied poetry in college, and spent much of his spare time writing verse. When he envisioned a new magazine, *Ms.* didn't come to mind; the *New Yorker* did. That was the inspiration behind *Christopher Street* magazine.

The shy and frumpy twenty-five-old made an unlikely candidate for publisher of an avant-garde publication. Before he launched *Christopher Street* in 1975, he had worked as a typist, a file clerk, and at a handful of other temporary jobs in New York City offices. But Ortleb could be extremely assertive and brash, and he was able to round up $10,000, enough to put out two issues. Then he promptly went into debt. He battled the red ink for four years, relying on

printers and suppliers who were willing to extend him credit. Meanwhile, Ortleb searched for a money-raising venture, and he thought
of the *Village Voice*. The alternative weekly had built itself a national reputation, and pulled in high profits. A gay version of the tabloid seemed almost certain to turn Ortleb's company around. So in the fall of 1980, he came out with the first issue of the twice-monthly *New York Native*.

Flash Point

Dr. Larry Mass was the *Native*'s part-time reporter who got the message from the tipster about the *Pneumocystis* pneumonia cases. The thirty-three-year-old Mass had been on the lookout for this kind of story. As an M.D. himself, he was intrigued by the explosion in the number of diseases that were circulating in the gay community. By 1981 gonorrhea, syphilis, herpes, and hepatitis were old familiars. New, mysterious maladies also were showing up. Amebiasis, for instance, a bacterial infection common in the Third World but rare in the United States, had been reincarnated as a sexually transmitted disease in the gay community. Stopping the bacteria was no easy feat. Treatment could drag on for months, while the unlucky host suffered with diarrhea and stomach pains. But Mass feared worse things were lurking.

Ortleb was often looking for copy to fill the fledgling *Native,* so it was not hard for Mass to convince him to give space to these kinds of problems. The doctor's excruciatingly accurate articles fit awkwardly in the pages full of gritty ads for bodybuilding salons and bathhouses. Mass was not a seasoned reporter or writer. He had a bachelor's degree in English from the University of California, Berkeley, but his first professional writing experience had been in technical journals during his medical training. He wanted to break into writing, and the *Native* was the most accessible publication.

His prose was rarely elegant, but in the gay papers where unprofessionalism reigned, Mass's careful reporting separated him from the young and reckless. Mass was intrigued about the lead he was given, but he was also cautious. Not until he got a second phone call corroborating the rumor, this one from a New York gay activist, did he decide to follow up on it.

Mass first tried to get a comment from a staff physician at St. Vin-

28 cent's Hospital, where some of the men were supposedly being treated. The doctor stalled, saying she couldn't talk about the cases until the following week. After asking around the New York City Health Department, he finally got hold of a doctor on loan from the Centers for Disease Control. The physician was careful to couch his terms in tempered bureaucratese to head off hysteria.

"Disease Rumors Largely Unfounded," Mass reported in the *Native* .on May 18, 1981. "Last week there were rumors that an exotic new disease had hit the gay community in New York. Here are the facts." He repeated a New York City public health official's claims that there was no wave of disease sweeping through the gay community, and that *Pneumocystis* was not unusual. But could it be, asked Mass, that "a new, more virulent strain of the organism may have been 'community acquired'"? After all, the public health doctor could not explain why young men in New York were getting the disease, which usually affected only elderly patients with advanced cancer.

At this point, the CDC had been gathering information for about a month on the outbreak that Mass's source was dismissing. The agency made official mention of *Pneumocystis* pneumonia affecting gay men in its *Morbidity and Mortality Weekly Report* only two weeks after Mass's May 18 story. Only years later did Mass realize he was the first journalist to write about the epidemic.

No other reporters followed Mass's lead. The six-inch story was easily overlooked on page seven of the *Native,* hidden away in a lower left-hand corner. Even if the scoop had been prominently played, as stories on the epidemic soon would be in the *Native,* Mass's piece would hardly have attracted much attention from the mainstream media. If journalists at institutions like the *New York Times* or Associated Press were reading the newspaper, none was admitting it.

The Death of Sex

As the number of gays checking into the hospital with this bizarre pneumonia continued to rise during the next month, Mass wondered why no one in the mainstream media was covering the subject. Why was nothing appearing in the medical journals? Maybe this story wasn't as important as he had thought. Then on July 3 the *New York Times* reported the outbreak of Kaposi's sarcoma (KS), as detailed by the *MMWR*. Like *Pneumocystis*, the cancer wasn't a novelty in New York. But whom it was striking—not the elderly and infirm but young, presumably healthy men—was news. Mass pursued the story with all the urgency of a cub reporter who had just had his first scoop confirmed by an ace journalist.

"Cancer in the Gay Community" read the *Native*'s July 27 front-page story. In a long lead that sounded like an introduction to a treatise on epidemiology, Mass asked, "What is it about male homosexuals—or a subgroup of male homosexuals—that distinguishes their susceptibility to this disease?" Inside, the gray columns of print were broken up by gruesome photos of KS lesions on hands and arms. Mass ran through the hypotheses being bandied about: one physician's belief that the new KS cases may be caused in part by genetic deficiencies, for example. Even *Village Voice* columnist Alexander Cockburn's observations were quoted: "subsequent enquiries seem to support the view that KS is associated with traumatic sex, or in less elevated parlance, such activities as fist-fucking." That was the first and one of the very rare utterances from the *Voice* in the first few years of the epidemic, even though it was widely held that as much as 30 percent of the newspaper's readers were gay. An openly gay *Voice* editor admitted that the publication's poor coverage of the issue in the early years was due in part to fears among the ultraliberal staff of offending the gay community. Some gay publications handled the epidemic with the same cautious silence.

Acknowledging the threat that sex posed, even before such a link had been proven conclusively, was hardly an easy step for Mass. "Sexual freedom was essential to being gay," he said. "And we [gays] were making headway in our progress for acceptance. I didn't want to go back to where we had been." What impact the health crisis would have on the political and social progress of gays remained to be seen, but it would clearly have an effect on sexual life-style. People like playwright Larry Kramer did their best to make sure of that.

Kramer's adaptation of D. H. Lawrence's *Women in Love*, which included a steamy wrestling-match scene between two of the male stars, had won him an Oscar nomination in 1970 and recognition in some quarters of New York's gay community. But ever since he had published *Faggots*, a 1978 novel about a gay man's tortured odyssey through the sexual underground of Manhattan's gay-bar backrooms and bathhouses, he had been a *persona non grata* in the same crowd. Many who had read the book, an all-out attack on promiscuity, considered him at best a spoilsport and at worst a "sexual fascist." No gay man had confronted the movement's credo of sexual excess as publicly as he.

Kramer read the *New York Times* piece and the *Native* cover story, both of which touched his life far more strongly than most New Yorkers, or even most Christopher Street denizens. A handful of Kramer's friends already had been diagnosed with KS. In early August Kramer called up Mass, and he and a small group of other alarmed gay men decided to hold a meeting. Dr. Alvin Friedman-Kien, a researcher at New York University who had been studying the disease, was invited to speak. In the months to follow, other doctors, including the CDC's James Curran, made the trek to the Village apartments of Kramer and his friends. All these medical experts brought the same scary news: the disease seemed to be striking only gays, and almost all those who came down with it were highly promiscuous.

Some of the men who gathered at the first meeting in late summer thought of the upcoming Labor Day weekend, and what it would be like on Fire Island, the New York area resort popular among gays. Sex would be as common as cocktails on the beach. Gays needed to be warned, it was decided. That evening the group agreed to make thousands of photocopies of Mass's article with the frightening KS photos and distribute them on the island. It was the first official act of the Gay Men's Health Crisis.

But Kramer did not imagine this grass-roots effort was going to go far enough to warn gay men against promiscuous sex, and to get the government moving to find a cause and cure. He wanted the kind of exposure that only a paper like the *New York Times* could give.

The AIDS Paper

By December 21, 1981, two new cases of Kaposi's sarcoma were being diagnosed each week in the United States. That day Mass logged the developments in a *Native* report: "The latest figures from the federal Centers for Disease Control in Atlanta strengthen earlier impressions that sexually active gay men are experiencing what's now being called 'an epidemic of immunosuppression.'" "Do Poppers Cause Cancer?" he asked in the same article, trying to keep up with the latest leads coming out of the CDC and the medical literature. The popular amyl nitrite, a fragrant, flammable liquid nicknamed for the popping sensation it caused when inhaled, used especially during sex, was thought to be a factor in the spread of the disease. In that issue, Kramer took on his critics, some of whom claimed that the playwright was reveling in the death of promiscuous homosexuals: "I am not glorying in death. I am overwhelmed by it. The death of my friends. The death of whatever community there is here in New York."

Kramer was desperately trying to get the word out through the major media. Almost daily he was on the phone attempting to get in touch with a producer at ABC, or he was writing a letter to the *New York Times* editor Abe Rosenthal or to a reporter there he had once met. He wracked his memory trying to come up with names of friends or acquaintances or even long forgotten fellow students at Yale, his alma mater, who might now be in a position of influence in the media. At the annual Halloween party thrown by his old friend, columnist Calvin Trillin, Kramer confronted, among others, NBC anchorman Tom Brokaw.

While Kramer was trying to get national attention focused on the epidemic, Mass's ambitions were much more modest. He wanted to reach the majority of gays in New York. The *Native*'s circulation of 14,000 did not even make a dent in the city's gay population, estimated to be between 600,000 and a million. It was the *Village Voice*'s gay readers Mass was aiming at, and so in the spring of 1982 he sent off an in-depth piece to the newspaper. He titled it "The Most Important New Public Health Problem in the United States." It was a much less clinical article than the one that had appeared in the *Native*, yet the paper said it was not a *Village Voice* kind of piece.

Mass's article wound up on the March 29, 1982, front page of the *Native:* "The Epidemic Continues," the headline read. "Facing a new case every day, researchers are still bewildered. . . . Sexually active gay men in the New York City area are currently being advised to see a physician twice a year for complete VD testing and at least once a year for a thorough physical examination," the article continued. "If your physician has not yet heard about the epidemic of immunosuppression, you should probably consult another physician." Dr. Curran, who had come to New York to speak to groups concerned about AIDS, was quoted extensively, and he even got his picture in the *Native*. Once again, the paper ran photos of KS lesions. Ironically, the story shared the front page with a first-person essay on one man's weekend experience with sadomasochism. Even as the *Native* was

becoming known as "The AIDS paper"—it was the first publication
32 in America to list high-risk behavior, to discuss the potential danger
of the disease being spread by a virus, and to list organizations to
help the epidemic's victims—it remained full of articles and ads that
glorified the sexually promiscuous life-style and the most dangerous
forms of risky sex.

The *Native*'s publisher never dealt straightforwardly with the
paper's contradiction, though in 1987 he finally pulled the publication's raunchy personals because of what he claims was pressure from
the *Times*'s Abe Rosenthal. (In a *New York Times* column, the retired
news executive pointed out that some in the gay press, including the
Native, were still promoting risky behavior through ads that solicited
dangerous sex.) Nonetheless, Ortleb was taking the epidemic very
personally, as the death toll rose dramatically among his readership in
mid-1982. This community under attack was the only home he had
known since leaving the Midwest and the only place in which he felt
comfortable. It had given him not just a place to belong to, but a title,
editor and publisher.

From his perspective, behind the lines in the onslaught of disease, it
was not hard to feel beleaguered. He knew scores of people with the
malady, and some who had died. Yet, the U.S. medical miracle machine was not coming up with any answers, much less a cure. Having
been a college student in the 1960s, and a gay man in the era of
Ronald Reagan's presidency, he did not trust the government and began to think the lack of progress was due mostly to a lack of interest.
Larry Kramer's bombastic entreaties also pushed Ortleb to speak out.

"The gay community has all too quickly adopted a polite wait-and-
see attitude toward the CDC," Ortleb wrote on August 16, 1982, in
his first of many editorials on the disease. "It has now been a year
since the epidemic surfaced as a serious health crisis, and we are no
closer to a cure or an explanation than we were a year ago. . . . If the
CDC exists for the purposes of monitoring this—or any—epidemic,
who exists for the purposes of monitoring the CDC? . . . Who can as-
sure us that not one ounce of homophobia is affecting the progress of
this investigation when we are all too familiar with the medical establishment's formal history of homophobia?"

The answer, of course, was that no one could. If the *Native* had had
greater resources and an editor with news savvy, probing the Health
and Human Services Department or the National Institutes of Health
or the President's Office of Management and Budget might very well

have yielded some interesting stories about how research on the crisis
was being impeded by the politics of test tubes and purse strings.   33

Ortleb was less a newspaperman than a philosopher. He labeled
himself a liberal Democrat, but he did not point to politicians as
people who framed his thinking. Instead he invoked the name of
Hannah Arendt, the German-born political theorist who wrote a hallmark study of the rise of totalitarianism and its destructive force, especially with regard to the Nazi extermination of the Jews. His animus
as a writer and editor was simpler: "I hate authorities." That attitude
would shape the *Native's* coverage more as Ortleb became increasingly
involved in personally overseeing the paper's AIDS reporting.

It was his hands-off approach in the early days of the *Native,* running
submitted articles almost verbatim, that attracted people like Mass to
contribute, even though Ortleb paid his writers next to nothing. By
contrast, Ortleb always insisted on a fairly high quality of writing from
contributors to *Christopher Street.* Because it was one of the few gay
magazines serious about fiction and criticism, it attracted some of the
bright lights among the homosexual literati. A typical issue featured
critically and financially successful authors like Andrew Holleran, author of *Dancer from the Dance,* and New York wit Quentin Crisp. Not
until a year and a half into the epidemic did Ortleb begin to take more
control of the newspaper and begin to accept less of what the writers
were offering. Finally, he had ambitions not just for his beloved magazine but also for the paper. As Ortleb saw it, there was a vacuum in
AIDS coverage that he and his staff could fill. In one particularly exu-
berant moment, he proclaimed, "I want to make the *Native* a legend."

The paper was far from that lofty goal. But by early 1983, after
most of the major media woke up to the epidemic when blood transfusions were revealed as a route of transmission, Mass had become a
source for some journalists in the mainstream press, including Dr.
Lawrence Altman at the *New York Times.* In a few short months, however, Ortleb's plan of building on the *Native's* coverage ran into serious trouble: suffering from exhaustion and anxiety as a result of
covering the epidemic and its deadly cargo, Mass stopped taking calls,
refused public speaking requests, and eventually quit writing for the
Native. He was later hospitalized with severe depression.

Mass had been recognized, even by scientists like the CDC's Dr.
Curran, as one of the most authoritative reporters covering the crisis,
and the *Native* was read by some doctors in the forefront of the epidemic. In this war, it hardly mattered if a comrade was working for a

34 homosexual rag that featured the lean torsos of sex-hungry men next to carefully researched science reporting. The *Native* seemed to be part of the solution. For some of its readers, however, the newspaper had become too focused on the gloom of AIDS. Circulation began to dip slightly. Even some committed *Native* readers began to question how the paper's intensity colored its coverage.

The AIDS Advertiser

Mass's increasingly infrequent reports were replaced at first by submissions from a variety of would-be writers, including doctors, doctors' assistants, and even gay men with no credentials but the fear they felt gripping their community. Some of the most important articles in the *Native* in those early years had nothing to do with the science of the disease, but rather its social consequences. "The AIDS crisis is a threat to every gay man," wrote Dr. Stuart Nichols on October 11, 1982. He had helped develop a support group for AIDS patients, and was now worried that "[the epidemic] is eating away at the sense of security that has been built up since Stonewall. This is no time to pull apart; we need to find a unity." Like any good newspaper, the *Native* was chronicling the major changes in its community, often in dramatic ways.

"We Know Who We Are" was the November 8 essay by two gay men who were declaring "war on promiscuity," as they put it. "Those of us who have lived a life of excessive promiscuity on the urban gay circuit of bathhouses, backrooms, balconies, sex clubs, meat racks and tearooms know who we are," wrote Richard Berkowitz and Michael Callen, a musician who organized New York City's People with AIDS coalition. "We could continue to deny overwhelming evidence that the present health crisis is a direct result of the unprecedented promiscuity . . . but such denial is killing us. . . . The motto of promiscuous gay men has been 'So many men, so little time.' In the '70s, we worried about so many men; in the '80s we will have to worry about so little time. For us, the party that was the '70s is over."

The most powerful of these entreaties came from playwright Kramer, who pointed the finger at the federal government, at New York City, and, most angrily, at gays themselves for not doing more to put a halt to the dying. His *J'Accuse*, "1,112 and Counting," ran on the cover of the *New York Native* on March 13, 1983: "If this article doesn't scare the shit out of you we're in real trouble. If this article doesn't rouse you to anger, fury, rage and action, gay men have no future on this earth. . . . The CDC is stretched to its limits and is dreadfully underfunded for what it's being asked, in all areas, to do. . . . With his silence on AIDS, the mayor [New York's Ed Koch] . . . is helping to kill us." Kramer was putting out the call, once again, to gay men to get involved in concerted and coordinated efforts to lobby government and change their own life-style. It was a tall order, especially in a city that attracted people who, above all, craved independence and individualism. At the end of the piece, Kramer listed the score of friends who had already died and declared: "I am sick of guys who moan that giving up careless sex until this thing blows over is worse than death."

By this point in the crisis, the *New York Native* may have had more influence three thousand miles from its editorial offices. A few weeks after Kramer's piece appeared in the *Native,* a vocal group of San Francisco political activists who had read his indictment sat down to draw up their own manifesto to fight the epidemic: "We believe it is time to speak the simple truth—and to care enough about one another to act on it," wrote Bill Kraus, an aide to the powerful Northern California representative Phil Burton and a member of the Harvey Milk Memorial Democratic Club. The organization was devoted to promoting the pragmatic politics of San Francisco's first gay supervisor, who had been murdered by a fellow politician five years earlier. Shortly after they penned the document, Kraus's antipromiscuity call to action was published in one of the local gay publications, the *Bay Area Reporter.* The creation of the statement was also covered by the *San Francisco Examiner*'s John Jacobs, who correctly portrayed the meeting as a turning point in the city's sexual politics. San Francisco's major dailies, the *Examiner* and the *Chronicle,* had been covering all sides of the AIDS issue for months, earlier than many gay publications. That sophistication in reportage of gays by the mainstream press was peculiar to San Francisco and due mostly to the fact that homosexuals had more political clout in that city than almost anywhere else in the world. In New York and Los Angeles, cities with far larger numbers of gays, the local media mostly overlooked them. The *New York Times* was an extreme case: for the first two years of the epidemic, it had virtually ignored the health crisis.

Because San Francisco's mainstream print media were so well informed about AIDS, they were describing many of the same changes documented by the *Native* in New York. San Francisco's fractious gay political parties, who were sharply divided on the question of whether gay leaders should speak out against promiscuity, also were violently split on whether these intracommunity fights should be broadcast in the daily newspapers. Nonetheless, in early 1983, one of the biggest political stories of the epidemic—in the *Examiner, Chronicle,* and *Native*—was the momentous steps being taken by the Milk Club on the West Coast and people like Callen and Kramer on the East Coast. Such actions by gays shook the cornerstone of the gay movement, which was sexual liberation, the freedom of consenting adults to have sex exactly as they liked. Many states, including New York and California, had legitimated that right only in the last two decades, but even earlier a huge gay business establishment of bars and bathhouses had institutionalized it.

By the early 1980s, many of those businesses were multimillion-dollar enterprises. The sex arcades, like New York's elaborate St. Marks baths, which wandered through floors and floors of private rooms and into a dozen different fantasylands, were especially profitable, and their best advertising vehicles were the gay papers. In some cities, bathhouse and bar owners were both publishers and advertisers. In New York, a sizable portion of the *Native's* $1 million annual revenue came from the ads placed by bars and baths. Often, that money helped cover the cost of free ad or editorial space for AIDS fundraising events, like the April 1983 Ringling Brothers Circus at Madison Square Garden, sponsored by the Gay Men's Health Crisis. But with writers ranting against promiscuity—the very obsession these businesses, in part, served—a publisher was forced to walk the line between fiscal sense and social commitment. This is the classical predicament of editors of small newspapers and magazines, which are often dependent on cigarette advertising. Curiously, Ortleb did not seem to be losing much sleep over the conflict. By mid-1983, he had other concerns on his mind, like finding the cause of AIDS.

AIDS and Pigs

Ortleb had his suspicions that the CDC and the government in general weren't doing enough AIDS research, and these grew stronger as day after day went by without a major breakthrough to a cure, or even a cause. By the time the third year of the crisis rolled around, he lost patience with the institutions the Kramers and Callens were trying to nudge forward. Like many gays, he had come to despise the Reagan administration for its seeming lack of interest in the rising death toll of gay men. In fact the president had yet to mention there was a crisis at all.

37

Kramer, who is Jewish, had once compared the Holocaust to the AIDS epidemic. But this time around, it was government *in*action that was murdering gay men. It was but a short leap for Ortleb to suspect that such a result might be the government's intention. If he were news editor of a major paper, he thought, he'd assign his best reporter to the story to investigate the hold up. Instead, since the departure of Dr. Larry Mass, he found himself relying on sincere but ineffective free-lancers. Then one of his editors met Dr. James D'Eramo. The thirty-five-year-old from Houston had gotten his Ph.D. in infectious disease at the University of Texas and came to New York in 1981 to match his science background with his urge to write. He had been making a living writing ad copy when Ortleb offered him a $100-a-week staff position to cover AIDS. D'Eramo jumped at the opportunity.

One of his first assignments was to look into a theory that had appeared recently in the prestigious British medical journal, the *Lancet*. Some doctor from Harvard, a reader told Ortleb, had found a connection between AIDS and a disease that killed pigs. The pork salesman's son was intrigued.

As it turned out, the theory was presented not in an article but in a letter in the April 23 issue of the *Lancet*, under the title "Could AIDS Agent Be a New Variant of ASFV?" Most medical writers knew the *Lancet* printed more letters on far-flung theories than did the *New England Journal*, the *Journal of the American Medical Association*, or *Science*. *Lancet* devoted an entire section, "Hypotheses," to provocative new ideas that had yet to be tested sufficiently. The writer of this letter— not a physician, but a Ph.D. in pathobiology, doing postdoctoral work at Harvard—had not done any AIDS research, or even work on the pig virus she was claiming was somehow connected to it. Her doctoral thesis was on the fertility habits of monkeys, and since then her work had focused on breast cancer. But thirty-six-year-old Jane Teas had done a lot of reading in other areas of late, and she was struck by the similarity of African swine fever virus (ASFV), which mainly affects pigs, and Acquired Immune Deficiency Syndrome. Both devastated the immune system and were extremely deadly. Biologically, these diseases behaved very much alike: they attacked the same cells in the immune system and destroyed them in similar ways. There was another coincidence that Teas thought important: ASFV had plagued pigs in the Caribbean for years. But in Haiti, it was first diagnosed only in the late 1970s, at the same time symptoms of what would become known as AIDS were being seen in humans. Teas wrote up her hypothesis and wanted to share it with AIDS and ASFV researchers who she thought might not have stumbled upon the connection. She sent the letter to the *Lancet* because she knew she had a better chance of getting it published there than at any of the major American medical and science publications. Days after the letter ran, she was interviewed by reporters in London and someone from the Physicians Radio Network. And then D'Eramo called.

He explained he was from a gay paper that had devoted extensive space to covering the epidemic, and he wanted to interview Teas about her theory. She had never heard of the *Native*, but she was willing to talk to anyone interested in the connection between AIDS and ASFV. The usually tightfisted Ortleb asked D'Eramo to make the trip to interview her in Boston, all expenses paid. He understood that Teas was not an AIDS researcher, that her credentials for doing this kind of hypothesizing were weak. That in part was why he wanted to pursue her. She was not part of the "AIDS Establishment," as he began labeling the CDC, NIH, and the doctors and scientists who worked with those agencies. The government, Ortleb decided, could not be trusted. He wanted D'Eramo to find out if Jane Teas was trustworthy.

On the May 23, 1983, cover of the *Native*, D'Eramo wrote his reply: "Is African Swine Fever Virus the Cause [of AIDS]?" he asked. And, in *Native* style, the story shared the front page with a strikingly handsome man—wearing a brief swimsuit—lean, chiseled, and posed to advertise the newspaper's Fitness section.

"A most uncommon, exciting and plausible theory has surfaced on the chaotic horizon of the AIDS mystery," the article began, sliding down the muscular back of the beefcake. "Dr. Teas has drawn a striking parallel between the first cases of AIDS diagnosed in Haiti in 1978 and the first confirmed appearance of ASFV in the Haitian pig populations in 1979." So what? Diseases in pigs, Teas knew, rarely jumped the species barriers into humans. Swine flu, the 1976 epidemic that never happened, was an exception. Dr. Teas conjectured in the pages of the *Native* that humans first came in contact with ASFV by eating undercooked pork. Humans could become infected only if the virus from the pig came in contact with their blood, which could happen if the pork eaters had tears in their gums, stomach lining, or digestive tract. Such ulcerations were common, especially in a disease-ridden, immunosuppressed population like Haiti's and Africa's. Humans could then pass the disease on to each other through sex. What proof did Teas have that any of this was correct? None, of course. It was complete hypothesis. Yet D'Eramo pushed on: "Dr. Teas' theory that ASFV is linked to AIDS may hold the answers to many of the questions that pertain to 'how the disease is spread.' [B]ut as yet, her theory has received only a very cool reception from official agencies and institutions."

If there was no evidence to date to prove that ASFV was the cause of AIDS, Ortleb believed it would be coming shortly. In mid-May, Teas had traveled to an international meeting of veterinarians in Florida, where one doctor told her he was interested in studying ASFV and had clearance from the government to work with the officially banned virus. A New York area researcher said he would be willing to supply human blood for the work. Then a doctor at the U.S. Department of Agriculture's research facility, Plum Island, said he thought the ASFV-AIDS connection should be studied. Finally, D'Eramo reported, "As the *Native* went to press, it was learned that the CDC in Atlanta had contacted the Plum Island facilities to request certain specially designed and treated microbiologic glass slides and cover slips necessary for studying aspects of ASFV." Could it be that even the CDC was beginning to study the ASFV-AIDS link?

This was the first time the *New York Native* diverged from the path of reporting the medical facts exclusively as they were seen by the medical establishment. It would never go back. D'Eramo continued to read the journals and attend the AIDS conferences, and to write stories from them. But ASFV became the *Native*'s cause. If Ortleb had his own doubts about Teas's theory, his delight in stumbling upon what just might turn out to be a major story convinced him to follow it doggedly. After all, the government had denied rumors about the spread of *Pneumocystis* when the *Native* first pursued that story. When, weeks after Teas had gotten positive responses from doctors at the Florida meeting, all the doctors reneged on their offers to help, Ortleb concluded a conspiracy by the government could be the only explanation. Uncle Sam had put his heavy hand on these scientists, had threatened to pull back their funding, or even to throw them out of their jobs, Ortleb thought. He was not quite sure why the government

40 would be doing this, but he was certain something nefarious was at work. He decided ASFV really must be the cause of AIDS. Now he had to convince the rest of the world.

It was easy to dismiss Ortleb, almost too easy. He was betting his newspaper's reputation, by now a well-respected authority on AIDS and its social impact, on a notion proposed by a scientist who had never done basic AIDS research. And Teas's theory itself played into Ortleb's own psychological struggles, like the conflict he had had with his father, the pork salesman.

Yet some shreds of evidence, while not proving the AIDS-ASFV link, at least pointed to some underhanded U.S. government involvement in the spread of swine fever. For instance, six years earlier two reporters for Long Island's *Newsday* uncovered a 1971 CIA plot to weaken the Cuban economy by killing the country's pig population with ASFV. The first modern outbreak of the disease had been recorded in Kenya in 1909, and ASFV had erupted in other regions of the continent for the next forty years. ASFV was spreading throughout the Caribbean by the late 1970s, which was about the same time AIDS began appearing there. Sometime later, so the theory went, this viral sabotage got out of control, and careened throughout the region. The United States and the rest of the world now had to pay for the sins of the CIA.

Ortleb's suspicion that the Reagan administration was homophobic, and thus uninterested in investigating the real leads in the AIDS story, was reinforced by the president's choices for public health appointments. Dr. Edward Brandt, for instance, the assistant secretary of health and human services, was not just a conservative, but a Baptist Sunday school teacher. The new director of the CDC, Dr. James Mason, was not just a Utah Republican, but a staunch Mormon. Both religions vehemently condemned homosexuality; why should any gay person trust these men, Ortleb often wondered aloud and in print.

Most suspicious of all, thought Ortleb, was the fact that the government had found no cause of AIDS yet. "Memos Show Administration Falsified AIDS Funding Needs," the *Native* reported on December 19, 1983, after a congressional study was released on "how the government conducted—and did not conduct—its campaign against the outbreak of AIDS."

"A stark portrait of government duplicity, which was quietly accepted by AIDS researchers in the Centers for Disease Control (CDC), emerges from the thirty-three page report by the House Committee on Government Operation." Ortleb was right, of course, about the CDC's collusion in the lie presented to Congress that no additional funding was needed for AIDS research in 1983. He was more certain than ever that the Reagan administration did not *want* to find the cause, or cure, for AIDS.

Convinced that he was one of the few people with enough insight and distance from the establishment to understand the epidemic, Ortleb began pushing others to pursue the swine fever angle. Teas, tired of being turned away by American doctors, went abroad to see scientists in Italy, Spain, and England. Ortleb contacted officials at the CDC, at the U.S. Department of Agriculture's Plum Island research facility, and at the New York State Department of Health. And he continued the weekly phone calls to reporters in the mainstream media. He was getting some reaction. The *Boston Globe*'s Loretta McLaughlin, a science reporter who had been covering the epidemic since 1982, followed up on the ASFV story, as did the *New York Times*, eventually.

Despite his year long crusade on what was being called the "pork connection," Ortleb was still taken seriously in some quarters. The *Native* was one of the most important records of AIDS information among the nonmedical press. Because public health officials considered it to be one of the best conduits to the gay community, the CDC's conservative Mormon director flew to New York specifically to talk to Chuck Ortleb, in early 1984.

Mason was quick to admit that he knew very little about homosexuality: "I knew what it was," he said, "but I had no idea what homosexuals *did*." That naïveté disappeared when he came to the CDC in late 1983. Mason's conservative credentials were indisputable, but so was his public health record. He wanted to reassure Ortleb that the government was committed to the battle. And he wanted to persuade the publisher that studying ASFV would not bring scientists any closer to discovering the cause of AIDS. "I tried to reason with him," said Mason.

Mason also had some exciting news for Ortleb. It could be a major scoop for the publisher. The CDC had been in contact with the laboratory of Dr. Luc Montagnier at the Pasteur Institute in Paris, which claimed to have found the AIDS virus. After extensive review of the work in the United States and abroad, Mason felt confident that the French had found the cause of the disease. They were calling it Lymphadenopathy Associated Virus, or LAV. It was an amazing gesture on the part of the CDC director. No major media outlet had

42

gotten such extraordinarily obliging treatment. Certainly none had been handed the kind of story Mason was serving up for Ortleb. The incident showed just how important Mason thought the *Native* had become. The publisher was hardly grateful: he buried the story in the back of the *Native* on April 9, 1984. Nonetheless, Ortleb's newspaper was the first lay publication in America to write about Montagnier's findings.

Nearly two weeks later, when the *New York Times*'s Lawrence Altman paid Dr. Mason a visit in Atlanta, the CDC director finally unveiled the news for a major medium. The story ran on the front page of the *New York Times* on April 22.

"[T]he *New York Times* took the LAV bait," was how the *Native* responded to Altman's story. Mason's expedition to New York solely to talk to Ortleb had impressed the publisher, but not in the way the CDC had hoped: "I knew we were on the trail," said Ortleb. "Why else would the government be sending its top guns" to a gay journalist? "He was trying to co-opt us." Ortleb greeted with equal cynicism the medical establishment's next major news: on April 23, Secretary of Health Margaret Heckler announced that Dr. Robert Gallo had discovered the AIDS virus, called Human T-Lymphotropic Virus Type III (HTLV-III). Gallo had previously discovered two other "isolates," HTLV-I and HTLV-II, which were not AIDS-related.

D'Eramo detailed the breakthrough with the same accuracy that characterized his monitoring of the journals, though he described LAV and HTLV-III only as the "probable cause" of AIDS. But Ortleb began mocking the scientist and his discovery in his publisher's column. On June 17, 1985, he titled his first lengthy editorial on the subject "AIDSGATE," declaring that Dr. Gallo was misleading America into the forest of AIDS research, and that his "discovery" of HLTV-III was in fact nothing more than the *re*discovery of the French team's identical virus. The piece was illustrated with an enlarged photo of the microscopic HTLV-III virus, with a graphic of a pig and with a photo of Fidel Castro. The dedicated *Native* reader would understand the Ortleb hieroglyphics: HTLV-III virus actually was the same disease found in pigs, and the virus had gotten out of control sometime after the CIA tried to undermine Castro by spreading it in Cuba.

Ortleb's tone was acerbic, but his ASFV theory continued to draw attention, even from National Public Radio. With the media response came a broader response from the medical community. Gallo was one of the first to call. Ortleb reprinted the conversation as he remembered it in the June 17 piece:

> [Gallo] told me . . . I had made a tremendous mistake, the mistake of my lifetime [in accusing him of fraud] . . . [that] I should "try to be a friend." I told Gallo a few of the basics about African Swine Fever Virus, and he thanked me. He seemed to know nothing about the virus.
>
> Gallo continually told me: "If you'd only read the science, if you only understood the science." I told him I wouldn't be browbeaten by him or his so-called science, even if most of the AIDS researchers in America are afraid of him.
>
> To borrow some of Gallo's own "scientific language," I think we have discovered two isolates: Gallo-I and Gallo-II. . . . Gallo-I is a reasonable scientist, who knows a great deal . . . (but not about African Swine Fever Virus). . . . Gallo-II is a fraudulent, vindictive, arrogant, anti-gay bully.

This was not the last time Gallo would be skewered in the pages of the *Native*. He became a favorite target and was even lampooned in one issue, in Carmen Miranda drag.

Ortleb had a similar skirmish with the New York State Department of Health, which had agreed to pursue the African swine fever theory as a result of his prodding. Since 1983, when the idea of a link between ASFV and AIDS had first appeared, scientists from Belgium, Holland, and Haiti had all done tests to determine if the pig virus was present in those with AIDS. None of those probes had found evidence to support the theory. Now, in 1985, the New York Department of Health came to the same conclusion. Of the ten samples drawn from people with AIDS, all were negative for swine fever but one, which showed "atypical reactivity."

The results hardly silenced Ortleb. The tiny positive response, in fact, encouraged him. "Heretofore, Swine Fever has been almost religiously declared *not* to infect human beings. . . . These findings strongly contradict that assertion." The September 30 piece in the *Native* was headlined "Antibodies to African Swine Fever Virus Found in City's Blood Bank."

Ortleb once again flipped through his overfilled Rolodex and got on the horn. Public health officials in New York state and at the CDC

44 shook their heads in dismay. Most journalists he was talking to, all of whom had heard his spiel before, listened only out of politeness or because of a fascination with Ortleb's obsessiveness. He often lost his patience: "You want gays to die," he screamed at *Newsday*'s B. D. Colen when the reporter, who had steadfastly been covering AIDS, refused to check out an Ortleb tip. Among some scientists, he earned the worst label of all: "a flake." From a high point during the early part of the crisis, Ortleb's credibility had sunk to a new low level. But the *Native* itself continued to be regarded by many gays as their most dependable guide to the crisis.

The Gay Press Comes of Age

The *Native* still delivered the important AIDS news, such as in-depth coverage of treatments. For instance, its January 6, 1986, "Guide to Antivirals and Immune Boosters" pulled together the alphabet soup of drugs that were being used to deal with the disease, including azidothymidine (AZT), which would become the most heralded of the treatments.

Ortleb did not believe that doctors developing these drugs to fight AIDS actually knew what they were battling, but neither did he stifle coverage of the issues. In fact, reading the *Native* could be confusing, what with the dutiful reportage of the AIDS researchers' latest findings sharing space with the publisher's aggressive accusations against those scientists, which sometimes spilled over from his editorial column into Ortleb-bylined articles in the news pages.

But by 1986, gays interested in the latest news about treatments had many other sources than the *Native*. Some major daily newspapers were covering the epidemic carefully, and the gay press, once disregarded as preoccupied with male sex—with pectorals and ass, as one former *Advocate* editor said—had become much more sophisticated. The *Advocate*, for example, assigned experienced journalists to cover the AIDS beat, including Nathan Fain, a widely published writer who later died of the disease. The magazine initiated a regular column, "The Helquist Report," in which reporter Michael Helquist tracked the latest developments in science and treatment. And Cindy Patton, an editor at Boston's politically astute Gay Community News, in 1985 wrote "Sex and Germs," an in-depth critique of how AIDS was viewed by America.

The *Native,* since the early days of Mass's painstakingly careful coverage, had always tried to assign someone literate in science to report on the disease. Even while Ortleb was targeting Gallo, he was also paying Ann Giudici Fettner—coauthor of the first popular book on the epidemic, *The Truth about AIDS*—almost $600 a week to do stories that included a lengthy interview of and in-depth rebuttal by Gallo. The *Native* also covered her expenses for a trip to Africa.

Just as Mass served as a contact for scores of journalists from the mainstream media during the early years, some of the reporters working for the gay press were being called on by traditional daily newspapers to cover aspects of the AIDS crisis. Michael Helquist broke the news about the founding of AMFAR, the American Foundation for AIDS Research, for the *Oakland Tribune,* in 1985. Randy Shilts, who worked in the gay press from the late 1970s and early 1980s before going to work for the *San Francisco Chronicle,* was regarded as one of the best-connected reporters covering the epidemic in America.

Those connections came, in large part, simply from knowing people in the gay community. That's why the gay press broke stories like those on "guerrilla" treatment centers, where people with AIDS were brewing up their own remedies from makeshift supplies not approved by the federal government; and that's how the gay press often came to report on the outcomes of certain drug trials weeks before the traditional media. These journalists did not have to scramble in unknown territory for sources. They almost always knew someone involved in the stories.

By 1986, some reporters in the mainstream media admitted to watching the gay press for tips on the epidemic. Scores of journalists across the country, like Associated Press science editor Paul Raeburn, said they regularly read the *Native* or other gay publications. Gay journalists became more professional during the AIDS crisis. They had to, because reporters for publications like the *Advocate* and the *Native* were now covering the life-and-death story of the decade. Gay journalism grew up, and got noticed.

Fear and Loathing

Ortleb continued to be on the lookout for new theories to undermine the idea that "Gallo's virus" was actually the cause of AIDS. He took up the argument of a New York doctor named Stephen Caiazza, who

46 contended that many cases of AIDS were not caused by the identified viral culprit, but by the "great masquerader," syphilis. The latter disease is considered a major problem in treating AIDS, because it often goes undiagnosed. The general practitioner, with an office in the gay-dominated Village and who is himself gay, was frustrated that he could do so little for his patients diagnosed with AIDS, until he met two West German doctors. They convinced him that they were having success treating the disease as syphilis would normally be treated, with penicillin. The *Native* told Caiazza's tale in a string of cover stories in 1987, the first of which asked "Is Syphilis the Cause?" Ortleb had not completely lost his ability to draw attention from the mainstream media. Kevin Kraus, an assignment editor at WSVN-TV, the NBC affiliate in Miami, was so intrigued by the syphilis-AIDS connection that he sent a crew to New York. They put together a two-part series, "Deadly Error," that aired on the Miami station in the spring of 1988.

Next, Ortleb began to promote Professor Peter Duesberg. In March of 1987, the University of California molecular biologist published an article in the obscure journal *Cancer Research,* outlining why the AIDS virus may not be the cause of AIDS.

For starters, the researcher explained, the virus infects such a small number of cells, it seemed unlikely that it could actually cause such a full-blown disease. And, he pointed out, viruses usually show their effects very quickly; with AIDS, the virus could linger for five to seven or more years before it had any impact. Ortleb, not surprisingly, quickly became a Duesberg champion. Because the scientist had good credentials—though he had not done AIDS research, he at least had done studies on viruses—he got some attention from the mainstream medical community after the appearance of the *Cancer Research* article. Scientists will attest that it is always easier to shoot down an idea than create one on one's own, and the few researchers who will actually talk about Duesberg said he has chosen the easier route. Duesberg did not claim that he knew what causes AIDS, just that traditional molecular biology and viral research do not support the current viral theory. Among the nonscientific press, Ortleb boosted Duesberg's publicity with another phone-calling campaign. In turn, the publicity helped push Duesberg into the pages of *Science* magazine, where he debated Dr. Gallo, among others, in articles that ran on July 29, 1988.

By the spring of 1988 Ortleb pronounced: "The AIDS crisis will be over in six months." As he saw it, the government was realizing exactly what it had wrought: the CDC put the number of Americans infected with the AIDS virus between 1 million and 1.5 million, while Ortleb believed ASFV probably had infected about half the American population, given the rate of U.S. pork consumption. The ailment, Ortleb believed, manifested itself in Chronic Fatigue Immune Dysfunction Syndrome, sometimes diagnosed as Epstein-Barre virus. A much smaller group of Americans were suffering from syphilis that was being misdiagnosed as AIDS, and a tiny percentage just might have AIDS, Ortleb allowed. But the country, and the world, was actually being devastated by ASFV. To rescue the U.S. from destruction, he said, the government would come out with its antidote.

And when the government atrocity was revealed, the *Native* would be more than just a gay newspaper that had dutifully tracked the epidemic from the beginning. It would be a legend, something the Midwestern boy fond of poetry had never dreamed he would be living. On the wall above Ortleb's desk in the *Native*'s grubby New York offices was a small postcard informing the sender that "Columbia University has received the Pulitzer Prize submission" from the *Native*. Did he really believe he might win print journalism's most coveted award? "At least I'll have introduced some more journalists to the *Native*."

"What would convince you that ASFV isn't the cause of AIDS?" Ortleb was asked.

"A bullet in the head," he shot back. Images and the words of the slain gay activist and San Francisco supervisor came to mind. "If a bullet should enter my brain," Harvey Milk had ominously pronounced shortly before he was shot down in the fall of 1978, "let that bullet destroy every closet door." Ortleb, a gay activist in his own right, clearly saw himself in that dramatic and righteous tradition.

There was another image, this one out of the annals of American journalism, that probably fit Ortleb best: the small-town publisher who believes that the hoods in Washington, the experts in the local state agency, and anyone outside his small community—which for Ortleb was New York's gay community—should not be trusted. It was with that distrust that he ran the *New York Native*.

Chapter 3
Frustration
on the wire

"A type of pneumonia found in five men, two of whom died, may be linked to 'some aspect of a homosexual lifestyle,' the national Centers for Disease Control said Friday." That was how the Associated Press (AP) introduced the mainstream media to the impending AIDS epidemic on June 5, 1981. By keeping close track of the reports from the CDC and the medical journals, the wire service set the agenda for early media coverage of the disease. It also beat out its closest competitor, United Press International, by months. But AP's approach impeded it from getting a handle on the real story for years and was one reason many newspaper editors and TV broadcasters who use the wire service did not begin to cover AIDS until well into the epidemic. Despite the professionalism of its reporters and editors, the best-trained journalists at any of the wire services, AP's method of covering the crisis also helped cause the epidemic's most frightening and unnecessary scare.

On the Wires

When AP managing editor Bill Ahearn decides to use the full force of the wire service to cover a story, he can call on 1,600 reporters located in almost every far-flung corner of the United States and the world. A tall, lean man in his mid-forties, he has a controlled frenzy about him, as though he is waiting on the edge of his chair for the next major news story to break. By mid-1981, Ahearn had not yet decided that this outbreak was a big story. Scattered cases of a strange pneumonia among gays in Los Angeles, and then an outbreak of a rare skin cancer in New York, San Francisco, and Los Angeles, were curious developments, certainly, and these conditions deserved to be followed as they were reported in the pages of the CDC's *Morbidity and Mortality Weekly Report* and the medical journals. That's how AP would cover them.

"Homosexual men who fall ill with unusual infections should receive fast, aggressive medical care because they may be victims of a baffling wave of fatal disease that has spread among homosexuals from coast to coast, a doctor says." On December 10, 1981, that dispatch went out to the 6,000 radio and television stations and the 1,500 newspapers in the United States that are members of the Associated Press. Some 180 cases of the illness had been reported since July, and seventy-five people were dead. The source of the story was the *New England Journal of Medicine*. Whether that publication had the inside track on most of the significant medical news was questionable. But publication in the *Journal* seemed to give news the American medical establishment's seal of approval.

In 1971, as a twenty-four-year-old newcomer to AP's Boston bureau, Warren Leary had helped start the tradition of the wire service following the *Journal* closely. Covering science from Boston, one of America's top biomedical centers, was no easy task. The *Journal* was a handy filter to help make sense of the latest medical research. Leary combed through each release of the weekly publication, generating an article about heart research one week, cancer the next.

United Press International, which was tougher competition in the early 1980s before the onset of its financial troubles, recognized that it was losing the battle for medical and science scoops. Soon the UPI correspondent in Boston was also covering the *Journal* every week. Stories that Leary dismissed were showing up on UPI's wire. And AP editors were getting nervous. "It became so competitive," said Leary, "that an executive directive was made in New York: Cover the *New England Journal of Medicine* like a glove." He became an even more careful reader of the somber publication, paying close attention even to the letters section. There some of the latest findings or most provocative research wound up, as well as the insignificant or sometimes frivolous, like the "frisbee finger" letter. With tongue in cheek, a West Coast doctor had described the ailment: an irritated digit common in aficionados of the plastic saucer. Leary's equally tongue-in-cheek story generated national attention. And at UPI, so the rumor went, reporters were ordered to keep an even closer tab on the *Journal*'s letter section.

As America turned increasingly health conscious during the late 1970s, the competition to put out science and medicine news increased. In Chicago, where the *Journal of the American Medical Association* (*JAMA*) is published, AP and UPI reporters were now scrambling to cover its releases. Consequently, the *New England Journal, JAMA,*

and the CDC's own publication came to define how AP covered the
growing AIDS crisis.

The Twenty-four Hour Deadline

For the modern reporter, who is pushed to go beyond the who, what,
where, and when of traditional journalism and into the why and how
of it all, the details of AP's December 10, 1981, story should have
spurred other stories. The number of cases were increasing hundreds-
fold each month, and the disease had a 40 percent mortality rate.
Didn't this suggest a mushrooming epidemic? Why were there so few
clues to this disease? And how were the 105 people known to be suffering from the malady—and their families and friends and lovers—
dealing with this outbreak? Those were all obvious questions, but
Associated Press was not asking them. That failure can be blamed
partly on the wire service reporters' extremely tight time constraints.
And they tend to cover a wider range of news than the average newspaper reporter. Young journalists learn to write fast and accurately
under this kind of pressure. That is why many papers consider a stint
at AP to be excellent training.

AP is a twenty-four-hour business, serving media outlets throughout the world. Along with its 7,500 American members, AP is found
in 10,000 other newspapers, magazines, and broadcast stations abroad.
UPI has only 2,500 subscribers, and the number is falling as it battles
insolvency. Reuters, the British wire service, has been gradually increasing the number of its U.S. bureaus and is popular on Wall Street,
where companies use it to track foreign markets. It is also becoming a
foreign news source for American newspapers. But the biggest challenge to AP and UPI are the "supplementals," the news and feature
services that sell to newspapers articles that have run in the *New York
Times, Washington Post,* and *Los Angeles Times* as well as in a score of
other newspapers.

AP is a success despite the competition because its reporters, editors, and photographers are seemingly everywhere delivering the
breaking news. From headquarters in New York, a skeleton staff of
journalists sifts the hundreds of stories and millions of words that
pour through the system daily and determine which stories will make
it on the "A" wire, the national wire that goes out to all members.

Newspaper editors and TV producers choose from the huge range of AP offerings. A wire service article can fill a tiny news hole or provide the only coverage an outlet might have of a breaking national or international story.

The offices of what is thought to be one of the world's most important news sources are poorly lit and cramped. The carpet is torn in places, and Bill Ahearn's corner office on the third floor does not have much of a view. In the winter, the large newsroom is drafty. The only impressive feature of AP's headquarters is its mid-Manhattan address. The wire service is the journalistic equivalent of the CDC: neither was built for comfort. Until very recently, AP focused almost entirely on covering the hard news from around the world. The wire services traditionally did not have time to ask the why and the how of the breaking stories, and "soft" life-style features didn't have much of a place there. But the role of the Associated Press has been changing along with that of America's newspapers.

As TV has assumed the function of providing Americans with their daily dose of the news, newspapers have been stretching to claim new territory. Increasingly, they are encroaching on the kind of life-style coverage and feature stories that have been the purview of magazines. The *New York Times*'s weekly "Home" section, for example, filled with the latest decorating tips and pictures of fashionable uptown apartments, is an attempt to pull in upscale advertisers that would normally appear in *Better Homes and Gardens* or even the tony *Town and Country*. Such sections are now seen in newspapers across the country. But the changes have not only occurred in the inside sections. Front-page space in the *Times* and other daily newspapers, previously reserved for breaking news, is being shared with lengthy feature stories that have no peg to that day's events. Only a few years ago, those stories would have been relegated to the inside pages, cozying up to the "Home" section. Although newspapers rarely can compete with television in the race to deliver the news quickly, they *can* win in the contest of providing more thorough life-style stories, as well as more analysis and features that have little to do with the midmorning train wreck or the president's afternoon press conference. That's how newspapers like the *New York Times* have transformed American journalism.

As newspapers change, as they slow down the news-gathering pace, so do the wire services. AP, UPI, and Reuters serve the newspapers, which are demanding more detail and accuracy. The wire services are also getting into areas once reserved for magazines and only recently found in newspapers: splashy graphics, figures and graphs and side-bars. Even the feature article is now a more important product of the Associated Press.

These factors helped to slow down AP's pace. And there was one other important influence: the decline of UPI. The also-ran wire service has struggled to survive for most of its eighty-one-year history. It has not run in the black since the early 1960s, but in the recession of the early 1980s UPI was faced with the worst economic trouble it had ever encountered: revenues dropped off drastically while costs continued to rise. The staff was cut back sharply, and well-paid, ten-year veterans were being replaced with recent college graduates. At a job where spirit and endurance are requisites, youth is usually no detriment. But UPI's pool of experience was being drained. Without an aggressive competitor, AP's scrappiness flagged.

That should have provided the perfect opportunity for the Associated Press to do more in-depth coverage of the incipient epidemic. But AP was not covering the crisis from San Francisco or Los Angeles or New York, where the largest number of cases were. Until October of 1982, AP stories were filed from the CDC in Atlanta, from Boston, from Washington D.C., even from Daytona Beach, Florida, where an American Cancer Society conference had broached the topic of Kaposi's sarcoma. The Associated Press was watching the tragedy unfold from the pages of the medical journals, the *Morbidity and Mortality Weekly Report,* and from the conference halls at science conventions. AP reporters were talking to the doctors, not to their patients who had the disease. As of late 1982, correspondent Warren Leary, who was filing most of AP's AIDS-related stories, had yet to meet a person with the disease.

Now You Read It, Now You Don't

What AP covers is decided largely by the reporters in the field, and none of those journalists were pushing the story of an emerging epidemic, according to Managing Editor Ahearn. No one at AP, it seemed, had yet been touched by the crisis. The lack of personal connection to the story became obvious in early 1982. In the first six months of the epidemic, after 180 people were stricken, AP had run five stories on the subject. That was a paltry total, to be sure, but by far the most written about the disease by any mainstream news organization. But then, suddenly, the coverage disappeared. What happened? The CDC's *MMWR* introduced no new data, and the journals, for the most part, released few new articles. Relying on those sources for new developments, AP had nothing to write about. At the wire service Ahearn can, theoretically, assign almost every member of his staff to any story. AIDS was no different. Everyone could cover it. But there was no single person thinking about exactly what that coverage should be. AP, which long has served as an agenda-setter for newspapers and broadcast outlets, went dark on the epidemic. So did the rest of the media, for the most part.

There were notable exceptions. Don Drake at the *Philadelphia Inquirer* and Long Island *Newsday*'s B. D. Colen, both well-respected science writers, independently began pursuing the story of the epidemic. For Drake and Colen, the crisis became something of a beat. But neither paper has the power or influence to set the national news agenda. As impressive as their work was, it mostly went ignored by the bigger media players.

Finally, on March 31, 1982, after three months of silence on AIDS, AP returned to the story. "Doctors alerted to unusually high incidences of some cancers among homosexuals have found outbreaks of two additional types of tumors among homosexuals in San Francisco," Warren Leary reported. The piece represented both the worst and the best of the wire service's approach to the news. Despite the fact that the crisis was unfolding in San Francisco, the news was coming from the mouth of a physician at a medical conference in Florida. However, typical of the AP and Warren Leary, the story was as thorough as that written by almost any newspaper reporter who generally would have more time to file the report.

"[M]any homosexuals are immunologically deficient, and this could make them prone to disease because their resistance is low. . . . Many homosexuals have a large number of sexual partners and this transient intimacy could be a factor in spreading around many infections," Leary wrote.

"There also are suggestions that recreational drug use may be a factor. . . . Notable among [this drug use] is the sniffing of amyl butyl nitrate, a practice which causes a temporary euphoric effect." AP prose was often less-than-compelling. But much of this information was new, and nowhere outside the gay press had it been pulled together in one article.

The average reader might notice the monotonous use of "homosexual" as a noun: AP management refused to allow reporters to employ the word "gay" as a substitute. "*Gay* rights" was acceptable, according to Managing Editor Ahearn, because readers would not be confused about the term in that context, but "gays protested" might disconcert readers. More likely, AP was less worried about confusing readers than offending the more conservative ones. Nonetheless, in 1988 Ahearn insisted that journalists had yet to reach a consensus about whether "gay" had become current enough usage among Americans to use synonymously with "homosexual," even though the *New York Times* and hundreds of other daily newspapers already had made that determination. The rigid language is part of the overall conservative approach to the news at AP.

By contrast, when UPI finally began covering the AIDS story consistently, in late 1982, it had no qualms about reporting the news from a gay leaders' conference: "The issue of a genetic predisposition [for AIDS] among homosexuals" has been raised, UPI reported on August 14, 1982. "But the truth is we really don't know," said Dr. James Wheeler, a Southwestern Medical School tumor specialist. "Why, for instance, didn't this surface among gays in the days of Michelangelo or Oscar Wilde?"

UPI's less conservative approach was also less conscientious. For example, on September 15, 1982, UPI science writer Jan Ziegler called the crisis the "Gay Plague," an inflammatory term that was also misleading, since the disease was known to be striking hemophiliacs, Haitians, and intravenous drug users as well. When "Gay Plague" finally grew out of fashion at UPI in late 1982, the wire service adopted other attention-grabbing monikers to describe the epidemic, such as "the nation's latest medical mystery." Making the disease as spooky as possible helped make AIDS a national issue, but it also fed on Americans' fears and did little to inform.

UPI, poorly staffed and suffering a chronic morale problem, was not only often late with the news; more often than AP, it got it wrong. "AID[S], a catch-all term for a mysterious medical condition virtually unheard of five years ago," was the way UPI described the epidemic on August 14, 1982. Of course, AIDS hadn't been heard of at all in 1977. And UPI said the CDC's study of the epidemic started in San Francisco. In fact, the first reports came from Los Angeles and New York.

AP was more circumspect. Ahearn dismissed any suggestion that he was uncomfortable seeing sexual matters discussed in an explicit way in the AP files. Yet during an interview for this book conducted in his office in 1988, he cut the conversation short when other editors began to debate how to cover the subject. However, Ahearn and his New York editors eventually did include straightforward language in AP copy when the medical news focused on taboo subjects like anal sex: "[A UCLA] study of 89 gay men is the first to show that those who practice 'receptive anal intercourse' are more likely than others to have immune system antibodies" to diseases common to AIDS victims, the wire service reported on April 5, 1984. AP went on to say that the findings "raise more questions about whether injury to the rectum might allow whatever causes AIDS to enter the bloodstream."

Sexual terms that might offend a "family" newspaper using the AP service had been strictly avoided in the wire service's AIDS reporting. But in mid-1984 and early 1985, "anal sex," "oral sex," and a closetful of other provocative terms finally began to show up in AP stories, a good two years after AIDS experts had begun to suspect that sex, and especially anal sex, was a likely way to spread AIDS. As usual, AP broke the news only after it appeared in a major medical publication, *JAMA*. Even with AP's lead, and *JAMA*'s seal of medical approval, UPI hung back. It did not mention anal sex as a means of transmitting the disease for another year and a half, not until December 3, 1985. Editors there could not remember why they had lagged so far behind. It was probably due less to modesty than to the wire service being beleaguered by staffing shortages and simply missing the story.

In the first year and a half of the epidemic, neither AP nor UPI had a sterling record of AIDS coverage. Associated Press was consistently accurate and technically complete, but its news decisions were still pegged to the journal releases. No one at the wire service was scrambling for feature stories. UPI was no more aggressive. By the end of 1982, with the tally of AIDS cases rising to nearly eight hundred, UPI had written a total of ten stories; AP had filed nineteen.

Small and medium-sized newspapers, most without full-time science or medical writers on staff, relied almost entirely on the wire service files. The scant reports that came through were often dismissed by the local editor as irrelevant to a small-town audience or middle-American readership. In late 1982 AIDS, when considered in the media at all, was thought of as a San Francisco and New York problem.

Even major newspapers, which sometimes had staffs covering science
and medicine exclusively, were depending on AP for their coverage
of AIDS.

That was the same attitude the networks seemed to bring to reporting on the epidemic. All the major news shows keep an eye on the
wire services, especially AP, to make sure no earthshaking event passes
them by. If a reporter cannot be dispatched to the scene quickly
enough, or if the news item isn't judged important enough to be covered independently, the anchor will sometimes "rip and read" the
stories almost directly from the wire. Often, these stories are taken
out of context by the TV news writers, producer, or anchor, and cause
minor misunderstandings to balloon into major blunders. A particularly absurd example is ABC anchor David Brinkley's dangerous mis-
reading of an AIDS transmission story in 1983, in which he claimed
that "heterosexual contact" was spreading the disease.

Until late 1982, there was little "ripping and reading" of AIDS
coverage, and even less original reporting. The December 10, 1982,
MMWR would change that. "A baffling killer disease that had been
thought to afflict mainly homosexuals and drug users now has shown
up in 20 children," the AP file read, with an uncustomary flourish of
language. All the networks but NBC followed up with the same scary
tone. The national shudder of fear these stories generated was but a
precursor to a larger event in May of 1983.

Spreading the Fear

"The mysterious and deadly AIDS disease may be transmitted by routine close contact in a family household," UPI reported on May 5. The
study in *JAMA* was bound to get close attention by the wire services. It
had all the signs of an accurate report, which meant journalists could
save some time by not checking the story with alternate sources. And
it *was* a shocking study. Dr. James Oleske, a New Jersey pediatrician,
one of the first doctors to diagnose AIDS in children in 1982, now
thought he was seeing the epidemic take a horrible twist. Watching
infants drown in opportunistic infections was horrendous enough,
but after monitoring the families of the children, the doctor concluded: "sexual contact, drug abuse or exposure to blood products is
not necessary for disease transmission."

Initially, AP hesitated to echo the *JAMA* report that with the new information in hand "the scope of the syndrome may be enormous." Instead, the wire service repeated the specific findings: "A study shows that children may have picked up the deadly immune disease AIDS from "routine close contact." But the next day, May 6, AP let loose:

"A study showing children may catch the deadly immune deficiency disease AIDS from their families could mean the general population is at greater risk," the lead paragraph asserted. No editor remembered why AP took that tack, but clearly the one wire service that usually led the rest was following this time. The other national media were swept along. The threat to the general population was the focus of the reports on the TV network news and in papers across the country. The stories had Americans asking exactly what was "routine household contact"? Sharing plates? Bathrooms? Hugs? And if it was so easy to catch in a household, how difficult could it be to get the disease in a steamy factory or on a crowded bus?

The concerns were real, but it turned out the news was not. It was true the babies had AIDS, and that they lived in homes with high-risk adults—intravenous (i.v.) drug users, for the most part. But there was a much more likely explanation of how these children had come to be infected: in their mothers' wombs. And there were pediatricians well-known for their work with AIDS babies who were eager to set journalists straight on this issue. Apparently, no one from a major media outlet bothered to ask them.

In the rush to get the story, the media forgot to get it right. Mistakes that happen in the scramble to report what appears at first blush to be big news tend to get amplified before they are corrected, if they ever get corrected. UPI's hyped presentation of the "casual contact" story forced AP to follow suit with one just as bombastic. Once these stories went out over the wire, and caught the attention of the networks, there was little chance that broadcasters were going to waste time trying to corroborate Dr. Oleske's findings. Hadn't that been done by the wires already? Even the careful and conservative *New York Times* took AP at its word: "Mere Contact May Spread AIDS" was the headline of the story run in the paper, until medical writer Dr. Lawrence Altman complained, and the headline was changed in the final edition. The epidemic rolled on, and the "casual contact" theory was discarded. Neither AP nor UPI followed up with a correction.

This story marked the first time a media firestorm erupted around

AIDS news. Newspaper and TV stations that had ignored the epidemic before suddenly took notice when word came over the AP wires that the disease might be spreading easily. That blast of interest died down quickly. Although Associated Press continued filing medical and science stories on AIDS, few media outlets used much of the material when the news had to do with gays or i.v. drug users, even when it was provocative. "Patient Zero," for instance, the man Randy Shilts made famous in his 1987 book *And the Band Played On,* was first written about in the major media by the Associated Press, on March 22, 1984. "Forty cases of acquired immune deficiency syndrome in 10 cities have been traced through a chain of sexual contacts to a homosexual man who may have been a carrier of the disease, spreading it across the country without knowing he had it," the wire service reported. The news that spurred sales of Shilts's AIDS book three years later appeared in only a handful of major papers across the country in 1984. Nowhere did it get prominent play back then, even though almost 4,000 Americans had been diagnosed with the disease.

The way the Associated Press's "close contact" and "Patient Zero" stories were featured in newspapers and on TV set the pattern for American media's response to this epidemic. As long as AIDS seemed to be confined to fringe groups like gays, i.v. drug users, and Haitians, it was simply a medical curiosity. The closer the threat of AIDS seemed to move toward the lives of the "average American"—that is, the average newsperson—the bigger the story became. Coverage of the epidemic illustrated the notion of journalist as surrogate for the reader or viewer: what the reporter found to be interesting or crucial or threatening was necessarily what the audience would find most vital. And what happens when the journalist misjudges what is important, or what is "news"? Crises can quickly become tragedies.

Chapter 4
Sex, death, and
Good Old Gray

One fall day in 1982, the talk in the newsroom was that Abe Rosenthal wanted to call a special meeting of his editors. That was one of the most powerful acts the very powerful executive editor of the *New York Times* could do. When he assembled his troops in his office, he was calling to order one of the most influential news machines in the world. But this meeting had little to do with newsmaking. The subject was personalities and people—gay people, specifically.

Rosenthal, sixty-one, was regarded as insecure and somewhat paranoiac. He started at the paper during his senior year of college in 1944, when he served as the correspondent for City College of New York. His competition was the other student correspondent from the Ivy League Columbia. He rose up the ladder quickly at the *Times*, but always seemed suspicious of those he had passed on the climb. Rosenthal did not take criticism lightly. And he had recently been stung badly in the pages of *Newsweek* for using his position to push for coverage of his friends. The article that prompted the *Newsweek* inquiry was a 6,500-word essay, extraordinarily lengthy for the *Times,* by media writer John Corry defending novelist Jerzy Kosinski. The Polish writer had been accused by the *Village Voice* of not being the sole author of works like his widely aclaimed *The Painted Bird*. Kosinski was a good friend of Rosenthal. The *Newsweek* piece, built on several anonymous sources inside the *Times,* was itself written by a former *Times* staffer who happened to be gay. So, the story went, Rosenthal said he wanted to find out which homosexuals at the *Times* had cooperated for the *Newsweek* critique.

Rosenthal denies he ever called such a meeting. No senior editor would say that he remembered such an event. Sources said one of the assembled editors convinced Rosenthal that from a legal standpoint it would be risky to confront the gay journalists, and the executive editor eventually dropped the idea. Whether the scenario was true or not, the tale swept through the *Times* and reinforced the idea that Rosenthal did not like gays.

In fact, what Abe Rosenthal *did* that fall day mattered less than what *Times* staffers believed he *thought*. At an institution where a negative comment tossed off at the daily 5:00 p.m. news meeting might be construed as an edict from the editor, perceived homosexual bias could not help but have an effect on how an epidemic largely affecting gays was covered. Successful reporters work to keep their editors happy, said one *Times* reporter. That is true at any well-run newspaper. But at the *Times,* which employs some of the most ambitious journalists in America, "almost everyone is out to get the story that's going to advance his career," said a current staffer. That is the story that could wind up on the front page, or the series given special play. Under Rosenthal, according to a number of top editors and reporters, homosexuals and the "Gay Plague" stood a poor chance of making it on the front page, or almost anywhere else in the *Times.*

"I've had people come to me and say 'I'd like to propose something with regard to AIDS or homosexuals,'" said Max Frankel, who became executive editor in 1986 when Rosenthal retired, "'and I no longer feel that it will reflect poorly on me.' The dark intimations were that if reporters [during Rosenthal's tenure] got to be known as excessively interested in homosexuals or were themselves thought to be homosexuals, something would happen to them."

"I'm sure that was true in some cases," Frankel added, "and not true in others."

Rosenthal defended himself by claiming he once had worked hard to hire an openly gay journalist. "I liked him very much," said Rosenthal, remembering the editor he interviewed almost two decades earlier for a job on his metro desk. Back then, all *Times* reporters had to take a psychological exam along with the required physical. And so, after Rosenthal pushed the paperwork through, the man went upstairs to see the staff doctor. Shortly afterward, Rosenthal said, the doctor bounded down the stairs and into his office. "We can't hire this man," the physician exclaimed, "he's a homosexual." Rosenthal said he knew that. "But don't you know that homosexuals are susceptible to homosexual rage?" the doctor asked. Rosenthal lost that battle.

In other cases, however, gay reporters have claimed that Rosenthal hardly supported them. When he found out they were gay, some said, their upwardly mobile careers at the *Times* seemed suddenly to slow down. A correspondent, for example, alleged he was called back from his foreign post when Rosenthal discovered he was gay. Others said the correspondent was not performing well abroad. Nonetheless, the rumors of Rosenthal's homophobia, seemingly substantiated by reports of his tossing off "faggot" and "queer" in some editorial meetings, in turn helped keep the epidemic from being reported in the *Times*. This was not the only factor, but combined with some of the paper's other characteristics it ensured that the story was virtually ignored for years by what is arguably America's journal of record.

Rumor- Rosenthal had homophobia

The Doctor on the Disease

Lawrence Altman is one of the best-educated science reporters in the nation: Harvard undergraduate, Tufts Medical School, a fellowship in epidemiology at the Centers for Disease Control, residency at the University of Washington. Well-qualified and well-connected, he provided comprehensive reporting of the 1976 Legionnaire's disease outbreak in Philadelphia, reporting which has been cited as one reason the culprit bacterium was found so quickly. Scientists working on the case knew they were under the severe scrutiny of the *Times*, which meant they had the attention of America's media establishment. Eighteen cases of Legionnaire's disease in a Philadelphia hotel resulted in a media blitz by the *Times*. By the end of the first week of the epidemic, the paper ran thirteen articles on the crisis, three of them on the front page; an even larger number of cases of Kaposi's sarcoma occurring, bizarrely, in healthy homosexual men, spurred but one article by Altman on July 3, 1981.

"Rare Cancer Seen in 41 Homosexuals," the headline read over the column-length article on page twenty of the newspaper's first section. Why was the story so obscured, compared with the Legionnaire's coverage? In part it had to do with the way the two crises developed: Legionnaire's exploded dramatically in one location in one city, whereas cases of Kaposi's were scattered in a handful of cities, from New York to California. Nonetheless, Altman the epidemiologist-cum-reporter should have recognized how newsworthy this Kaposi's outbreak might be. Instead, working off of the CDC's *Morbidity and Mortality Weekly Report*, a journal he had helped write during his days at the agency more than a decade earlier, Altman stretched to downplay the spread of Kaposi's sarcoma: "The cause of the outbreak is unknown," he wrote, "and there is as yet no evidence of contagion." Then he struck up a theme that would be repeated throughout his reportage: "The sudden appearance of the cancer . . . has prompted a medical investigation that experts say could have as much scientific as public health importance because of what it may teach about determining the causes of more common types of cancer." The forty-four-year-old reporter had the drive and dispassion of a trained epidemiologist. He had been attracted to the CDC for much the same reason that he was lured from medicine by journalism: it was the hunt for information, for clues, whether the conundrum be reporting on a new outbreak of disease or tracking research into new lifesaving devices. He tried to make sense of the senseless death he witnessed, in the same way many doctors and scientists do. He distanced himself from the person struck by the malady and asked "what can this tragedy teach us about illness?" That is a powerful and useful tool, and a limiting one. It helps clarify the science behind a medical story but badly distorts the story itself. Because medical news is essentially about the struggle to save individual lives, it should be some of the most person-centered journalism the media produces.

Altman had a great deal of freedom to chase the leads he found most interesting. He is a hardworking, intense, and self-assured journalist who was not likely to be very concerned about Abe Rosenthal's alleged biases. Altman joined the newspaper in 1969, making it the only American newspaper at the time to have a science reporter with a medical degree. In the subsequent years he built a reputation for being dependable and *accurate,* a *New York Times* legacy that was the top editor's mandate ever since Tennessee publisher Adolph Ochs bought what was then, in 1896, a provincial paper with 9,000 paid subscriptions. Altman fit into a long tradition of science coverage at the *Times,* established in the early part of the century by men like Carr Van Anda, who had sought out Albert Einstein and became the first newspaper editor to publish his work.

That was the kind of investigation and reporting that Altman had done in the past. He took a hands-on approach to his beat, often going on patient rounds with doctors so he could keep abreast of the latest medical trends. During one such visit to Bellevue Hospital in the early spring of 1981, he came upon cases of Kaposi's sarcoma among young men. He also knew Dr. Alvin Friedman-Kien, the New York University researcher who was gathering information on the strange disease affecting gays. Instead of filing a story, Altman was suddenly

called away to monitor President Reagan's health after the assassination attempt in March. Six weeks later he was just as suddenly dispatched to Rome to report on the physical devastation that another
assassin's bullet caused Pope John Paul II. While in Italy, Altman
tripped over a chain-link fence and broke both his elbows, making it
almost impossible for him to write. Finally, with help he put together
the article on Kaposi's on July 3.

Events seemed to be conspiring to keep Altman from reporting on
the epidemic, but the crisis itself was not intriguing him as other
medical mysteries had. After that first story, the spread of the disease
would warrant only two very brief mentions in the newspaper throughout the rest of 1981. "KS was an oddity," said Altman. "What were we
supposed to cover? The body count?" Tens of thousands of Americans die each year of heart disease. Thousands are killed by tuberculosis and influenza, which today mostly affect the poor. Yet those
maladies are rarely covered except when major advances in treating
the diseases have been made. That was the case with hepatitis B, another threat to gays, which got its biggest boost of publicity when a
vaccine was developed.

The Kaposi's epidemic, however, was worth covering just because it
was new. At the very least, the *Times* might have done the same reporting as the Associated Press. That is, Altman could have stayed on top
of research as it appeared in the *MMWR* and the medical journals.
But Altman, unlike his colleagues at AP, has never been tied to those
publications. He has a confidence in his medical knowledge that few
other reporters can match, and usually his judgments are correct.
Consequently, his opinions about what is medical news are rarely
framed by what the medical establishment is calling newsworthy. What
intrigued Altman most in the early 1980s was the progress being
made on the artificial heart. He thought development of that device
would prove to be the story of the decade.

Turf Battles, but Who's Fighting?

In the army of journalists that make up the *Times,* Altman was hardly
the only reporter who could cover the AIDS story. The newsroom on
the third floor is home to almost three hundred reporters, scores of
editors, and a handful of department editors who oversee the product

of the different *Times* staffs. There was the world-famous foreign desk, one of the most desired domains in American journalism. And the prestigious national desk. It had broken such major stories as the Pentagon Papers, Secretary of Defense Robert McNamara's secret history of how the United States had gotten increasingly entrenched in the Vietnam war. Although the *Washington Post* broke the first Watergate stories, the *Times* national desk caught up fast and pushed the investigation forward. The section covers more than politics. Because it oversees the domestic bureaus as well, the national desk files stories on social and even scientific developments from throughout the United States. In the early 1980s, it was the first major publication to investigate intensively the feasibility of Star Wars, President Reagan's space-based defense system.

And then there was the metropolitan desk. In 1963 Rosenthal came back to New York from abroad to take over and turn around this hitherto lackluster part of the paper. He succeeded in bringing a new respect to the metro desk, pushing the staff to investigate New York City as he had New Delhi, Warsaw, and Tokyo. In the early 1960s Rosenthal seemed to be open to all manner of stories that previously never would have been considered for the Gray Lady, as the *Times* has been dubbed. For instance, a few months after he took over, the *Times* ran a front-page feature on gays: "Growth of Overt Homosexuality in City Provokes Wide Concern" appeared on December 17, 1963. It was hardly a progressive look at gays by today's standards. The article framed the issue in terms of "the problem of homosexuality" and described gay bars as "notorious congregating points for homosexuals and degenerates." A synonym for "homosexual" was "deviate." The police commissioner was quoted frequently: "The police jurisdiction in this area is limited. But when persons of this type become a source of public scandal, or violate the laws, or place themselves in a position where they become the victims of crime, they do come within our jurisdiction." But the extensive piece also quoted a half dozen gays, giving some insight into their struggle for basic rights. The article covered the issue of homosexuality in America as no other newspaper had. Seven years later, a year after the riots of Stonewall, the *Times* ran another front-page feature, "Homosexuals in Revolt," chronicling the emerging gay movement.

But in 1981 and 1982, neither the metro nor national desk editors remembered any reporter asking to take another look at the gay community, in New York or beyond, as it was trying to cope with the onslaught of the disease. David Jones, who oversaw the national desk, had been reading the impressively thorough coverage of the epidemic by Don Drake in the *Philadelphia Inquirer*. No other medical reporter in America, not even Altman, had more freedom than Drake. He generally spent several months and as long as a year on a story of his choosing, and then generated a series of articles or one major feature. The fifty-three-year-old family man had thought little about the epidemic striking gays until early 1982, when an *Inquirer* reporter asked him a question regarding the disease that he could not answer. Drake began looking into the epidemic, and the subject fascinated him from the start.

At the *Times,* Jones wondered whether the topic really did warrant the kind of space that the *Inquirer* was giving it. New York had the highest percentage of cases of the disease anywhere in the United States, and Philadelphia had only a tiny fraction of New York's total. "Were we off-base, or were they?" asked Jones. Almost no one at the *Times* paid attention to Long Island's *Newsday* or the *San Francisco Chronicle*, which had begun to cover the crisis. Even the *Los Angeles Times* was covering the disease, though only irregularly. Downtown at the *Wall Street Journal*, reporter Jerry Bishop's stories on the epidemic were being turned down repeatedly, on the grounds that the disease was affecting such a small group of people. More important, the *Times*'s biggest national print news competitor, the *Washington Post,* was not doing much more on the epidemic.

Even though the largest number of New York cases were in the city itself, metro editor Peter Millones, with almost a hundred reporters at his disposal, was not moved by the story. The paper overlooked the birth of a major social service organization, the Gay Men's Health Crisis, established not only by muckrakers like playwright Larry Kramer but also by respected business people like insurance executive Paul Popham. And the *Times* seemed to be oblivious to the fear that was gripping much of Manhattan. Millones said he assumed the science desk, floors away from the main newsroom, was handling coverage of the disease. Science editor Richard Flast, who has a Pulitzer prize-winning staff of ten to call on, said he believed Altman was covering the story adequately. "He was the one who was carrying the ball," said Flast.

Perhaps the *Times*'s news staff simply believed the epidemic was being covered, and that it would be impolite, or impolitic, to step on turf supposedly claimed by Altman. But several *Times* editors echoed

Frankel's thoughts on the subject to explain why their reporters, or they themselves, were not proposing more angles on the story. If Rosenthal was not outright hostile to the idea of covering a "Gay Plague," he was certainly uninterested. By the end of 1982, with 881 confirmed cases and another 200 suspected nationwide—more than a third of that U.S. total was in New York—the *Times* had run only five stories on the disease. Only one of those, written by Altman, provided an in-depth look at the crisis. In a piece dated May 11, 1982, "New Homosexual Disorder Worries Health Officials," he included reporting on a congressional hearing in which a National Cancer Institute spokesman said the disease was "of concern to all Americans." It was one of the most important warnings the government had delivered to date, but it was placed in the "Science" section of the paper, far from the front page. In 1982, the scourge of gays never made it to page A1, although that same year the *Times* ran four front-page articles on the Tylenol scare. The newspaper ran more than fifty articles on the three-month ordeal that left seven people dead.

What runs on the front page is decided every evening at the paper's 5:00 p.m. news meeting, attended by the editors of the various departments and presided over by the executive editor. Top national and international news will certainly wind up on the front page. But newspapers are increasingly placing more than just the news of the day on that page. The breaking news usually has been reported at least in part by the electronic media before it appears in the papers. An exclusive on a less timely piece, however, will set a paper apart from the rest and make it a more compelling read. Thus feature stories increasingly appear up front. The New York Times has led the way in this trend. So it is hard to explain why the first two years of the AIDS crisis prompted no front-page story in the *Times* on the epidemic.

The editors who gathered at the last meeting of the day often argued with Rosenthal about his choices for the *Times*'s face. But they did not challenge him on his front-page decisions regarding the disease that, despite its appearance in hemophiliacs, Haitians, and drug addicts, was still being labeled "gay-related immunodeficiency" by the *Times* in 1982. Editors were not pressuring Rosenthal, many of them said, in part because their subeditors and reporters offered them no stories on the epidemic. "The Rosenthal sensibility," as one editor called it, was so seemingly well understood that no one at the *Times* thought a story on the social or cultural impact of the epidemic would get by the chief. So it was not proposed. By the end of 1982, the paper had established a pattern of looking at the disease in much the same way it viewed calamities in obscure foreign countries. Occasional flare-ups such as a coup in Guinea-Bissau during the early 1980s would be covered, but for the most part that tiny nation's turmoil, like the gay epidemic, seemed just another instance of faraway and easily forgotten chaos.

On March 28, 1983, a deadly virus claiming lives did make it on the front page of the *Times*. The horror was unfolding in a small town in Austria, where the Associated Press was covering the carnage. The newspaper ran the wire service's compelling story about the thirty victims who had already died. Who were these famous foreigners who warranted such play in America's paper of record? The dancing Lipizzaner stallions, a Vienna tourist attraction.

Altman continued to file an occasional story on AIDS. His reporting was not extensive, though he had an insider's view on the petty squabbling that was breaking out between labs investigating the epidemic, and how that ill will and suspicion were slowing down the research process.

"Scientists involved in the research have been reluctant to discuss their findings, even at scientific meetings, much to the displeasure of some colleagues working on AIDS," he reported on May 1, 1983, in the article "Rare Virus May Have Link with Immunological Illness":

> At a meeting at New York University in March, members of Dr. Gallo's group discussed aspects of their work without disclosing specific data, even when questioned repeatedly by participants. . . .
>
> "People hissed and booed," one participant said.
>
> Dr. Gallo said in an interview that he did not attend and did not release data because the scientific meeting was open to the press and he wanted the data to be published in a scientific journal first. . . . Dr. Essex was willing to discuss the findings . . . but then said he would not discuss them because Dr. Gallo would not.

Altman's incisive look at the turmoil was the best reporting done on the subject. Unfortunately, neither he nor anyone else at the *New York Times* was looking beyond the purely scientific aspect of the disease. As if to articulate just how distanced he and his newspaper were from the personal side of the crisis, many of Altman's articles included his by-now familiar coda, "Medicine may learn from the tragedy."

A Day at the Circus

The fact that the Lipizzaner stallion story was given better coverage in the *Times* than the AIDS epidemic outraged some of the more vocal members of the gay community. In early 1983 playwright Larry Kramer wrote to Rosenthal about it and followed up with other letters directed at *Times* officials throughout the organization, including Max Frankel. He got no response. He knew it was impossible that no one inside the *Times* was being touched by the disease. In a city with an estimated gay population of between six hundred thousand and one million, a good percentage of the paper's reporters and editors either were gay or had friends who were gay and frightened of the epidemic. Kramer himself knew gays on staff and kept pushing them to write about AIDS. In one bold attempt to grab the attention of someone at the *Times,* he sneaked past the guards on duty in the lobby. He made his way to the second floor and tried to search out a popular columnist who wrote about the New York scene. He went to the columnist's desk but couldn't find him. In frustration he lit into the reporter closest at hand, cursing the *Times* for its poor AIDS coverage.

"A lot was going on on the clinical side," said Abe Rosenthal. "I didn't think much was happening on the social side to cover." However, one event in the spring of 1983 was hard to miss.

On March 14, the *Times* reported in its chatty "Day by Day" column that "for the first time in at least five years, all 17,597 seats at a performance of the Ringling Brothers and Barnum & Bailey Circus in Madison Square Garden have been bought by a single group for resale as a benefit." The group was the Gay Men's Health Crisis, and the money-raiser was to aid support services for the five hundred New Yorkers with AIDS. It was the single largest event to date to generate funds to fight the epidemic. Regardless of the cause, the circus to take place on April 30 and headlined by conductor Leonard Bernstein would be news, simply because it drew almost eighteen thousand people together at a charity event. Much smaller fundraisers, from Boy Scout boxcar derby races to banquets of the Daughters of the American Revolution, got covered by the *Times*. What made the circus even more newsworthy, besides its celebrity host, was that it was the first of its size for AIDS.

Almost all of New York's major media followed their news instincts and covered the story: from the local TV stations to Long Island *Newsday,* the *Daily News,* and even the *New York Post,* which had a reputation for being virulently homophobic. The *New York Times* was conspicuously silent on the circus. Kramer, who had helped organize the event and was embittered by the *Times*'s lack of coverage, grew more hostile and shrill about the newspaper. Feeding off his anger, he began writing a play about the early years of the epidemic.

Soon after the circus, in the spring of 1983, a group of gays decided to confront the behemoth *Times* themselves. Virginia Apuzzo, executive director of the National Gay Task Force, New York gay activist David Rothenberg, writer Andrew Humm, and local civil court judge Richard Failla sent a letter to the paper's publisher, Arthur Ochs "Punch" Sulzberger, requesting a meeting. They also delivered a threat of a picket and boycott of the paper. Apuzzo may have had some added influence because she was a political friend of Governor Mario Cuomo. Sulzberger's assistant, Sydney Gruson, whose job included hearing out disgruntled groups representing some segment of the readership, agreed to meet with the four. Gruson listened politely to their complaints, but no promise of action came out of the meeting. Then Humm contacted the *New York Post,* which relishes every chance to tweak the nose of the establishment *Times.* The paper ran a brief of the meeting in its gossipy "Page Six."

Gruson was incensed at the publicity. But shortly afterward, the group, excluding Humm, was invited to meet with Rosenthal. The *Times* publisher, as well as his assistant, are not involved in the day-to-day working of the newsroom, and only rarely is a decision by the executive editor overturned or vetoed by the top office. But when a request comes down from Sulzberger's office, it is usually acted on promptly. Rosenthal hosted a lunch for the trio days later. "We told him the *Times* was missing the story—not just the Circus, but the whole AIDS story," said Apuzzo. "And that the *Times* was missing the news that gays and lesbians were building institutions like the GMHC. . . . It was Gays and AIDS 101." For the executive editor, these stories were new territory. He could be accused of being homophobic, but no one could honestly level the charge that A. M. Rosenthal, as he was known in the business, did not have good news judgment. On a hundred other stories, from White House maneuverings to backstage

Broadway intrigue, the paper was more often than not on top of the
70 news, in large part because Rosenthal demanded it. He began to demand more on AIDS.

Another Voice at the *Times*

Even before Rosenthal recognized AIDS as a news story, articles on
the epidemic did show up in the *Times*, but in the section of the paper
he had no control over: the editorial pages, under the aegis of editor
Max Frankel. "Federal officials seemed to approach the epidemic with
embarrassment," began the April 22 opinion piece by New York physician Kevin M. Cahill. "Almost without exception, public leaders
evaded the epidemic issue, avoiding even the usual expressions of
compassion and concern. The victims' sexual orientation apparently
made involvement risky, and the politicians directed their courage
and energies elsewhere." There is no way to judge what effect strong
words on an opinion page have, but when those words appear in the
New York Times, one of the most influential audiences in America—the
Washington, D.C., elite and the intelligentsia from coast to coast—will
be reading them. Probably even more important, though, is what the
paper asserts in its editorials, also Frankel's purview, which run on the
page opposite the opinion pieces. There, on May 15, 1983, the *Times*
chastised the federal government for its lack of concern about AIDS:

> Assuredly frightening, the disease has caused too much alarm
> among some groups at risk. But it also has caused too little in the
> Federal Government. . . . The Government's Centers for Dis-
> ease Control responded immediately to AIDS. . . . But the Fed-
> eral research agency, the national [sic] Institutes of Health, has
> been less prompt. It has done little to mobilize biomedical re-
> searchers, despite the high theoretical interest of AIDS, and was
> slow to fund research in the field.
>
> To compensate for NIH's inertia, Representative [Henry]
> Waxman has proposed a . . . research fund for AIDS or other
> medical emergencies. The Reagan Administration, with inap-
> propriate apathy, opposes the measure.

Long gone were the days when a press baron like William Randolph
Hearst could use the editorial pages of his influential *New York Journal*

and other papers to push the U.S. government into war. But the *Times'* editorials helped wake the federal government to the public relations problem it was creating.

Dr. Edward Brandt, assistant secretary for health and human services, had been trying to squeeze adequate funds out of the department's various agencies to fight the epidemic. It was obvious to most of those who understood the scope of the problem that the federal government needed more money to do the job, but asking for more funds was a step, or a misstep in the Reagan administration, that Brandt was not willing to take. Instead, he simply announced on May 25, 1983, a heightened concern on the part of the government: AIDS had become the U.S. Public Health Service's "No. 1 health priority." It was the kind of news item perfectly suited for the *Times,* which always reports carefully on officialdom and pays particularly close attention to anything that emanates from Washington, D.C. For the first time, the paper ran a front-page story on the epidemic.

Brandt's announcement had obvious news value in and of itself, something editors across the country including Rosenthal could not ignore, which accounts for at least a part of the upturn in news coverage nationwide during the spring of 1983. But the way the *Times* played the story signaled its national importance. The paper does not set the news agenda for the nation's media by itself. But because of its influence and diverse readership—the paper has twice as many readers in California, for instance, as in parts of New York City, such as the Bronx—its one million weekday circulation has a far greater impact than well-respected newspapers with larger distributions, such as the *Los Angeles Times*. And newspeople watch the papers's coverage closely, because the *New York Times* has a history of a conservative and trustworthy approach to the news. If it is in the *Times,* it is widely regarded as fact. Broadcast executives at all the national news networks—ABC, NBC, CBS, and CNN—said that the paper, especially its front-page news, is required reading. The paper often serves as a guide for their own evening news programs.

Gays, AIDS, and Old Gray

Shortly after his meeting with Apuzzo, Rothenberg, and Failla, Rosenthal called a handful of editors and reporters into his office. He wanted the *Times* to take another look at the gay community, much as it had done in the early 1960s and again in 1970. It was obvious that there were stories there. How was AIDS affecting gays in New York? In the spirit of a paper that considered itself the record of the nation, Rosenthal also wanted the *Times* to find out how AIDS was affecting gays throughout the United States.

On June 16 and 17 he got his answer.

"In neighborhoods throughout the city and across a broad spectrum of New York life, the influence of homosexual men and women is being seen and felt more than ever before," wrote Michael Norman of the metro staff, one of the two reporters assigned to the story. But the AIDS epidemic "has also created anxiety and caution in the homosexual community at large among those who lead a variety of life styles—individuals and couples whose lives are moored by work, home, family and friends." It had been thirteen years since the *Times* looked at the gay community in New York so closely, and it had never looked so honestly.

The next day, national reporter Dudley Clendinen, a Boston correspondent for the *Times* assigned to cover the issue nationally, introduced readers to people like Paul DiAngelo. "[His] adult life has been a quiet reflection of the progressive reach for self-respect and for public acceptance of homosexual freedom." The epidemic "has struck at an ethos still in evolution."

And there was Chuck Morris, from San Francisco:

Three years ago, when he was diagnosed as having AIDS, Mr. Morris was publisher of *The Sentinel,* a newspaper for homosexuals. Now, he says, he has more than 30 active symptoms, has had three brain seizures in six months, is unable to work and is abandoned by friends of years' standing. Twice he has been forced out of his apartments, both times while in the hospital.

The second eviction, he says, took the form of a phone call from one of his roommates, who called to tell Mr. Morris that he would kill him if he moved back. He moved out.

"I was standing on Castro and 18th Street with a little plastic bag with all my possessions that I could grab, and all of a sudden the enormous horror of all this hit me," he says. "At this point I had been working for 25 years, and I felt that the year before I was a reasonably wealthy man. I had my own newspaper, and now here I was, standing on the street, homeless and broke, and I had no idea where I was going to stay. It was the first time

that I realized that this had caused my whole world to crumble
around me."

It was a moving anecdote from a newspaper that had stolidly ignored the mounting deaths in the gay community. Near the end of
the article, Clendinen even dipped into the funding controversy: describing a congressional proposal to put $12 million into research on
AIDS, he wrote, "this is the third time that Congress has moved on its
own to appropriate research money for AIDS. The Reagan Administration has requested none, suggesting instead that money be taken
from other health projects." It was the most prominent press mention
to date of the funding debate in which the CDC and Capitol Hill were
embroiled.

Neither Norman nor Clendinen were gay, but like any good reporters, they brought to the assignment a strong curiosity and a good
eye for detail. They were talented journalists. But they also had other
connections to the story. A mentor of Norman's on the paper happened to be gay; a favorite college professor of his was too. As it
turned out, so was a close relative. Clendinen initially became interested in the story because a physician friend in Boston had treated
one of the first cases in that city, a former football player in his early
twenties who was married. The young man's ordeal was powerful material, and Clendinen was surprised that the *Times* was not covering
stories like this, but only the clinical side of the disease.

"This thing is killing people," he remembered saying to himself,
"and we're still treating it like some foreign war."

Both Norman and Clendinen were aware of the *Times*'s reputation
in the gay community, and they faced some hostility at first. "The re-
sentment was earned," said Clendinen. "But I also told [people being
interviewed] that we were trying, that we had to get on with it."

AIDS increasingly could not be avoided as a news story. By early
1983, the epidemic had reached into almost every segment of the
population, from gay men, hemophiliacs, and i.v. drug users at first to
women and children later. By May of that year, the false alarm that
AIDS was spreading by casual contact, set off by the *Journal of the
American Medical Association* and then sent out by the wire services, had
been picked up by most major media and a majority of the smaller
dailies and radio and TV stations. In the summer and fall of 1983
American media's coverage of the epidemic leaped almost 600 percent over the previous six-month period.

Journalists were finally reacting to the news, in part because Assistant Secretary of Health Edward Brandt had announced that the epidemic was on the national agenda. But as one midwestern editor put it, with the report by AP and UPI on the casual contact story, "now this disease seemed to be creeping toward 'average' Americans." Certainly, most journalists did not know anyone who was affected. For that matter, they couldn't even be sure whether they knew anyone in a risk group: gays in all but a handful of major cities were generally culturally invisible and i.v. drug users lived in neighborhoods that metropolitan newspapers routinely ignored. But if AIDS could strike even children, then at last this thing could be seen as a real threat to people editors and reporters knew, to their audiences.

Not only did the reporting increase, it also changed. Those newspapers and broadcast outlets that were doing their own stories on AIDS—not the majority, but a growing minority—were not simply covering the science leads that AP and UPI were generating; they were filing pieces on the personal tragedy. The *Los Angeles Times*, which had produced the first front-page story in the mainstream media in May of 1982, began running features on the crisis. The *New York Native*, of course, had been doing that from the beginning. National Public Radio, just months into the epidemic, produced a compelling report on how the gay community was being wracked. But among the major print media, *Newsweek* in April of 1983 was the first magazine to do an extensive feature on how AIDS was affecting Americans: not just gays, but hemophiliacs, i.v. drug users, and children. The *New York Times* reporters said they were not heavily influenced by the *Newsweek* story. It is much more likely that the magazine was encouraged to do its follow-up story in August exclusively on gays because of the *Times* series, since *Newsweek* tends to follow major national newspapers rather than lead them.

AIDS demanded that mainstream news organizations deal with formerly taboo subjects like homosexuals. But just as the lack of coverage by the mainstream press in the early years of AIDS reporting distorted America's view of the epidemic—it seemed to be something happening far away, or perhaps in a laboratory, like so much white-mice research—this new focus on gays was also blurring the real picture. Homosexual men made up 71 percent of the cases in New York. Intravenous drug users accounted for the second largest percentage of cases, and Haitians made up a sizable portion, as well. If the former CDC hand Dr. Lawrence Altman had investigated the agency's figures, he would have discovered that blacks and Hispanics were being hit by the disease disproportionately hard. In the two articles that appeared in the *Times* in 1983, each running approximately 3,500 words, the fact that groups other than homosexuals were being affected was mentioned only twice and in passing. Neither the children nor spouses nor lovers of i.v. drug users were mentioned as at risk. The AIDS story had finally made its way from the science section and the back pages of the news, but it was still reported as almost exclusively a gay disease. At the *Times,* covering gays and AIDS had been the assignment Rosenthal handed down. But for journalists across the country, gays were almost always the focus largely because these men were accessible. Unlike i.v. drug users, they did not have to be sought out in unpleasant neighborhoods. And, important especially for TV and radio, they were often articulate and willing to talk. By this point, the gay community had spent two years trying to get the word out about the disease, and many of those with AIDS who were interviewed expressed a desire to publicize what activists like Kramer were calling a "gay holocaust."

These factors made the journalist's job much easier and contributed to defining the disease as a malady spread by certain types of people rather than certain types of behavior. By the spring of 1983, the CDC realized the problems such a misunderstanding might cause. Married men who would not identify themselves as gay, but who nonetheless occasionally participated in anal sex with other men, for instance, might not consider themselves at risk. Yet it was far more probable that they would be the ones to spread the disease into the larger population. Very few journalists, and no one at the *New York Times,* were trying to clear up the potential confusion by using explicit language to describe just how the disease could be spread.

Although Norman and Clendinen portrayed homosexual relationships in sophisticated and unblushing terms, their articles ducked the issue of how these men were becoming infected. "AIDS seems to be spread through male sexual contact" was the way they hinted at anal and oral intercourse and the exotic menu of other sexual practices common in the gay community. Even Altman the clinician was less than forthcoming: "intimate contact between homosexuals" appeared often. At other times, he used even less specific, and more confusing, terminology: "most cases have occurred among homosexual men, in particular those who have had numerous sexual partners, often anonymous partners whose identity remains unknown," he reported on May 11, 1982. Who were these mystery "partners"? Was this disease being spread by a group of wandering fugitives? the casual reader might have asked.

Later that year, after interviewing CDC officials, Altman wrote: "sexual contact with patients with GRID syndrome does not lead directly to the breakdown of the immunological system but simply indicates a certain style of life. 'The number of homosexually active males who share this life style'; [according to the official], 'may be much smaller than the number of homosexual males in the general population.'" What did it all mean? For any reader who was not well versed in the latest AIDS research, the obvious questions arose: Did intimate and sexual contact include kissing, masturbating, caressing? And what "style of life" was the doctor writing about? Was it a promiscuous sex life? Did it include anal sex, oral sex, hugging, kissing? By mid-1982, the CDC had plenty of facts about what behavior was endangering gays and the sex partners of i.v. drug users, hemophiliacs, and others infected with the virus. But the agency was very circumspect about detailing explicit sex acts. The *Times* offered few clues, as well.

"I always felt that people knew what homosexuals did," said Altman's editor, Richard Flast. He admitted he was a bit uninformed. But even as Flast's naïveté faded, as he began reading reports of bathhouse sex in other media, the *Times* did not become much bolder. Katherine Bishop, a national reporter based in San Francisco, remembered covering that city's bathhouse controversy in 1984. She tried to describe the sex guidelines established by the social service organization developed to deal with the epidemic, the San Francisco AIDS Foundation: no oral or anal sex without a condom. But she could not get the straightforward language approved by the copy desk. Instead, she was forced to use the almost amusingly obtuse descripton, "safe sex as defined by the San Francisco AIDS Foundation."

The *Times* also shied away from using the term "gay" in place of "homosexual" when used as anything but part of a proper name, as in Gay Mens Health Crisis, though it could be used as an adjective in a commonly used phrase, like "gay rights." (The institutional phobia of the noun was one of the gripes the activist threesome of Apuzzo, Failla, and Rothenberg had brought to Rosenthal at their spring meeting.) Some inside the *Times* claimed the rule, enshrined in the newspaper's style guide, was established in the mid-1970s, after the *Times* Sunday travel section ran a provocative piece about an ocean-liner trip. "The All-Gay Cruise: Prejudice and Pride," written by a free-lancer, was a funny and revealing look at a freewheeling week-long voyage taken by several hundred gay males and lesbians. Publisher Punch Sulzberger, whose mother was supposedly offended by the bawdy tone of the piece, was allegedly furious. Rosenthal was said to be none too pleased, either. The editor of the Sunday *Times,* at that point Max Frankel, thought to be a challenger of Rosenthal's in the paper's political arena, was harshly reprimanded. "Gay" had to go.

Rosenthal explained the ban differently: "'Gay' was a politicized term," and with its use the *Times* would seem to be politicizing the issue. Nonetheless, a journalistic rule of thumb has been to describe groups of people by the terms they choose to call themselves. In a society that places a high value on individualism and self-determination, it's a reasonable guideline, and the media usually follow it. For example, when vocal "Negroes" shunned that term and chose "blacks" instead, most newspapers eventually complied.

But the change was gradual. "We try to follow the usage of literate America," said Allan M. Siegal, a *Times* editor and one of the architects of the paper's language usage during the 1980s. After Reverend Martin Luther King's death in 1968, Siegal claimed there was a shift in attitude with regard to the term "black" to describe a race of people. By the early 1970s, there was a general consensus, which the *Times* joined.

"People at the *Times,* especially reporters, tend to be more avant-garde," Siegal asserted. "The fact that almost all of us have friends who call themselves 'gay' doesn't mean we should force that term on our readers." How would the *Times* determine when literate America was comfortable with the term "gay"? Cautiously, conservatively, said Siegal. "We'd go out to look at small papers in the South, at *TV Guide,* at other similar publications, to see how they were handling the term. We would try to correct for the fact that we were avant-garde."

Cutting Edge in the Executive Suite

Avant-garde was hardly a state of mind Rosenthal was wrestling with in the executive suite. The gay activists who had visited him in the spring of 1983 had an impact because they played off his news judgment. They did not believe he had much of a desire to be on the cutting edge of culture. Neither had they tried, as Kramer did, to convince the executive editor he had some moral responsibility to cover gays and AIDS. Rosenthal rarely responded to such outside pressure or suggestions of someone meddling in his domain. "I don't have to do it," he was quoted as saying in a 1982 magazine article. "What are they [critics] going to do? Bust me to civilian? You can't do anything to an editor on the *Times*."

The most virulent attack on Rosenthal and AIDS coverage in the *Times* came in April of 1985, when the play Larry Kramer had been working on, *The Normal Heart,* opened at the Public Theater in New York City. The entire production, from its strident dialogue to the set, was designed to shock. The theater walls were plastered with statistics such as the number of AIDS cases in the United States, the tiny sum Mayor Koch had appropriated for the crisis—$75,000 up to 1984, compared with San Francisco Mayor Dianne Feinstein's $16 million. And then there was a detailed description of the coverage the *Times* had given to the epidemic: seven articles in the first nineteen months.

In the melodrama, Ned, the self-righteous hero, shouts at a *New York Times* reporter: "Do you know that when Hitler's Final Solution to eliminate the Polish Jews was first mentioned in *The Times*, it was on page twenty-eight." The first story on AIDS, as a wall poster in the theater informed the audience, ran on page twenty.

The *New York Times* could hardly ignore the play. In his review, theater critic Frank Rich called it "a fiercely polemical drama about the private and public fallout of the AIDS epidemic. [T]he playwright starts off angry, soon gets furious and then skyrockets into sheer rage." All in all, a fair description.

In addition to Rich, the *Times* sent two representatives from the paper's corporate side to view the play. Their rebuttal ran just below the review: "charges in 'The Normal Heart' that *The Times* suppressed news about AIDS are untrue. As soon as *The Times* was informed about the existence of the disease, a member of the science staff was assigned to cover the story." It was the paper's responsibility to review the play. It took the prerogative to "set the record straight" in the same news space the same day. That was a luxury afforded no other institution or individual criticized in the paper's pages. Apparently, it was reserved for Punch Sulzberger and Abe Rosenthal.

No one inside the paper was openly faulting Rosenthal on the *Times*'s AIDS coverage, though it was increasingly frustrating to those reporters and some editors who thought the AIDS story should be getting more prominent play. In the late winter of 1986, correspondent Jon Nordheimer, then based in Miami, proposed a story on how AIDS was affecting heterosexuals, and whether bisexuals were acting as a conduit between the infected population and those not yet infected.

He got the OK from editor David Jones and began his odyssey across the country: "In California, in New York, and to a lesser degree in urban centers all around the nation," he wrote, "growing numbers of heterosexual men and women are asking questions that seem destined to dominate the dialogue between the sexes for the rest of the decade. "Will you infect me with an incurable disease if we have sex? How can I protect myself?"

It was one of the first articles on the subject. Heterosexuals, bisexuals, and AIDS became a big story the following year, covered by almost every major metropolitan daily and TV stations nationwide. Whether the disease was rapidly making inroads into the majority of the heterosexual population that did not use i.v. drugs was an issue debated for years to come. Nordheimer didn't come up with any clearcut answers to that question for the frantic heterosexuals he met. At the time, he probably couldn't have. The warnings that Surgeon General C. Everett Koop was issuing—that everyone who did not practice safe sex or did not take other basic precautions was at risk—were not based on hard data. Because the virus could remain in the body for seven to fifteen years before causing disease, any figures on how many untested heterosexuals were infected were simply guesswork. Nonetheless, the article included trend-setting reporting, and Nordheimer, former chief of the coveted London bureau, said both he and national editor David Jones thought it was front-page material. Rosenthal was less than enthusiastic about featuring the article prominently. Nordheimer suspected Rosenthal didn't want to run it at all. The correspondent finished the piece in February, yet by mid-March it was still languishing in the *Times's* reserve file. It finally ran, on March 22, 1986, buried in the back of the paper's Saturday edition. At the same time, a gay editor proposed another series on the social impact of AIDS. Rosenthal was not interested, so the story died.

Breaking AIDS news made it into the paper regularly. However, even as the *Los Angeles Times* was devoting more of its resources to covering the crisis—highlighting a dramatic series on one man's struggle with AIDS, for example—the epidemic was not considered a Rosenthal priority at the *New York Times*. Consequently, there was little or no coordination of the coverage, and the *Times* sent out mixed signals. On March 21, 1986, metro desk reporter Ron Sullivan wrote an article headlined "City Data Show Reports of AIDS Leveling Off." A month later, Erik Eckholm on the science desk reported "New AIDS Cases Up Sharply in City," citing data that had been available at the beginning of February, well before Sullivan wrote his story. The error could not entirely be chalked up to the *Times*. The city Health Department was providing no clear evidence about where the disease was heading. And Rosenthal's paper was not the only news source contradicting itself on the latest findings. But putting science and metro reporters in close contact, or at least one person on the copy desk overseeing AIDS news, would have helped avoid such confusion.

That kind of coordination also might have encouraged the *Times* to use straightforward language to talk about how AIDS was spread. Instead the modesty line was first broken by health columnist Jane E. Brody on February 12, 1986, almost five years into the crisis: "AIDS, as many health experts have repeatedly asserted, is not a very contagious disease. It requires intimate contact, probably through the blood stream. Thus, infected semen can spread it through intercourse in which the virus comes in contact with broken blood vessels or lesions in the anus or vagina. Theoretically, it could spread through deep kissing if infected saliva contacted mouth sores or bleeding gums."

Brody went on to detail "How to Protect Yourself": "Avoid anal intercourse and any sexual activity that might cause injury or tears in body tissue. . . . If you suspect that you or your sex partner may have been exposed to the AIDS virus, use condoms in every sexual encounter and avoid oral-genital contact, deep kissing and contact with any body fluids (semen, blood, feces, urine and the like)."

None of this information was news, but it was new to the *Times*. Because the guidelines came from a highly respected columnist at the paper, rather than a correspondent in one of the less prestigious bureaus, such as Katherine Bishop in San Francisco, the language got through the copy desk. Also, with Dr. C. Everett Koop's increased publicity around the topic, and his increasingly strident calls for all Americans to be as informed as possible about the epidemic, there was a "growing consensus," as the *Times*'s language guru Siegal would describe it, to become more explicit. The breakthrough allowed Jon Nordheimer in his piece on heterosexual and bisexual AIDS a month later to offer some similarly explicit advice. "Many experts now recommend that non-monogamous men and women should insist on the

80

use of condoms, and the presence of any open lesions or bleeding should serve as a warning for either partner to avoid sexual contact." 81

Changing *Times*

Not until Abe Rosenthal retired in November of 1986, and was replaced by editorial page editor Max Frankel, did the *Times* begin to take a coordinated approach to covering the epidemic. Shortly after his arrival in the executive offices, Frankel wrote what became known as his "AIDS memo," calling for increased reporting and recognition that the disease was one of the most important stories of the decade. It was the first of a series of such mandates sent to staffers that would change the tone of the *Times*. In December of that year, another memo circulated, this time from the office of style-watchdog Allan M. Siegal. Breaking a long tradition of extreme propriety in the obituaries, Siegal wrote: "We can mention a live-in companion of the same or the opposite sex in the course of the narrative. . . . Generally we should mention an unmarried companion if associates of the deceased ask us to do so."

Six months later, another Siegal memo did away with the final barrier that had so annoyed the activists who visited Rosenthal four years earlier: "Starting immediately, . . . *Gay* may refer to homosexual men, or more generally to homosexual men and women."

Behind all these changes, of course, was Max Frankel, the man who a decade earlier had been harshly reprimanded for the use of "gay" in his section, and whose editorial pages had recognized the political and social issues surging beneath the surface of the epidemic before the news desk made the story a priority. Just how far the *Times* had come was illustrated by the obituary written for GMHC-cofounder Paul Popham on May 8, 1987. It described the forty-five-year-old executive's Vietnam record, his career, and his involvement in AIDS activism. Along with his surviving mother and sisters, the *Times* listed Popham's lover: "His longtime companion was Richard Dulong."

On the same page that featured Popham's obituary, the *Times* printed the death notice of Congressman Stewart McKinney, who had been suffering from AIDS, as well. The liberal Connecticut Republican was married and had five children, but in Washington he was widely reputed to be a promiscuous homosexual. In the twenty-four-inch obituary, however, the *Times* made no mention of those rumors, even though the *Washington Post*, the *Boston Globe*, and the *Los Angeles Herald Examiner* had reported it. Instead, the *Times* simply repeated the claim made by McKinney's doctor that the representative probably had been infected by a blood transfusion during heart surgery in 1979.

"There is a custodial consciousness at the *Times*," said one former reporter. "The newspaper is not interested in breaking new ground." Indeed, in interviews with a score of *Times* editors, almost all of them described themselves as being "conservative" journalists. If there has been an activist among them in recent history, it is Frankel himself. Yet even he, like Rosenthal, is a product of the newspaper where both men began their careers.

The emphasis at the *Times* has always been on covering officialdom. "All the news that's fit to print," as the paper's time-tested standard goes, has always included the details of government and politics. The *Time's* best work has been done not on breaking the news but on following it up thoroughly and accurately. No story proved that rule more than AIDS.

All the News about AIDS
That's Fit to Print

After nearly two decades at the paper, Larry Altman, like Rosenthal and Frankel, saw himself in the *Times* tradition. What he considers news, for example, is most often an event in officialdom: a research project the government has sunk millions of dollars into, turmoil in the leviathan of federal research institutes, a scuffle in the corridors of science. When the AIDS story took on those shadings of importance—after Congress had invested millions, and the major researchers began squabbling, and the formal civility in the halls of science was shattered by shouts of "liar" and "thief"—then the full weight of Altman's journalistic prowess came to bear on the story.

That was April of 1984. Gossip was circulating in AIDS labs around the country that some researchers were close to discovering the cause of the disease. Ever since the epidemic had first been recognized three years before, this achievement had been the goal of scientists throughout the United States. Many in the field placed their bets on Dr. Robert Gallo's labs at the National Institutes of Health. He was an aggressive doctor who in the 1970s mistakenly claimed he found the first viral form of cancer. Now, many of his colleagues believed he wanted to redeem himself by discovering the cause of AIDS.

Meanwhile, the French continued with their research, trying to substantiate their hunch that Lymphadenopathy-Associated Virus (LAV) was the cause of AIDS by working with other laboratories doing work on the virus. Montagnier and his colleagues sent samples to the CDC in Atlanta, where Dr. Donald Francis had been pursuing the cause of AIDS. They also sent blood samples to Gallo. Altman had spoken to Francis about the validity of the French work after the Pasteur group presented their data at a meeting in Utah. Initially, the CDC researcher was not impressed. But the more Francis probed the French find, the more interested he became. "They found it," he began telling his co-workers and his boss, Dr. James Mason, in the spring of 1984.

By mid-April, the research was too exciting to be kept quiet. The French seemed to have discovered the virus. But Mason was intent on parceling out the news. One of the first batches went to the *New York Native*, as a goodwill payment to the gay paper that was lambasting the CDC and the government's response to the crisis in general.

The *Times*'s Altman did not learn about the CDC endorsement of the French finding until he made a scheduled trip to the agency, to interview Mason for other stories. By April 20, the Associated Press had picked up on the story, and even TV stations from San Francisco to New York were preparing stories. But the biggest play came on April 22, when the *Times* ran with the news on the front page.

> Dr. James O. Mason, head of the Federal Centers for Disease Control, said today that he believed a virus discovered in France was the cause of acquired immune deficiency syndrome, or AIDS. . . .
>
> Dr. Mason said he based his opinion on findings made in recent weeks by the researchers who discovered the virus at the Pasteur Institute in Paris last year. Dr. Mason said his opinion was also based on additional findings made by scientists at the disease centers here and the National Institutes of Health in Bethesda, Md.

84 In fact, as Mason would later admit, he knew almost nothing about the NIH work except what he had read in a press release sent out by the Institutes days before Altman's article ran. Gallo had isolated the AIDS virus—that was the gist of the release. No mention had been made of the French or the CDC. A press conference was scheduled for Monday, April 23, Altman reported, "presumably to discuss findings made by . . . Gallo and his colleagues . . . concerning a retrovirus they have reportedly called HTLV-III, for human T-cell lymphotropic virus."

By the time Health and Human Services Secretary Margaret Heckler took to the podium that day in Washington, Gallo's finding was no longer news. But the way Heckler framed the doctor's research was: Gallo had been able to mass-produce the virus, a necessary step in developing a blood test for it and eventually a vaccine, and something the French had not been able to accomplish. Despite Mason's claims in the *New York Times* that the Pasteur Institute had found the virus first, the French were only perfunctorily credited by Heckler. LAV, she said, "will prove to be the same as that identified by Dr. Gallo." The Health and Human Services Department had been harshly criticized for its slow response to AIDS. Now, she boasted, "the arrow of funds, medical personnel, research and experimentation . . . has hit the target." Heckler went on to assert that a blood test would be available in six months and a vaccine would be tested in two years.

"Today we add another miracle to the long honor roll of American medicine and science," she said. "Today's discovery represents the triumph of science over dread disease."

Almost none of the researchers entrenched in AIDS work were as optimistic as Heckler. In fact, a blood test for the virus would not be widely available for more than a year. And the projection that a vaccine would be available by the mid-1980s was probably a decade too ambitious, most scientists thought. Nonetheless, most papers throughout the country reprinted Heckler's claims without questioning them. The major networks all featured her on the nightly news, without rebuttal from more sober authorities.

Altman and the *New York Times* focused more squarely on what was erupting as an international battle for the scientific credit: "Even as the French and American researchers' confidence has grown . . . the tension of the exhaustive search was apparent. . . . Dr. Robert C. Gallo of the National Cancer Institute, who headed the team that is reporting its findings in four papers in the journal *Science*, said that if the two viruses turn out to be the same, 'I will say so.'"

The ownership stakes in this particular competition were quite high: international recognition and lucrative patents for a blood test, perhaps even the Nobel Prize for Medicine for unlocking the mystery of the worst scourge in recent history. There would be no rush to share the credit. The *Times* was one of the first media sources to recognize the U.S. government was taking this approach, and chided Heckler for it in an editorial three days after the press conference:

> The commotion indicates a fierce—and premature—fight for credit between scientists and bureaucratic sponsors of research. Certainly, no one deserves the Nobel Peace Prize.
>
> In the world of science, as among primitive societies, to be the namer of an object is to own it. . . . The French will claim prime credit for finding the virus while the American team will get credit for doing the substantial extra work needed to develop diagnostic tests.

It was through that kind of compromise that international negotiators, led by the famous virologist Jonas Salk, eventually got the two sides to agree to share the glory. And the AIDS virus—formerly called either LAV or HTLV-III, depending upon which side of the Atlantic you were on—became "HIV," Human Immunodeficiency Virus.

The *Times* had the sobriety to say: "The discovery is not yet 'the triumph of science over a dread disease,' as Mrs. Heckler puts it. . . . It is only the nomination of a prime suspect."

The *Times* Legacy

"At first AIDS was a gay story," said a senior *Times* editor, describing the news evolution of the epidemic at the *Times:* "And then it became a scientific story. And finally, it was a story about government." Only in that last phase did AIDS become an important ongoing story that reporters throughout the newspaper were covering. Finally, the epidemic had become a *Times* story, no matter how Abe Rosenthal might have wanted to dismiss it.

Ironically, when Rosenthal retired in 1986 as executive editor, and began writing a column for the newspaper, he suddenly saw the epidemic loom in importance. His column—officially called "On My Mind," and unofficially dubbed "Out of My Head" by *Times* reporters—has frequently been devoted to AIDS issues. Despite the harsh nickname given to his words of wisdom, his opinions on the matter are generally progressive and well informed. It's a topic he clearly has finally warmed up to. Just how important is the issue to the man who once kept it from being reported at all? "AIDS," Rosenthal declared in 1988, "is the story of the decade."

Chapter 5
A killer on the
cover *Newsweek*, New York

TO: Broyles, Parker, Sheils, Clark
FROM: Atlanta, Coppola
RE: STORY ADVISORY
November 26, 1982

There's a very major story developing on several fronts that we should plan on covering.

Consider this: Since 1979, more than 600 people have contracted a mysterious, deadly and thus far incurable affliction known as the Acquired Immunodeficiency Syndrome. Half of them are dead or dying . . . And three new cases are being diagnosed every day.

AIDS first struck and predominantly strikes young homosexual men (75%). But it has spread to the general population. . . . AIDS is truly a nightmare epidemic. . . . [Its] victims are utterly defenseless against recurring diseases (Pneumocystis pneumonia, a virulent form that can knock off 100 lbs of body weight, Herpes Zoster with eruptions the size of oranges. . . .) No one knows how to treat these people. . . . I'm convinced doctors have sent scores of AIDS victims to their deaths by using chemotherapy.

The reaction of the gay community may be what pushes all this into a cover story.

Vincent Coppola was taking the usual route to lobby for a major feature story at *Newsweek*. The four-page memo excerpted here was sent to editors throughout the magazine's hierarchy, including Editor-in-Chief William Broyles, and it gave enough facts to outline a story, with enough pathos to make it dramatic. Coppola did not have to go far to find the pathos: his brother was dying of AIDS.

Driven to save his brother's life, the *Newsweek* correspondent spurred one of the most aggressive efforts to cover the epidemic. Caught between fraternal responsibility and his journalistic instincts, Coppola used his personal involvement in the crisis to help frame the approach the magazine took to the story.

"I Have This Thing Affecting . . . Homosexuals"

Vincent Coppola finally got his parents to come to Atlanta, where he and his wife and child lived, and where he worked for *Newsweek*'s Southeast bureau. His folks were working-class people who had raised four sons in a cramped Brooklyn home. It was during that visit in the summer of 1982 that Vince's brother Thomas called from New York to tell his family he was sick. "I have this thing affecting Haitians, drug addicts . . . and homosexuals," he said.

Coppola had not known his brother was gay. Thomas was twenty-eight years old, a tall, blond struggling model who wanted to be an actor. He lived in New York's Greenwich Village and had a collection of "artsy" friends: rockers, dancers, actors. Vince, thirty-four at the time and the eldest in the family, had worked for *Newsweek* since 1978. He was considered an aggressive and bright reporter who could stretch to handle general assignment work with some distinction. He broke into *Newsweek* as a stringer covering international news from London. Back in the United States, he landed the assignment to cover political comer Mario Cuomo. Most recently, he had been assigned to report on the Southeast from Atlanta.

After Coppola got off the phone with his brother on that summer night, he headed for the reference books. He looked up immune deficiency and Kaposi's sarcoma, the telltale brown spots that the doctors had found on Thomas's feet. Thomas had beaten other illnesses, including a bout with cancer as a teenager and a thyroid problem when he first began modeling. He was going to win this one, too, Vince decided.

In the next few days, Coppola read everything he could about Gay Related Infectious Disease: some medical journal articles, a scattering of newspaper and magazine clips. *Newsweek* had done only one piece, on December 21, 1981.

The news magazines—the three most influential are *Newsweek*, *Time*, and *U.S. News and World Report*—generally do not follow the wire services as the newspapers do. "Has the *New York Times* done it yet?" is a question writers and correspondents are often asked when they propose stories. A negative response can veto a too-new idea. Besides the *Times*, the magazines rely for their leads on the *Washington Post,* the network news programs, and, increasingly, even *USA Today.* Their traditional role, set by Henry Luce when he founded *Time* magazine in 1923, has been to put the news in perspective. Their seven-day news cycles are, of course, seven times longer than the daily newspapers', so the magazines rarely break major stories. They often completely disregard fast-fading "minor" news, like the outbreak of *Pneumocystis* and Kaposi's sarcoma in the summer of 1981. When one writer at *Newsweek* persisted in proposing stories very early in the epidemic, she was met with the most frustrating cliché in journalism: "If this is so important, why isn't anyone else doing it?" Checking their coverage against their competitors, and their idols, is one way editors believe they keep their news judgment sharp. Too often, that habit dulls their news products. "Pack journalism" is always in dogged pursuit of some notion of professional consistency.

Newseeek's first story, "Diseases That Plague Gays," a brief two-column article that ran in the back of the magazine, was prompted by a *New England Journal of Medicine* issue earlier that month devoted to the new immunosuppression diseases affecting homosexuals. The maladies had drawn the attention of the *New York Times* in July. *Time* magazine produced a piece similar to *Newsweek*'s and it appeared the same day.

Frustrated by the lack of information, Coppola decided to travel to the other side of Atlanta, to the Centers for Disease Control. It was a steamy Georgia day when, without an appointment, he marched into the office of Dr. James Curran, who was overseeing the newly formed AIDS task force. The *Newsweek* connection helped get Coppola past Curran's secretary. It tumbled many more obstacles in the future, as the reporter scrambled to learn about the latest research, determine which therapy was the most promising, and get his brother into little-known treatment programs.

Cuisinart Journalism

Atlanta, home of the CDC, was a good place to be based if you wanted to track the epidemic. To spend his time pursuing those leads without drawing the wrath of his bosses back in New York, however, Coppola realized he had to generate more interest in the AIDS story. Senior writer Matt Clark, a well-respected medicine reporter, and his researcher Marianna Gosnell wrote *Newsweek*'s first piece in December of 1981. Nine months later, they were finally working on another one.

Based at the magazine's mid-Manhattan offices, Clark and Gosnell were part of a team of specialized writers who focus on technical areas, such as medicine, business, and science. Most of the *Newsweek* staff, including correspondents like Coppola who are stationed in bureaus throughout the United States and the world, are expected to be able to report on politics one week and the ramifications of a medical breakthrough the next.

Up to this point, putting together a story for a news magazine is similar to producing a newspaper article. Then the process gets much trickier. When the correspondents finish their reporting, they write up "files" on what they saw and heard. These documents can be as complete as a fully crafted newspaper story or as terse as a laundry list. From these sources, a writer back in New York then sits down to compile the piece. Sometimes he or she has to draw on as many as fifteen files. Regardless of the correspondents' eloquence, or lack of it, only shreds of what they send to headquarters will get into the magazine. "Cuisinart journalism" is the way one longtime *Newsweek* editor described the process.

The story then moves through the hands of an editor before it is finally sent to the "Wallendas," the magazine's top editors who sign off on the copy before it goes to press Sunday. The nickname, borrowed from the high-flying circus family, was first used to describe the group of editors who ran the magazine in the 1960s, and who prided themselves on running risk-taking features that attempted to track the rapid cultural changes shaking the United States. During that time, the magazine produced some provocative covers, including the 1968 "The Negro in America: What Must Be Done" and "Vietnam: A Reappraisal," which in 1968 called for a U.S. withdrawal from the Southeast Asia war. These days, one of the riskiest tightropes the "Wallendas" have to walk is making sense of the news after it is mulched and reconstituted by the editing process.

The whole procedure usually starts with a memo to get the lower-level editors interested in the proposed idea. For a potential cover story, the "Wallendas" have to be hooked, as well. With his sights on an AIDS cover, Coppola penned his memo on November 26, 1982.

That fall Thomas was hospitalized at New York University for

treatment of his Kaposi's sarcoma lesions. Chemotherapy was the pre-
scribed regimen, and Coppola began calling up every newly develop-   91
ing source who might have any information about the success of that
procedure. The CDC's Curran warned him off chemotherapy: that
treatment further debilitated an already weakened immune system.
Coppola was told about promising interferon work being done at Memorial Sloan-Kettering Cancer Center.

So, Coppola went to New York, pulled his brother out of the NYU
hospital, and got him enrolled in the program at Sloan-Kettering. Not
only did his job allow him extraordinary access to information on the
latest treatments, but it also served to help get Thomas into the programs. The *Newsweek* connection eased their odyssey through the
blind alleyways of early AIDS research. Thomas' struggle to stay alive,
a battle being fought by dozens of people Coppola had met as he
moved his brother from facility to facility, was providing the correspondent with vast material for the story he proposed.

Inside *Newsweek*

When the magazine was founded in 1933 by Thomas J. C. Martyn,
the original foreign news editor of *Time*, it was leaner and feistier than
Henry Luce's publication. More than fifty years later, after *Newsweek*
was folded into the *Washington Post* Company, its editors still embrace
that image. The fact is, the two magazine giants—*Time* has a larger
circulation, 4.7 million, compared with *Newsweek*'s 3.3 million, but
Newsweek has more advertising pages—mirror each other's complex
bureaucracy. They also have shared the tumult of the 1980s during
which all three of the national newsweeklies, including the also-ran
U.S. News and World Report, with 2.4 million readers, scrambled to re-
organize in order to compete more effectively.

In 1981 *Newsweek* publisher Katherine Graham hired thirty-seven-
year-old William Broyles as editor-in-chief to help her do that. The
New York media establishment bristled at the choice. The intellectual
Broyles was from out of the blue: that is, from out of the light and
fluffy *California* magazine and the irreverent *Texas Monthly*, both of
which he ran for a time. Broyle's own selections to fill some of the top
editor slots were no less provocative: *California* magazine's Meredith
White and *Rolling Stone*'s Terry McDonell, for example, as senior editors in charge of the life-style sections of the magazine.

For some at *Newsweek,* these changes represented a move to make
92 the magazine more hip: "trend" stories and life-style features were
gaining more prominence, while breaking the news was becoming less
of a priority. For others, like Vince Coppola, the new guard was opening up the magazine to fresh ideas.

Broyles lasted eighteen months. That brief stint was long enough
for him to earn the ire of some staffers, who admitted he was extremely bright, but claimed his hands-off approach hindered the
magazine. "He's the only journalist in America who combined the
work habits of Ronald Reagan with the character of Jimmy Carter,"
said one *Newsweek* editor.

Coppola defended Broyles and said that without him and people
like McDonell and White in place, his memo on why the magazine
should cover the plague that was predominantly striking homosexuals
never would have gotten the attention it did. In late 1982, for instance, the epidemic still had not been featured prominently in the
New York Times. Getting it on the cover of *Newsweek* would mean taking
some risks.

By December of 1982, there was strong interest among a few other
Newsweek staffers to look beyond the medical news about the epidemic. At least one of the editors had a gay friend who was terrified
by the epidemic. The December 27 article "AIDS: A Lethal Mystery
Story" quoted Larry Kramer: "to be a gay man in New York today is
like living in London during the blitz." The playwright, reviled as a
sell-out by many gays, was now being cited so frequently that he became the single most important source for mainstream journalists on
gays and their community. That is less a testament to Kramer's press
savoir faire—though he was a tireless promoter of media interest in
the epidemic—than an example of journalists' laziness in uncovering
new and unique sources. Kramer clearly was not the only gay person
who could have given *Newsweek* insight into how the community was
being affected. He may not have been the best.

At least *Newsweek* was attempting to provide readers with some
understanding of the epidemic's impact. *Time* did not write about how
AIDS was devastating the hardest hit group, gays, until the spring of
1983. Senior editor Claudia Wallis, who was involved in most of *Time*'s
AIDS reporting and remembers lobbying for more coverage in the
early years, says there was resistance even to the term "gay." "Editors
insisted on 'homosexual,'" she said. That inhibition was odd, given
that *Time* had done an in-depth look at gays in 1979. Since then, how-

ever, the top editor's slot had changed hands. Like *Newsweek,* the entire magazine was in flux. In a six-year period, *Time*'s science editorship turned over five times.

Coppola was not the only one at *Newsweek* pushing to feature AIDS on the cover. Senior editor Meredith White also thought the story was important, and she even penned her own memo to her colleagues. There was growing interest among lower-level editors like Jean Seligmann, who covers medicine. She was a close friend of Coppola's. Washington, D.C.-based science reporter Mary Hager, whose beat included the National Institutes of Health, kept sending memos about the evolving science story.

Coppola's fervor, however, was overwhelming. Some *Newsweek* staffers, including the Wallendas, knew his brother had AIDS. He was commuting regularly between Atlanta and New York to oversee Thomas's treatments, and when he dropped into the offices of *Newsweek,* he detailed the horror stories to some of his colleagues: how he went with his brother to Sloan-Kettering where Thomas got interferon injections; how Coppola sat in the waiting room feeling the heavy tension of men battling death; how he could barely look at one of the patients whose face was contorted by a ravaging skin cancer.

If Coppola had been working at one of many other major media outlets, that extraordinarily personal connection to the tragedy might have disqualified him from covering the story. Could he report accurately on treatments when he had so much personally invested in their success? Could he be fair in writing about the political battleground around AIDS funding? If those questions were being asked at *Newsweek,* Coppola was not being forced to answer them. "Where objectivity is not a sham, it is boring," declared the famous British journalist Walter Bagehot. His words of wisdom run against the grain of most American journalists. Perhaps the Wallendas trusted that "Cuisinart journalism" would mix out misleading bias. "The AIDS Epidemic" was scheduled for the spring.

A Killer on the Cover

Although Coppola had predicted that the gay community's reaction to the crisis would be the story *Newsweek* featured, the piece actually focused on something else he had mentioned in his memo: "Atlanta's

Centers for Disease Control . . . is trying to track and uncover the cause of AIDS. But also note that generally, funding for research on AIDS is not coming through."

The cover story of April 18, 1983, was optimistically subtitled "The Search for a Cure," even though most of the experts working on the disease were still not certain about what caused it, much less how to go about looking for a cure.

"Since it came into public view in 1981," the article began, "derisively called 'The Gay Plague,' AIDS (Acquired Immune Deficiency Syndrome), which ravages the body's immune system, has stricken 1,300 Americans—more than half of them in the last year."

"AIDS is creeping out of well-defined epidemiological confines," said Dr. Anthony Fauci of the National Institute of Allergy and Infectious Diseases. Despite Coppola's strong rhetoric in his memo, the fact that the epidemic was claiming more than just gay lives undoubtedly helped convince the Wallendas to put AIDS on the cover.

Written by Jean Seligmann and reported by Coppola, Hager, and Gosnell, the article reflected a levelheaded understanding of the disease: "Ninety five percent of AIDS victims have identifiable risk factors; the disease doesn't strike at random, and does not seem to be spread by airborne droplets of a cough or sneeze, like influenza. Most physicians agree that extremely intimate contact—or exposure to blood—is probably necessary for infection."

The *Newsweek* piece also did what no other article on AIDS had done up to that point: it gave a clear picture of all the groups being infected with the disease. There was Tom Biscotto, a gay man who was a stage manager for Chicago's Goodman Theater. "His life was full, his future bright. Today Biscotto, 35, doesn't know if he has a future at all." And Destiné, a twenty-six-year-old Haitian. "His right side is now paralyzed and he lives in constant pain. Yet somehow he is stoical about what has befallen him. 'I think God wants me more close to him,' he whispers. 'That's why he gives me disease.'" Hemophiliac Walter Scott had thought factor VIII, a clotting agent, was the "'most wonderful thing that ever happened.' . . . Now he's too weak to talk much and rarely leaves his wheelchair." And toddler Ahmad Carlisle was once "big and healthy and easy to please. Now he was wasting away from AIDS, and his mother was suspected of having the disease."

Finally, at the end of the seven-page section, Coppola wrote about "The Change in Gay Life-Style":

> The four young men sat in the semi-darkness of the deserted ward waiting for their weekend shot of interferon at New York's Memorial Sloan-Kettering Cancer Center.
>
> They tried not to look at the fifth man, the law professor. His face was swollen and disfigured by purplish Kaposi's sarcoma (KS) lesions; his frail body, wracked for months by pneumonia and other recurring infections, weighed no more than a child's. He was beyond hope, beyond terror. They fought not to see their fate in his. And again they fought the old fears and doubts. Their life-style was not sinful. AIDS was not a gay plague sent down upon them.

The lead came directly out of Coppola's own experience: Thomas was one of the four young men.

The magazine's April 18 cover story was hallmark AIDS coverage, but *Newsweek* quickly slipped away from the high standard of reporting it set in that piece. On May 16, 1983, a science writer summarized the latest theories of transmission, including the scarifying—and false— "close personal contact" claim. Nonetheless, in the article "The AIDS Hysteria," dated May 3, *Newsweek* saw fit to chastise the media for "a spate of sensationalized publicity suggesting that the disease may not be limited to the previously identified high-risk groups." *Newsweek*'s contribution to the hysteria was not mentioned. Even in the article of May 30, the magazine was guilty of fanning the flames by sloppily reporting another case of mysterious transmission that was under investigation: "A New York sanitation worker who reportedly contracted the disease when he picked up garbage that contained a contaminated syringe." Had he been stuck with the needle? Or was the disease so contagious that just being near a contaminated device might cause infection? *Newsweek* gave no clue.

Time Plays Catch-up

Although a *Newsweek* cover story rarely sets the national agenda for news, the magazine's impact on the AIDS story in 1983 was significant. For the first time, a national publication was giving the epidemic important play. Not until months after the AIDS cover story appeared did the *New York Times* and Associated Press prepare lengthy features on the disease. *Time* magazine, which had been debating when to come out with its own cover on the epidemic, followed up on July 4, 1983. "Disease Detectives" ran nine pages, reporting on the work by scientists to uncover the AIDS mystery. "At the outset of each new inquiry, they may not even know the description of the quarry, but its power is often all too evident." For the next six pages the reader was shown the detectives' trail in pursuit of the elusive AIDS, focusing on the efforts of the Centers for Disease Control. What was noticeably missing, however, was any mention of work being done beyond the United States.

"'We've looked at a lot of suspects [as the cause of AIDS],' says Dr. Anthony Fauci of the National Institutes of Health (NIH), 'but we have not come up with enough grounds for an indictment.'" Overlooked was Dr. Luc Montagnier's team of scientists at France's Pasteur Institute, who had published an article in *Science* identifying the AIDS agent a full month before the *Time* cover appeared.

Time's story uncovered little "news." The article carried much of the same information as Newsweek, even down to the sidebar, "The Real Epidemic: Fear and Despair."

"AIDS isolates many of its victims and is changing the gay lifestyle," the subhead read. "As the deaths from AIDS-related diseases continue to rise, so does hysteria about possible contagion. AIDS victims and members of high-risk groups—male homosexuals, Haitians, hemophiliacs and intravenous drug users—are being shunned by their communities, their fellow workers, and sometimes their friends and families."

Despite *Time*'s initial hesitation to use the word "gay" in place of "homosexual," in its first cover story the magazine was explicit about possible forms of transmission. "Repeated exposure to the herpes virus, or to sperm entering the blood after anal intercourse," *Time* explained, could begin the process of suppressing the immune system. But behind the scenes, some editors at both publications continued to have blushing reservations about otherwise clinical langauge: in *Newsweek*'s first cover story, a top editor reading the galleys a final time asked that a description of how the semen might enter the blood system during anal sex, through a tear in the rectal wall, be replaced with "sperm . . . absorbed by the body during frequent oral or anal intercourse." Not wrong, of course, but not exactly right, either.

Nonetheless, both magazines were helping to redefine the bounds of "appropriate language" for American journalists. The more explicit terms found in *Time* and *Newsweek* were still being resisted by many "family" newspapers, and such language was implicitly censored at the networks. The newsweeklies have more leeway in part because, unlike newspapers, they are not tied to one single community and thus are not confined to narrowly perceived standards of prudery. Unlike television, which is broadcast into almost every home in America, magazines go to readers who are self-selected: they can far more easily choose not to encounter errant language.

Newsweek initiated the change in AIDS coverage and language, but it did not always take the lead. The two magazines often move in tandem: so much so that, despite *Time*'s very conservative roots planted by founder Henry Luce and *Newsweek*'s more liberal tradition, sometimes the two publications print nearly identical covers the same week. The looks of the magazines also change together. For instance, as newspapers began developing news features, thus elbowing into the territory that used to be exclusively controlled by the newsweeklies, *Time* and *Newsweek,* along with *U.S. News,* had to adjust. As a result, the magazines are using more pictures and graphics. That leaves less room for prose and encourages even more *Newsweek* speak and "*Time*-style": sentences clipped by colons and semicolons to save space. For example, from *Newsweek:* "Kaposi's sarcoma strikes in about a third of all cases; others get the deadly PCP (average survival after diagnosis: seven months)." Lost in the tailoring process is some of the complexity that might better explain difficult issues. For example, those diagnosed with *Pneumocystis* [PCP] often had only months to live in 1983, but those with Kaposi's generally lived much longer. How much essential information about the spread of the disease, like the garbage collector's infection, was distorted this way? The language crunch was a major impediment on TV, and now it was affecting the newsweeklies.

Undeniably, *Time* and *Newsweek*'s most important influence in American journalism is on each other. But the feature treatment the two national newsweeklies gave the epidemic—coupled with their willingness to write about *all* the groups initially affected by the disease—helped break down obstacles to broader reporting. It is impossible to pinpoint exactly what kind of interest those two cover stories generated among newspaper and broadcast journalists, but they clearly helped move the story from the science beat and expand the audience for AIDS information.

98 Why *U.S. News* Ignored the Story

In the interval between *Newsweek*'s and *Time*'s first AIDS cover stories, *U.S. News and World Report* made its first mention of the disease, on 3 June 1983. "AIDS Epidemic" was included in a roundup of health news with other short pieces on a glaucoma treatment and an improved rabies vaccine.

"With four or five new cases reported every day, AIDS—Acquired Immune Deficiency Syndrome—had become a major public health problem," the article began. A virus may be behind the infections, the magazine suggested. "It appears that this mysterious agent can only be transmitted sexually from males or through blood and blood products." The language was not only oblique, but wrong. The most recent data showed that AIDS could be spread by both men and women. More important, the *U.S. News* reader was offered much less information than *Time* and *Newsweek* provided, and it was presented in language more circumspect than that used by some of the most sensitive daily newspapers. *U.S. News* veterans recalled how squeamish the top editors were about featuring almost anything having to do with sex, much less gay sex, in the pages of the magazine. If the topics and langauge that appeared in *Time* and *Newsweek* were somewhat circumscribed by concern for what their audiences—middle Americans—would be interested in reading about, *U.S. News*'s smaller, more homogenous readership—often described as conservative businessmen—had an even tighter grip on its news focus.

U.S. News also was in a state of flux. Shelby Coffee, the young editor from the *Washington Post* (and now the executive editor of the *Los Angeles Times*), had been brought on board to pull the magazine out of its doldrums. He steered it toward "news consumers can use." And *U.S. News*'s idea of the kind of consumers it was reaching did not include gays. Not surprisingly, the first feature the magazine did on the epidemic, on July 25, 1983, addressed the issue of the danger posed by blood transfusions. "As AIDS Scare Hits Nation's Blood Supply" summed up *U.S. News*'s approach: "The baffling and lethal disease that destroys the body's immune system is frightening people away from giving and receiving blood." Another factor determining how *U.S. News* covered the issue was the magazine's Washington, D.C., location. The publication always has been more influenced by Capitol Hill than have the other two Manhattan-based newsweeklies. And in the first few years, when AIDS was a low-priority issue for legislators, the epidemic was not generating much press from D.C.

Another Coppola Memo, Another Cover Story

By the summer of 1983, Thomas Coppola was getting daily injections of interferon. The powerful antiviral drug makes the patient feel as though he or she were experiencing the onset of the flu with each injection. Sick and exhausted, Thomas retreated to his parents' home in Brooklyn. Coppola was spending more of his time in New York so he could be with Thomas. As his brother's friends from the Village would make their way to Brooklyn for afternoon visits, Coppola gained increasing insight into the gay community and how it was reacting to AIDS.

He had glimpsed the responses when he wrote about the gay lifestyle for *Newsweek*'s first cover story. Since those early months of turmoil following his brother's diagnosis, Coppola began to think about the epidemic as a journalist. True to the *Newsweek* mindset, he thought of the trends. It was probably too early to tell how AIDS was affecting America and its social institutions, but a look at the impact on Gay America was certainly timely.

Coppola's second memo was sent to editor-in-chief Rick Smith, senior editors Sheward Haggerty and Terry McDonell, and medicine writer Matt Clark.

HOMOSEXUAL ADVISORY:
We live in a tense and economically unsteady America with aggressive fundamentalists, a conservative president and very nosey neighbors. Gays have won many victories. . . . But in many places, especially urban centers, gays have become Ugly Americans. . . . Word of . . . bathhouse rituals, S&M, the terror of AIDS, is spreading.

"You sound like a raving Jehovah's Witness," Coppola was told by Shu Haggerty, a longtime *Newsweek* hand, cautious and conservative. He, along with many editors at the magazine, knew how personally involved Coppola had gotten in the story. Again, Coppola wrote

about the issue convincingly enough to suggest he would make dra-
100 matic contributions to an article. By this time, he could also point to
the similar feature the *New York Times* had done. Coppola converted
Haggerty, and shortly after had approval from the other top editors
as well. On August 8, 1983, *Newsweek* ran its second cover story on the
epidemic, "Gay America: Sex, Politics and the Impact of AIDS."

"A turning point has been reached, and AIDS may mean the party
is over," the story was summed up. But there was a political edge to
the piece as well: "As some leaders of the gay community tacitly recognize, moreover, the long escape into hedonism has most of all been a
reckless diversion of Gay America's energies—energies that must now
be directed into winning political gains, and winning hearts and minds
of men and women who, in many communities, live right next door."

Coppola did not write the cover story, but his reporting was woven
throughout, as were the sentiments from his memo. Another sensitiz-
ing influence resulted from the *Newsweek* practice of circulating articles for minority review: stories about blacks are read by blacks on
the staff before they hit print; likewise stories about gays get a read
from open homosexuals; and stories about women, even when they
are written by a woman, have to be read by a female staff member.
The process serves to maintain a kind of political correctness in the
prose. This is as close as any mainstream media get to watchdogging
potential antiliberalisms. The routine, however, also helps weed out
stupid errors. Newspapers use it frequently, in cases such as a City hall
reporter covering a medic rescue of a heart attack victim. Before the
article goes to press, the medical reporter is often asked to make sure
the clinical facts are correct. Unfortunately, *Newsweek* and most other
publications were not using the same care with AIDS reporting. In
1983, there was no "authority" on hand at *Newsweek* reading through
the complex material on the epidemic to prevent mistakes.

Disappearing Epidemic

At first, the interferon treatment seemed to be working for Thomas:
the Kaposi's had disappeared; he felt healthier. He even moved back
to the Village. But by the winter of 1983, it was clear the drug was not
a cure. Once again, his brother sought out the next promising treatment, and before the end of the year Thomas was enrolled in a new

program at the National Institutes of Health in Bethesda, Maryland, where patients got regular doses of interleukin 2, an immune system therapy.

For months afterward there was no major medical news, and as at most publications, the AIDS story vanished from the pages of *Newsweek*. Dr. Robert Gallo's AIDS-virus discovery, in the spring of 1984, and the subsequent feud between the Americans and the French, got some coverage. But then months passed when nothing was written about the epidemic. By the spring of 1985, the disease had struck more than nine thousand Americans. Coppola wanted to go to Africa to cover the AIDS story, believing that the secret to the cure might be found there. As his brother's health worsened, however, he became less interested in tracking the epidemic. Coppola was losing hope.

One night, close to Thomas's death, Coppola searched his brother's face for any remnants of the handsome man whom he had known. Thomas's blue eyes were swollen shut, his blond hair now a dull, ash gray. The initial radiation treatments had turned his legs to leather. Because lesions blocked off all of Thomas's lymph nodes, the body's natural filtration system, he was swelling up with infection. Coppola did not recognize his brother beneath the layers of disease, but the face was chillingly familiar. Suddenly it occurred to him: Thomas looked like the man Coppola had written about in *Newsweek's* first cover story, the one the four young men had turned away from.

The Glossy Approach

Often the news doesn't get told until someone in the newsroom is affected by it and is willing to admit the connection. Associated Press and the *New York Times* proved that. *Newsweek* might have found that link without a Vince Coppola, especially after the *Times* set the agenda. *Time,* which was debating when to run its cover story before *Newsweek* came out with its own, undoubtedly would have delivered eventually. *U.S. News,* simply because of the increased Washington exposure to the issue, would have had to pay attention, too. But all that probably would have happened later if one concerned *Newsweek* correspondent had not pushed for more AIDS coverage. In that way, the magazines are not all that different from the rest of the world of American media.

Throughout mainstream journalism, from the newsweeklies to the picture and opinion magazines and even newspapers, the way the news is framed is changing. Strong anecdotes and sharp pictures are used to convey the sense that the news is close enough to touch, and poignant enough to touch your soul. Often, it is not a story until it is a drama. Is that doing justice to the news? Probably not.

This approach can also lead to exaggeration and outright distortion. *Life* magazine's July 1985 issue is a prime example of editors stretching to make the story compelling until the story itself has been stretched. "Now no one is safe," the red letters shouted, and beneath them a terrified family looked out at the reader. Inside, the writer claimed that because the blood supply was infected, and because the virus was infecting more than just gays and i.v. drug users, all Americans needed to be on guard. It was generally good advice. Read in the *Life* magazine context, however, it was much more likely to put the reader on the defensive, running scared.

Even a staid feature magazine like *Atlantic Monthly* came to report the epidemic in sensationalistic ways. The publication's September 1987 "AIDS and Insects," for example, was a 16,000-word treatise devoted to the already debunked hypothesis that the disease could be spread by a bug bite. There were scores of other magazines that could not quite find "their angle" on the epidemic. For instance, the painfully politically correct *Nation,* which bills itself as the guardian of America's leftist sensibility, was silent on AIDS for years. Finally, in 1987 a group of gay activists contacted its editor, Victor Navasky, to set up a meeting. When they arrived, the magazine's meeting room was packed with staffers, but Navasky was not among them. He was in Chicago, at a conference on McCarthyism.

The Face of AIDS

After Thomas died in the spring of 1985, Coppola wanted nothing to do with the AIDS story. When *Newsweek* finally began covering the epidemic again in 1987, after an almost media-wide hiatus of twenty-four months, it resurrected the dramatic approach Coppola had taken. Reporters and writers were not having to search for some connection to AIDS anymore. There now were well-developed sources and even AIDS foundations that provided names of people with the disease who were willing to talk to journalists.

In the next three years, *Newsweek* produced seven AIDS cover stories, including a powerful yearbook of 302 men, women, and children who died in a single twelve-month period. "The Face of AIDS," which ran August 10, 1987, was clearly inspired by *Life* magazine's gripping photo essay two decades earlier of young men killed in Vietnam. In San Francisco, the *Chronicle* had prepared a smilar collection of the fallen some two years earlier. But *Newsweek's* cover uniquely framed the tragedy in the national mind's eye. Some magazine staffers by now understood that the epidemic was pummeling the American psyche as powerfully as Vietnam had. Peter Goldman, one of *Newsweek's* premier writers, was in that group. He had come up with the faces cover idea, with the help of his close friend, editor-in-chief Rick Smith. By late 1987, AIDS had become a part of the *Newsweek* institution.

The Masters and Johnson Debacle

Unfortunately, the same commitment to covering the epidemic that allowed powerful cover after cover to be written—specifically, a strong interest among top editors like Rick Smith—also was the cause of the magazine's most embarrassing AIDS coverage. Senior editor David Alpern, who was in charge of book excerpts for the magazine, was approached by the publishers of a new work by the well-known sex therapists Dr. William Masters and his wife, Virginia Johnson, and Dr. Robert Kolodny.

Crisis: Heterosexual Behavior in the Age of AIDS was being sold as a provocative piece of scientific research that refuted all the experts' wisdom about the disease: Masters and Johnson claimed the virus was being spread through the most casual of contact.

Publishers routinely seek out Alpern in hopes of getting their books into *Newsweek*. The magazine can provide a national showcase to sell a given book; and the book makes an "exclusive" feature story that sells magazines. That was the reason Bob Woodward's 1987 *Veil,* a look into the Central Intelligence Agency, allegedly backed up by deathbed interviews with CIA chief William Casey, made a *Newsweek* cover.

The decision to run a book excerpt as a cover story does not go through the traditional channels. The editor-in-chief makes the call, and his fellow editors are later informed about it. In the case of AIDS, a complex story with the potential to strike terror nationwide, the "normal" turn of events set up the magazine for some dangerous maneuvers.

Rumors had been running through the *Newsweek* offices for days that Masters and Johnson were going to be on the cover, that the book was exploitative, and that Rick Smith was not going to be swayed. He was fascinated with the epidemic. His wife, a social scientist with the World Health Organization, was doing AIDS research. His colleagues seemed always to be chatting about the subject. And he knew people with the disease. Admittedly, he was not well versed in the technical apsects of AIDS, but Masters and Johnson seemed qualified experts. Certainly, their thesis was dramatic.

Only days before the book excerpt was scheduled to appear did anyone at a level lower than a Wallenda—that is, anyone who actually covered AIDS—get to read the Masters and Johnson claims. Smith said the agreement he signed with the book publisher included strict confidentiality provisions, to minimize leaks to the public. Finally, days before it was to run, senior editor Terence Monmaney was asked to write an introduction to place the piece in context.

"The Masters and Johnson book sounds an alarm about a crisis whose true dimensions won't be known for years," Monnamey ended the carefully worded introduction. The passage reminded Vince Coppola of how *Newsweek* introduced its exclusive on the "Hitler Diaries" in May of 1983. "Now the appearance of Hitler's diaries—genuine or not, it almost doesn't matter in the end—reminds us of the horrible reality." The documents turned out to be forgeries, and it *did* matter. A major national magazine had been fooled and thus had in turn fooled the nation. The precious commodity of journalistic credibility was devalued once again, when the Masters and Johnson book appeared as a cover story.

Ironically, one of the most insightful critiques of the Masters and Johnson controversy and *Newsweek's* role in it came from *U.S. News and World Report*. By early 1988, with new management in place, *U.S. News* was finally following the AIDS epidemic as a serious news story.

Touched by the Plague

Rick Smith and Vince Coppola had been moved by the epidemic, both essentially for personal reasons. Coppola was trying to save his brother's life, and Smith was trying to understand the fear and fascination he sensed all around him. The drive to react to those signals is one of the best instincts a journalist can have. That motivation also needs to be tempered, by editors and fellow writers who can help put "hunches" in perspective. Because Coppola was a correspondent, whose memos had to make their way through layers of editors before they were accepted as cover ideas for *Newsweek*, his work was honed and improved through that process. Smith, at the top of that process, had no one to check him. The *Newsweek* system did not fail; Smith simply refused to use it.

Epilogue

A crowd of *Newsweek* editors and writers were on hand at the funeral of Thomas Coppola in the spring of 1985. The casket was closed, but a picture of the handsome young man lay atop it.

Vince Coppola still lives in Atlanta. He got divorced soon after Thomas's death. And he no longer works for *Newsweek*. He is remarried now and has another child. His name is Thomas.

Chapter 6
Controlling what we know

The babies Dr. James Oleske treated in his Newark, New Jersey clinic during the first months of 1983 came from some of the poorest and most drug-infested neighborhoods in the United States, where AIDS was breeding with epidemic efficiency. Despite these circumstances, Oleske was surprised to find the disease creeping into the infant population there. By all appearances, these children were not being infected by dirty intravenous needles used to shoot drugs or by sexual contact, the two most likely ways to get AIDS. But almost all of them were living in households where someone had been diagnosed with the disease or was at particularly high risk of coming down with the ailment, usually because of i.v. drug use. This was the evidence, Oleske claimed, in the May 6, 1983, *Journal of the American Medical Association* (*JAMA*), that suggested America's worst fears about AIDS were coming true: the disease was spreading by routine close contact.

AIDS and babies was a hot topic in the medical journals that season. Only six months before, some of the first cases of the disease in infants had been reported by the CDC's *Morbidity and Mortality Weekly Report*. Since then the *New England Journal of Medicine* had featured correspondence on the subject. Now *JAMA* was showcasing Oleske's piece. Not only was the study placed in a prominent position in the magazine, but *JAMA* also ran an editorial by the National Institutes of Health's Dr. Anthony Fauci warning that the findings could mean "non-sexual, non-blood borne transmission is possible." It hardly needed to be said that if such transmission were occurring, "the scope of the syndrome may be enormous." *JAMA*'s press release focused on that possibility, hyping the publication's May 6 issue. "Evidence Suggests Household Contact May Transmit AIDS" ran across the top of the release.

The press release was parroted by most of the media in the firestorm that followed, even though the study it was promoting was dangerously wrong. True, babies who lived in homes with high-risk adults were coming down with the deadly disease. They were not being infected by the touch or kiss of a drug-addicted parent with AIDS, argued physicians like New York's Dr. Arye Rubinstein, chief of the Albert Einstein College of Medicine's pediatrics department. After all, people who lived with and cared for adult AIDS patients were not catching the disease through household contact. No, it was much more likely Oleske's babies were being infected in their mothers' wombs, where there would be some transfer of blood.

Unfortunately, almost no journalist was seeking out experts with an opposing viewpoint, something every reporter is taught to do in Journalism 101 or the first day on the job. That opposition would hardly have been difficult to find. An article by Rubinstein on how the disease might be transmitted in the womb was carried in the same May 6 issue of *JAMA*. The evidence was quite clear, he wrote: "The mothers of five of the seven children are sexually promiscuous and/or drug addicts." But the journal did not bother to highlight this article. It was, clearly, less dramatic, less newsworthy.

JAMA played this scoop as many newspapers and magazines would, but perhaps with a bit more calculated marketing in mind when it sent out the press release announcing the story to journalists across the country. That approach to AIDS news made sense in the extremely competitive environment of the medical journals. When prestigious publications like the *New England Journal* and the British *Lancet* were vying to be first with the most interesting research in medicine, such dramatic packaging was inevitable.

But mainstream journalists were not used to thinking about the information that comes out of these sources in such a light. Rather than viewing *JAMA* and the *New England Journal* as competitive publications that sometimes, just like the media everywhere, get the news wrong, reporters often read these magazines as though they are "the holy writ," as one science writer mockingly called them. "Covering the journals is almost a religious experience for some [journalists]," said Ben Patrusky, a nationally known authority on science writing. "The journals come down from the mountain with the word each week," and the media dutifully transcribe what is handed them.

Patrusky overstates the cooperativeness of the media. Many studies presented in the major journals are overlooked altogether by mainstream reporters. But once a story has made it onto the agenda of the national media, the journals' detailing of new findings or "breakthroughs" is usually followed closely, sometimes slavishly. That was the case with *JAMA*'s "routine household contact" story.

The power instilled in the medical journals, and fostered by the publications themselves through rigid rules about the way medical information will be disseminated to the mainstream press, has often dictated how technical AIDS news is communicated to Americans. That power undermines what should be essential characteristics of a journalist: cyncism and a drive to question authority. The medical journals also play havoc with another basic element of the modern media: the free flow of information.

Medicine's Holy Writ

Only a handful of publications make up the core of journals that inform much of the world about the latest findings in medicine and science. *JAMA* is on that list. Its circulation of 700,000 is bolstered by the requirement that every doctor who chooses to join the American Medical Association also must pay part of his or her medical dues for the weekly magazine. Its releases, meant to tip off the press about articles running in the publication, help maintain its high profile. Others in that group of most important magazines include the *British Medical Journal* and the *Lancet*, the *Annals of Internal Medicine* and the *New England Journal of Medicine*. All these technical publications, with claims to be academic journals, sell themselves aggressively through media kits to encourage advertisers to buy space. The *Lancet*'s pitch is that it is "the most authoritative international medical journal," which ostensibly makes up for the fact that it has a relatively small circulation, 45,000. The *New England Journal*'s eighteen-page advertising booklet promotes the publication's 245,000 subscribers as the top of the top-doctors list.

Among journalists at major newspapers and magazines, the *New England Journal* is the single most important source for medical news. During a forty-month period, the *Journal* was quoted five hundred times by major U.S. print media. That's more than twice as much as any other medical- or science-oriented publication.

The offices of the *New England Journal of Medicine* are in the Harvard Medical School, home of some of the most renowned doctors and scientists in the world and one of the most impressive research facilities. Even Harvard is less a symbol of the American medical establishment than the magazine.

Founded in 1812 as "*The New England Journal of Medicine and Sur-*

gery," it was one of the first publications of its kind in the United States. The magazine boasts other firsts, from the initial clinical descriptions of angina in the early 1800s to the original announcements in the late 1980s that the drug AZT was successful in treating AIDS. Today, like most of the major medicine and science journals, the weekly is a glossy magazine thick with advertising. Its articles run in sober black and white, two wide columns of print splitting every page of type. The editorial format is dull, all the better to help highlight the four-color pharmaceutical ads that make up nearly two-thirds of each issue.

"Being published is acceptance," said one young researcher. Being published in the *New England Journal* has become a significant stepping stone for scientists and doctors who want to devote their lives to research. With a *Journal* imprimatur comes credibility, a cachet that often translates into support from places like the National Institutes of Health, one of the largest supporters of research in the world. Although funding has grown dramatically in the 1970s and 1980s, spurred by major government research programs like the "War on Cancer" in the early 1970s, the ranks of scientists scrambling for those dollars have also exploded. Between 1976 and 1986, the number of scientists in the United States jumped from 959,500 to more than two million, according to the National Science Foundation.

Because of the crush of new material being sent to the *Journal,* the magazine was able to become far more discriminating. The publication was receiving hundreds of manuscripts each month; it published only a handful in each weekly edition. The surplus of manuscripts at the *Journal* allowed then-editor Dr. Franz Inglefinger to demand an "exclusive" on every article that appeared in the Journal. The publication would run no manuscript that had been reported in detail anywhere else, including the popular press. As a result, articles could be backlogged for months before they were reviewed and eventually published.

In the fields of astrophysics or geology, disciplines in which the professional journals have now adopted their own versions of the "Inglefinger Rule," such a restriction makes some sense, if only to guarantee the quality of research and avoid redundancies. Scientists, after all, should not be striving to make the front page of the daily newspaper, but instead should be working to advance scholarly information.

In medicine, however, when a new technique or finding could save huge amounts of money and lives, such a rule can slow the research process to a deadly pace. By the early 1980s, the *New England Journal* was not the only publication to have a lengthy review period. All five of the top journals had some waiting time to review articles. At most of the publications, that period ranged from a few months to two years. The dramatic 1981 study by UCLA's Dr. Michael Gottlieb of the first appearance of Kaposi's sarcoma in healthy gay men made it into the *New England Journal* more than half a year after it was first submitted. The one magazine that bucked this trend was the *Lancet*.

The British Maverick

Long considered the most provocative of the traditionally staid publications, the *Lancet* often features ideas so unconventional they would never see print in the *New England Journal*. The British magazine reserves an entire section for "Hypotheses," ideas proposed by a doctor or scientist who cannot do the research to prove them. The *Lancet* is considered by some Americans to be a sanctuary where they can air unorthodox medical notions that never would be published at home by the *New England Journal* or *JAMA*.

The *Lancet*'s openness made it the first of the major medical journals to print a study of the new outbreaks, on September 19, 1981. "Kaposi's Sarcoma in Homosexual Men—a Report of Eight Cases" was written by a group of researchers that included New York University researcher Dr. Linda Laubenstein. (She was the scientist who was the model for Larry Kramer's heroine in his play, *The Normal Heart*.) The first articles on the growing crisis finally made their way through the *New England Journal*'s labyrinth in the winter of 1981. Almost three months after the *Lancet* ran its first piece on deadly disease among gays, the *Journal* featured four articles on the subject, including an editorial calling for doctors to be on the lookout for the maladies. The CDC's *Morbidity and Mortality Weekly Report* had run three major articles on Kaposi's and *Pneumocystis* before the *Journal*'s presentation. But it was only after the December 10 issue of the weekly magazine that, according to science writers and doctors across the country, the outbreak became an issue. Before the *Journal* featured it, the crisis was easily overlooked. It was still being disregarded by most of the other major medical and science publications. *JAMA*, *Science*, and *Nature,* which considered themselves on the cutting edge of their fields, did not publish any articles on the subject until late 1982.   **111**

Who Gets Published, and Why

If the *Lancet* editors believe an article is particularly important, the review process can be as short as ten days. Getting the piece into print generally takes another week and a half. Getting published in the other top medical publications is a good deal more involved. The first step of the review process at most of the journals is similar to the decision-making process at almost any publication. If the topic interests a particular editor, either because it is newsworthy, innovative or somehow touches his or her life, it will get a full reading, and then perhaps a second by another editor. However, if the article survives that stage at the *New England Journal,* it then must weave its way through a kind of old-boy network of doctors and scientists. The process, called peer-reviewing, is supposed to help determine how valuable the new study is. The physicians who read the piece are chosen primarily because of their connections to the journal editors, whether personal or professional. Such networking is an obvious approach to the arduous task of finding qualified people to critique the material.

Reacting to criticism from researchers, all the top journals, excluding the *Lancet,* agreed in mid-1983 to speed up the process. They shortened from months to weeks the amount of time spent on reviewing high-priority AIDS material. Still, some doctors, including a few of those who did groundbreaking work, believed even the expedited system often shut out some of the most innovative ideas. Research was overlooked, or so the complaint went, simply because it had not been done by well-known scientists or doctors somehow connected to the National Institutes of Health. Even worse, some say their submissions were thwarted because a particular reviewer had a personal or professional vendetta against the author or his or her institution.

Dr. Donald Francis, who directed the CDC's laboratory effort against the disease during the early years of the epidemic, was one physician who suspected obstacles to publication of his and his colleagues' work were being thrown up by a political enemy. The problems arose after the controversy surrounding the discovery of the AIDS virus exploded, in mid-1984. Francis and other CDC staffers

early on had argued that the French, led by Dr. Luc Montagnier, deserved a large amount of the credit for the find. After all, they had
announced the breakthrough of isolating the virus a year before Dr.
Robert Gallo of the National Institutes of Health went public with his
very similar results. Francis said Gallo was so angry at the CDC's endorsement of Montagnier that he threatened "to take care of" people
there. His dislike for Francis was allegedly even stronger because the
CDC doctor claimed Gallo had not followed usual protocol in dealing
with the French discovery. Shortly after that conflict, Francis recalled,
articles that had his name attached to them would be sent back from
the journals with conflicting messages. According to Francis, one reviewer wrote, "It's worth running, but these minor things need to be
worked out." A second critique of the same piece contained scores of
questions about small details.

Because conflicting reviewers' reports are quite common in science
and because the reviewers' names are kept confidential, Francis could
not say for sure whether the overly negative critiques were coming
from Gallo's lab. The NIH researcher, of course, was being called on
repeatedly to review papers for the journals, because he was considered one of the leading experts on the epidemic.

The kind of investigative reporting necessary to unlock some of
these intrigues surrounding the AIDS story was almost nowhere to
be found in the mainstream media's coverage of the epidemic. The
medical and science journals themselves did not report the turmoil.
They held fast to their "academic" purpose.

Covering the Doctors

By the late 1970s, Americans seemed obsessed with medical news.
The nation's population was growing older and was more interested
in maintaining its health. As a result, medical news was playing a
bigger part in the mainstream media.

Science also was drawing a growing audience. The modern media
fascination with the subject began with the establishment of NASA, in
the early 1960s. By the time Apollo 10 was hurtling into outer space
with the world's first moonwalkers in 1969, every kid in America who
ever wanted to be a cop or firefighter or airplane pilot now wanted to
be an astronaut. The nation's media were equally giddy over the en-

tire event. Newspapers across the country ran "Countdown to the Moon" series, which featured beaming portraits of the astronauts and of the technology that would take them into space.

The American media were almost completely unprepared to cover a science story having the magnitude of the landing on the moon or the establishment of NASA. Few reporters who fought their way onto the prized assignment actually had any science background beyond the obligatory biology course in high school. As a result, journalists relied almost exclusively on NASA itself to frame the news. Its press conferences focused on the "wonder of American science" and the seemingly wholesome personalities of its astronauts. The reporters on hand at the Cape Canaveral launch never asked the kinds of questions they might have thrown at a government official proposing a multi-billion dollar Health Department program, or a Transportation Department plan to build a road around the world. Consequently, far from the news headlines were NASA's internal struggles, funding questions, and technical concerns that were at the center of the Apollo event. Most of those who covered the first moon flight earned the title of "Gee whiz" journalists from younger, better educated reporters who covered the same beat in the 1970s and 1980s. That "Gee whiz" crowd, however, set the pattern of science coverage for years to come. Those covering NASA almost never posed the tough questions, such as whether a particular space flight was safe, and what were the political motivations behind the timing of launches. Better reporting may not have prevented the horrible Challenger tragedy of 1986, in which the space rocket exploded and killed its seven passengers, but journalists would have been much better able to explain to Americans exactly how such an accident could have happened. The image of the explosion's stream of white smoke against a pale blue sky is etched into the national memory, but how NASA works is still grossly misunderstood. During the AIDS epidemic, as during the NASA launches, the word of the scientist would go largely unquestioned.

Science and medicine deserve to be covered as aggressively as defense, foreign affairs, and even City hall, if only because the tab for science and medicine is increasingly being picked up by the taxpayer. By the early 1980s, for example, government spending on the National Institutes of Health—just one item in the colossal Department of Health's budget—was about $3.6 billion, more than the funding for the entire Department of Justice.

Following the taxpayer's money is in the best tradition of American journalism. That is one reason the *New York Times* and the *Washington Post* have staked their reputations on covering Washington D.C., and why well-respected reporters at both papers are now assigned to cover the U.S. Department of Health and Human Services. For the same reason, the *Times's* medical reporter, Dr. Lawrence Altman, closely tracked huge spending programs like the one on the artificial heart.

That is how government spending helps set the news agenda. In the early 1980s, the lack of federal funding to investigate the AIDS epidemic and stem its spread served to define the disease as a low priority news item, even for newspapers like the *Times* and *Post,* with highly skilled and educated science and medicine reporters.

Return of the "Gee Whiz" Crowd

Because general science and medicine were becoming more important political issues in Washington, more newspapers and TV were making it news. By the early 1980s, ABC had hired on a science correspondent, George Strait, and NBC had an immunologist, Bob Bazelle, on its reporting staff. One of the pillars of a new twenty-four-hour news program, the Cable News Network, was this kind of reporting, which CNN's creators hoped would attract and hold the graying American audience. Still, most media outlets relied on journalists with at best a minimal science background—a biology, physics, or calculus course in college, or just a strong interest in the subject. In turn, those reporters depended heavily on the technical journals to figure out which breaking news was important, and which was not. Few questioned what they were fed by these publications, especially in the complex and confusing world of retrovirology, one of the branches of study that AIDS eventually fell into. That unquestioning acceptance helped further fortify the *New England Journal's* reputation among the mainstream press. For the science- and medicine-hungry media, these publications made their jobs easier.

Some medicine writers were more demanding than others. For example, National Public Radio's Laurie Garrett, who was trained in immunology, frequently served as a conduit for immunologists on either side of the country who had not yet read about their fellow researchers' studies. UCLA's Dr. Michael Gottlieb was one of the few scientists eager to talk to the media. Unfortunately, that kind of interaction was routinely discouraged by the existence of the Inglefinger Rule and other pressures. In Gottlieb's case, his colleagues and superiors let it be known that his frequent appearances in the mainstream press were somewhat unbecoming an academic. Publishing a study in the *New England Journal of Medicine* was appropriate, and extremely helpful for rising up the university ladder. A quote in the *New York Times* or on National Public Radio, on the other hand, was not going to shorten the path to tenure.

Trapped by the Inglefinger Rule

By the early 1980s, mandates similar to the *New England Journal*'s had been adopted by about three hundred major biomedical publications throughout the world. The Inglefinger Rule prohibits researchers from publishing any part of their findings, from graphs or tables to paragraphs, anywhere, including the mainstream press. As competition grew among doctors and scientists for space in the prestigious *New England Journal,* the otherwise sensible rule seemed to hang over the heads of researchers, who feared one whisper of their results would cut them off from the publication for good. Dr. Arnold Relman carried on the Inglefinger tradition when he became editor of the *Journal,* in 1977. Relman has said that the *Journal*'s rule is not meant to prohibit the flow of information: "The only 'flow' we attempt to discourage is the premature dissemination to the public of unsupported and unreviewed claims," he wrote in a *Journal* editorial. "We have never objected to any form of exchange among scientists or to presentations at meetings . . . but premature publicity . . . does not promote the free exchange of scientific information."

Whether the rule is misunderstood or not by researchers, doctors point to the chilling effect the *Journal*'s restrictions have on research, though few would do so on the record. The history of the AIDS epidemic is studded with incidents of scientists concealing information, or refusing to detail their findings, even when giving presentations at medical conferences, for fear that once their studies were revealed they would not be published in the more prestigious journals. Even top researchers with international reputations claimed to be sensitive to this prohibition. Dr. Robert Gallo refused to share data at a 1983 AIDS conference for that very reason. From minor findings of how the disease was spread to how the body reacts to the virus, the proprietary instincts that rules such as Inglefinger's served slowed the sharing process essential to good science. "Relman has scared the hell out of researchers," said Bruce Dan, a senior editor at *JAMA* and critic of the mainstream media's medicine coverage.

Few disciplines are as competitive as medicine. And almost no other technical publications vie for scoops and exclusives as the medical journals. It is, of course, done in a far more subtle way than the brawls among newspapers, magazines, and broadcast outlets in the mainstream media. But it is done for the same purpose: to beat out the competition. "Relman is ambitious," said Dr. Uwe Reinhardt, a health economist at Princeton University and one of the authorities on the medical journals. "He wants the *Journal* to be the most prestigious publication in the world." As a result, "he manipulates the flow of data, supposedly for the sake of peer review. It's actually about profits."

Relman undoubtedly isn't the only journal editor with that ambition. Yet the mainstream media have traditionally accepted the rules handed down by these chiefs without a challenge, even while some journalists recognize that the vaunted review process and the stifling of discussion it causes have contributed to debacles like the routine household-contact story. The fact that the journals generally do not correct their errors, as newspapers and magazines are sometimes obliged to do, tends to perpetuate mistakes. The *JAMA*-Oleske affair is just one example. Another notable incident occurred in the *British Medical Journal* in 1985, when it published a study by NIH's Dr. Robert Biggar. The researcher claimed as much as 20 percent of some parts of the Kenyan population had been infected with the AIDS virus. Biggar discovered shortly thereafter his findings had been skewed by so-called sticky serum, blood damaged by heat and humidity that often incorrectly registers a presence of the AIDS virus. The article prompted loud protests from Kenyan officials, who were understandably alarmed that their country was being pegged as the AIDS center of the world. As a result, some scientists were shut out of the country, and some news reports were banned. Nonetheless, the *British Medical Journal* never ran a correction.

Defenders of the medical journals' restrictive rules have argued that eventually the debate on many of the most divisive issues is aired, because the publications often run opposing viewpoints. In fact, the boundaries for such a discussion are often so narrow that the debate is nothing more than a muffled dialogue on obscure issues. And the most provocative voices are silenced because their views have not been sanctioned by the American medical establishment. Many claim that this is what happened with the discovery of the AIDS virus by scientists at the Pasteur Institute in Paris.

The French finding was first published in the United States in the journal *Science*. Considered one of the most groundbreaking publications in its field, it nonetheless has little effect on the science news agenda. The work *Science* publishes is often far more technical than what is found in the *New England Journal* or *JAMA*. Seldom do articles have as an immediate impact on the lives of Americans as, say, news of the dangers of cholesterol that appeared in the *Journal*. *Science* also does not produce carefully crafted press releases to grab the attention of journalists, as *JAMA* is known to do. The publication's feeble influence is no better illustrated than by its May 1983 issue, featuring the French discovery of the AIDS virus. No sooner was it published than it disappeared. American scientists did not begin to discuss this discovery until months later, when the finding was presented at a conference in Utah. Only a full year later did the cause of AIDS become a major news item, with the federal government's announcement that an American, Dr. Robert Gallo, had discovered the virus.

The University-Industrial Complex

The "Gee Whiz" attitude that still pervades American journalism's medical and science coverage seals off huge territories of the research complex. For instance, there is a growing collaboration of science and industry, which one expert in the field, Ohio State University Professor Martin Kenney, has called "the University-Industrial Complex." Like the behemoth military-industrial complex that President Eisenhower warned the nation of in the 1950s, this new research establishment is creating a very new dynamic in the world of research and technology. Just as scandals have plagued the collaboration between business and the military—with industry unduly influencing government and "disinterested" parties benefiting from the corruption—so too, Kenney senses, a dangerously cozy relationship between scientists and business is emerging. Unfortunately, journalists have rarely felt comfortable enough with science and medicine to pursue this connection.

As a result, the science and medical establishment goes as unquestioned as the findings that are presented as Truth from institutions like the *New England Journal of Medicine* and *JAMA*. No one in the mainstream media has probed the business interests of scientists doing AIDS research and how the publicity of their work affects the corporate world. For instance, Dr. Max Essex, a pillar of the journal-review process, held shares in a firm called Cambridge BioScience. Does the pull of commerce distort the goals of basic scientific research? As the university-industrial complex grows, these questions loom in importance. Yet they simply are not being asked.

Instead there is a pervasive sense that the medical and science establishment *owns* the news: that is, research, even though it is often supported by American tax dollars, should be doled out according to guidelines set up by the powers that rule the establishment.

Who Owns Science News, Anyway?

In the university-industrial complex, the *New England Journal's* Dr. Arnold Relman is clearly one of those powers. The Inglefinger Rule is just one way his publication controls the flow of news. The other is through "the embargo," a mandate that the news media may use no information on articles that will appear in the currently released issue until Wednesday at 6:00 p.m. eastern time. Those major outlets that abide by this agreement receive an advance copy of the *Journal*, usually delivered on Monday, rather than on Thursday when most subscribers get it. (Copies of *JAMA*, along with press releases highlighting particularly provocative articles, are sent out ten days in advance of the date on the cover.) About 250 journalists throughout the United States get an advance copy of the *Journal*, which is supposed to give them time to select and prepare stories, to gather the resources they might need to make sense of complex medical and science news.

At least that is how Relman claims it works. And to some extent it does. For important breaking stories in the *Journal*, reporters have a lead of up to two full days in which to write about them. Of course, the embargo does nothing to solve the problem of scrounging up sources to comment intelligently on the articles. A scientist who was not directly involved in the research—indeed, a scientist who might be willing to criticize a researcher's findings—would not yet have the new issue of the *Journal* when the reporter comes calling. As a result, the most important sources for a particular article are that article's authors. The predicament is similar to giving advance notice of a debate, but only allowing the audience to read what the advocates will say, and not their opponents.

Despite this frustrating situation, few journalists have challenged the embargo. The most publicized flare-up came in the spring of 1988, when the *New England Journal* published an article on the protection aspirin might provide for those who had not suffered from a heart attack. Claiming the wire service had gotten the story from sources other than the *Journal,* Reuters's executive editor in North America, Desmond Maberley, decided to run with the story on the Tuesday before the publication sanctioned its release. Almost immediately after Reuters published the news, and it was sent out across the news wires, news organizations nationwide followed up, so as not to be completely beaten out on the story. By the end of the day, Relman's embargo was meaningless.

For that transgression,. Relman withdrew Reuters's advance copy of the *Journal.* Maberley hardly was contrite: "We have an obligation to get the information," he said. Reuters is widely used on Wall Street and in financial markets throughout the world. Early notification could mean money for the service's subscribers. Maberley points out that many researchers knew about the results before the *Journal* was released, as did the federal government, which funded the research. Even drug companies were all prepared for the news, having known about the study for months. "The only person who didn't know about it was the average citizen," said Maberley.

Maberley is probably less concerned about the average American getting the information than he is about his Wall Street clients having it. Nonetheless, he has a point. Often, hundreds of researchers are aware of the latest major discovery months and sometimes years before it is made public. Even interested investors and manufacturers are likely to know about advances before the average taxpayer gets the word. Yet, the odds are good that the taxpayer paid for the research in the first place.

Dr. George Lundberg, *JAMA*'s editor, called Relman's revenge silly: "Reuters will get information about research to be published in the

Journal one way or the other." Reuters's Maberley said he was called by Relman soon after the incident. The doctor said he wanted to talk about getting the wire service reinstated on the list for advance copies. Maberley said he was not interested, that he could get the magazine's articles from other sources.

Forty Thousand and Counting

A reasonably well-connected journalist can certainly find his or her way around a *New England Journal* embargo easily enough. But once a reporter gains access to the articles, or to the information before it is published, how many physicians are willing to risk their chances of being published by talking to journalists about their research or breakthrough studies? Some AIDS doctors eschewed the technical journals entirely to get out their message. Los Angeles-based Dr. Neil Schram, for instance, was a widely published expert on the disease, but his work appeared almost exclusively in mainstream media like the *Los Angeles Times*. Such provocative appeals to readers, usually calling for them or the government to act on funding or other issues, would have been unheard of just a decade earlier.

For those scientists doing laboratory work, the popular press remains out of bounds. When will the research institutes remove the taint they place on scientists who have no qualms about dealing with the media? Seven years into his tenure track appointment, Dr. Michael Gottlieb, one of the first to describe the epidemic and one of the only researchers willing to work with reporters on almost every aspect of the story, left UCLA because he realized his chances for a full professorship were slim, in large part because he spent too much time explaining his work to the mainstream press. Experiences like that do not bode well for young researchers who would break down the barriers between scientists and the media.

Probably the best hope for progress toward that goal is in the explosion of specialty science and medicine journals. There are now forty thousand such periodicals published throughout the world. Since the beginning of the epidemic, fifty publications have sprouted up in the United States dealing with AIDS itself. The exclusivity rules of magazines like the *New England Journal* are continuously being challenged. Contrary to Dr. Relman's claims, science and medicine news is not hindered by the work of journalists probing these territories as they would the Environmental Protection Agency or the Pentagon. Science and medicine reporting is getting better. The fact is, the biggest disservice journalists can do is to echo unquestioningly the faulty data or overenthusiastic claims of a researcher.

Science and journalism are both driven by the same force: the desire to uncover the hidden secrets, to get to the bottom of things. The sense of shared motivations, along with awe for the achievements of researchers, has made reporters approach the white coats with more reverence than is healthy. Science is not about discovering the Truth. Rather, the endeavor is the slow progress that endless trial and error generate, and scientists are subject to the same quirks and passions and uncertainties as every other human being. Reporters should understand that and be particularly cynical of any institution or individual who purports to be offering something no scientist can ever produce.

Chapter 7
The unphotogenic epidemic

The avuncular David Brinkley faced ABC's "World News Tonight" audience on June 18, 1983, with the latest findings reported in a medical journal: "The terrible new disease, AIDS, first seen among homosexuals, drug users, Haitians and hemophiliacs, is now appearing among people who are none of these. A study in the *New England Journal of Medicine* says apparently the disease can be spread by contact between heterosexuals—and there's no cure in sight."

It took twenty seconds for Brinkley to read the news item and days for the phones to stop ringing in scientists' offices throughout the nation. The *Journal of the American Medical Association,* with the help of the media, recently had scared Americans into believing that people with AIDS could spread the disease through casual contact. Was this more proof of that? And what exactly did Brinkley mean when he used the term "heterosexuals"? Weren't most hemophiliacs, Haitians, and drug users heterosexual? Or was this latest finding more evidence that AIDS was spreading like wildfire anywhere people congregated: on the bus, in offices, in schools?

None of this was true, but this time the medical journals were not to blame for the confusion. The *New England Journal* article stated that sexual partners of heterosexuals with AIDS, not surprisingly, could be infected by "sexual contact." That route of transmission, especially from man to woman, was thought to be possible, even before this study. But just how important it would prove to be in the future of the epidemic, no one could say for sure.

Reporting the story correctly would not have taken up much more air time. Brinkley could have tucked in the word "sexual" before "contact between heterosexuals." The senior broadcaster was not known for his sexual straight talk. Neither was the network.

In its first year of reporting on AIDS, ABC had not built a reputation for conveying its subtleties. In interviews with everyone from frontline reporters to executive news directors, the same complaint was echoed: the thirty-minute network news format (which commercials whittle down to only twenty-two minutes of airtime) does not allow for reporting the day's events in any detail. "That's what news- **123** papers are for," said one ABC executive.

Increasingly, however, Americans are not filling in the gaps of the six o'clock news by reading daily newspapers. In 1987, the Roper TV poll showed that for the first time since the invention of TV, a majority of Americans were getting their news *only* from television. The survey also found that Americans are believing what they are being fed in the medium's twenty-second snippets. This made getting out accurate AIDS information extremely difficult during the early years of the epidemic.

The Talking Heads Spread Confusion

A month after the Brinkley newscast, the network reported on its ABC/*Washington Post* AIDS poll: 80 percent of the people surveyed had heard of the disease, a rather astounding number, considering that surveys have shown only a slightly larger percentage of Americans can identify where California is on a map of the United States. (Asked what they knew about this new disease, however, and their answers varied widely. As late as 1987, one in four Americans surveyed believed they could gets AIDS from *giving* blood.)

Later in that 1983 newscast, ABC reporter Ken Kashiwahara went on to detail how hysteria was sweeping across the country: First-aid classes in Coronado, California were suspended because people feared getting AIDS from the resuscitation dummy. Funeral directors in San Francisco were refusing to deal with the bodies of AIDS victims. Two nurses in San Jose quit rather than treat AIDS patients. Even journalists were struggling with the hysteria; a San Francisco TV station had attempted to interview a person with AIDS, but the studio technicians refused to have him come on the set for fear of contamination. He was interviewed by phone from his home.

Kashiwahara did not touch on the fact that the media had contributed, if not largely created, the unnecessary fear. The epidemic was not spreading by the touch of an infected individual or the sneeze of a person with AIDS. The CDC's Dr. James Curran repeated that information at every media opportunity he got. Elected officials, from New York's Mayor Ed Koch to San Francisco's Mayor Dianne Feinstein, spoke out loudly on the subject to help calm public fears. Even Secretary of Health Margaret Heckler, who had been ineffective in pulling together any coordinated effort on AIDS, showed up at the bedside of a patient when the TV cameras were rolling. With her fluffy blond wig slightly akimbo, as was her unwitting trademark, she held the young man's hand to show Americans that being close to and even touching someone with the disease was not something to be feared.

But every time David Brinkley delivered a misinformed tidbit about "heterosexual contact," or Dan Rather looked into the camera gravely and pronounced that the disease was being spread by "household contact," months of reasoned public health education were undone. A single network's evening news show reaches about thirteen million people. Combined, the three major programs are seen by almost one-fifth of the nation. Napoleon had feared the journalist's pen far more than the sword; the TV camera is a media weapon for the atomic age.

Kashiwahara's report ran for two minutes (two minutes and fifteen seconds is the average time allotted to most features on network news programs). Max Robinson, the first black anchor at one of the three big national programs, gave his own summary: "Fighting the fear of AIDS is as important as fighting the disease itself." He delivered the line without a hint of irony.

Bad Blood

"Since deadly Acquired Immune Deficiency Syndrome first appeared in 1979," CBS's Dan Rather began the August 30, 1983, report, "there has been concern about the possibility that it could be transmitted in a blood transfusion." Bad blood and the casual-contact scare made AIDS a nationwide story for TV. Rather had the perfect lead-in for the second half of the "Evening News," when broadcasters are most likely to lose their audience's attention to pots boiling over on the stove or to dinnertime conversation.

The story that reporter Terry Drinkwater unraveled that night attempted to trace a vial of a blood product tainted with the AIDS virus. He started with the Southern California hemophiliac who allegedly had been infected by the product, and followed it back to a blood donor who had been healthy when he gave blood, but who later died of AIDS. "Two hundred hemophiliacs across the country could have received transfusions from that infected plasma," he reported. It was a sophisticated story, moving from blood donation centers to warehouses apparently filled with cases of the plasma. There were eye-catching graphics that detailed the distribution of the product nationwide, and personal interviews with frightened hemophiliacs dependent on donors whose blood might kill them. Then, in a dramatic move, Drinkwater held up the as-yet-unnamed suspect: "5,592 vials of this," he said, were contaminated and on the market in the United States. "This" was as close as Drinkwater ever came to revealing the name of the product. Even when he aimed the vial at the camera, the print on its label was obscured so badly that no viewer could identify the medicine.

"Already the product has been put on sale throughout the country," said Drinkwater. Now it was being frantically recalled. The camera panned a hemophiliac's refrigerator, stocked with what those very familiar with the product might recognize as factor VIII, a blood extract prepared by Cutter Laboratories that provides hemophiliacs with the clotting ability their blood lacks. Because hemophilia affects only about twenty thousand Americans, the average viewer easily could have overlooked the story. But for any hemophiliac, there was an obvious unanswered question: was Drinkwater's poisoned vial of "this" actually factor VIII?

The following night, in nearly the same time segment as the hemophiliac story had run, Rather read a clarification: "Last night we reported the recall of a blood byproduct that could have been tainted by an AIDS victim. In the course of that report, we also showed a picture of Cutter factor VIII, a generic blood plasma widely used by hemophiliacs. For accuracy and fairness, we want to emphasize that byproduct is not the subject of a recall." So what was "the subject of a recall"? Unbelievably, Rather never said.

Journalists sometimes don't give the complete story—the names of victims of violent crime, for example, are often withheld—to protect those who might be harmed by the news. Network executives could not remember why the decision had been made to play the story the way it was presented. "Protecting" hemophiliacs, whose doctors should be telling them that the drug they were using might be contaminated, was the broadcasters' best defense. A more likely reason was that Drinkwater, and Rather, had waded into the unfamiliar waters of AIDS reporting with their better judgment overwhelmed by the situation. Often during the epidemic, broadcasters have ceded to "officialdom" the critical responsibility of warning Americans. In this case, it was assumed that doctors or the government or someone else would somehow take care of the crisis, making sure that no new hemophiliacs were infected, and that those with the drug were prevented from taking it. All the broadcasters had to do was hint at the problem. It was an absurdly trusting position for Dan "The Shark" Rather to take, and it would be embraced throughout the AIDS crisis by journalists who knew better. But fear of the unknown also adds to hysteria. Even nonhemophiliac viewers would have reason to be frightened by the confusion.

No One's Beat

Network news is a beat-the-clock game. Time to get the story and tell it right is always in short supply. That is true because TV news is much more immediate than print news, and because the nightly program is so condensed (the twenty-two-minute format has room for about the same amount of words that would fit on a half-page of a daily newspaper). In addition, the networks generally use fewer reporters than the print media equivalents. For example, NBC "Nightly News" has fifty-four correspondents, reporters, and producers, whereas the *New York Times* has five times that many reporters and editors. The imbalance is due in part to the fact that broadcast journalists cost more. Most make more money than even the most highly paid newspaper reporters. ABC's medical correspondent George Strait, for example, is paid about $90,000 per year, which is considered an average salary for network news. The scale can rise as high as Dan Rather's reported $3 million annual paycheck. What's more, for each correspondent in front of the camera reading the news, there are at least two more people behind the lens, including the camera operator and a producer, who help pull the story together and get it on the air. Subtract all the expensive high-tech equipment that goes with telling the TV story, and the cost is still more than three times higher than what the newspaper incurs for the same news item.

No wonder, than, that the networks generally did not invest in "experts," except for political coverage, as the larger newspapers and magazines had done for years. Thus when AIDS became a news story for TV, there were few broadcasters who could report it with any sophistication. And no reporter was claiming it as a personal beat. By the end of 1983, no fewer than thirteen journalists had reported one or more of the eighteen AIDS stories CBS did. The other networks 127 had fewer reporters working on the story. At ABC, George Strait did most of the reports, and he at least had some background in science, a master's degree in biochemical genetics. NBC has a reputation among the networks for hiring specialists. Its Supreme Court correspondent, Carl Stern, has a law degree, for example, and Irving R. Levine, the business correspondent, was trained as an economist. For most of its stories on AIDS, NBC turned to Robert Bazell, who had nearly completed a Ph.D. in immunology at the University of California at Berkeley before becoming a journalist.

Only ABC has two full-time medical reporters, George Strait and Dr. Tim Johnson. Johnson was one of the first doctors to do medical reporting on the air back in 1972, when the American Medical Association still had tight strictures on M.D.s appearing on broadcast outlets. Johnson encouraged early coverage of the AIDS epidemic, and he was the first broadcaster on the major networks to feature an interview with anyone connected with the crisis: the CDC's Dr. James Curran got a fleeting forty-five-second spot on "Good Morning, America" in December 1981. Johnson also was the first TV journalist to report on the crisis for a major network, with another morning show segment on pneumonia cases among gay men, on February 23, 1982. Johnson, a conservative doctor who also teaches at the Harvard Medical School, works out of Boston. He rarely travels beyond the Northeast to file stories because, according to sources, he is afraid to fly. Some of his critics claim that phobia helped keep much of ABC's AIDS coverage confined to the Northeast corridor between Washington, D.C. and Boston, despite the major news occurring in Los Angeles and San Francisco.

Whereas an individual network's morning show reaches upwards of eight million viewers, the evening broadcasts can bring in audiences twice that size on particularly heavy news days. Despite ABC's early start and talented bank of medical reporters, NBC's Robert Bazell was the first reporter to broadcast an AIDS story on the influential evening news, on June 17, 1982. That was a late start, to be sure, but it beat out ABC by four months, and CBS by half a year. By June of 1983, the NBC "Nightly News" had done thirteen stories. ABC had reported only eight, and CBS had filed a scant six.

Why did the networks come to the crisis so late? Some reporters have claimed that until the epidemic began moving beyond gays, drug

abusers, hemophiliacs, and Haitians—that is, into the larger population—it wasn't a story that interested the average viewer. That attitude, as translated by a score of broadcasters, meant the network
powers did not want to see stories about junkies or homosexuals.

Sally Holms, senior news producer at ABC, remembers the resistance she ran into when trying to get some AIDS stories on the air.
A feature she wanted done on New York's Gay Men's Health Crisis
was criticized for "being too soft on gays." Another, on minorities with
AIDS, was picked apart so thoroughly by upper managment that the
segment almost died before airing. She also remembers having trouble
with the technical crew: one cameraman refused to go into the room
of an AIDS patient.

Such opposition was not limited to broadcasters, of course. Resistance to AIDS news, or news about gays and i.v. drug users, kept the
epidemic under-reported for years. During that first part of the crisis,
the lack of AIDS news in the print media, especially in the *New York
Times,* helped set the agenda for the networks. According to Ernest
Leiser, former executive producer of CBS "Evening News" and one
of the architects of the networks' news format, "Two-thirds of the
stories that the networks cover are picked up from newspapers and
magazines, and most of those stories run first in the *New York Times.*"
NBC's Robert Bazell became interested in the epidemic only after
reading an article by the *Times*'s Dr. Lawrence Altman that ran in the
back of the paper.

The news wires—Associated Press, United Press International, and
Reuters—are also important agenda-setters for the networks, especially for science and medical news. "All the networks are driven
by the wires," said Bill Lord, former executive producer of ABC's
"World News Tonight." "[The wire copy] is in front of us. It has the
appearance of fact, even if it's wrong." The only medical or science
journals widely read among those covering the beat for TV are the
New England Journal of Medicine and the *Journal of the American Medical
Association.*

The networks occasionally work to reverse the agenda-setting cycle
by promoting stories they are about to break. That was done, for example, when NBC's Robert Bazell put together a piece in the spring
of 1983 on the research into the cause of AIDS at Harvard and in Dr.
Robert Gallo's labs at the National Institutes of Health. The news report aired almost exactly a year before the work would become major
news with Gallo's announcement of the discovery of the AIDS virus,
labeled HTLV-III (for Human T-Lymphotropic Virus, Type III). Ex-

cept for technical reports on the French discoveries in *Science* magazine, followed up by the *New York Native,* Bazell's story was the first
word on the work in the United States. Minutes before the story was
to air on NBC, print reporters like the *New York Times's* Altman were
called by the network. With the warning, such reporters would have a
chance to do their own stories, crediting NBC, of course, with breaking the news. (Altman was never able to confirm the lead NBC gave
him. A key scientist allegedly had his teenage son tie up the phone so
he would not have to talk to any more reporters, and the *Times* could
not run with the story.)

That kind of interest in AIDS news, however, was as rare at the
networks as it was at the *Times* in the early years of the epidemic. At
these institutions, journalists had a strong incentive not to propose
story ideas on the epidemic: "The whole focus of the day's activities
[for the broadcaster] is getting on the air," said ABC's Lord. "If you
can keep up your appearance on TV, it looks like you're productive."
Covering AIDS was not going to get a journalist that precious space
on the front page or time on the nightly news. What's more, most
broadcasters, especially in science and medical reporting, follow the
news rather than break it. Producers will most often assign a story
from the *Times* or one that has come over the wire. "The idea isn't to
get something new," said one TV reporter; "it's to make sure we're not
beaten out."

"We're good leeches," explained Lord.

Nonstop News

The TV outlet that was on top of the AIDS story almost from the start
was Cable News Network, founded by Ted Turner and on the air only
since June of 1980. The single most important force behind that coverage was Reese Schonfeld.

Cheap and smart. That's how colleagues of the former CNN president describe him. Those two qualities undoubtedly helped the old
UPI hand get the job at CNN, where he was given a modest sum of
money to do a huge task: start up a national network to compete with
the three established giants in the broadcast news business.

The enterprise was begun with a clear strategy. It would serve
up the news when and how the audience wanted it. As Schonfeld and
Turner had discovered through viewer surveys, that meant twenty-

130 four hours of programming every day. It fit the increasingly varied life-style of many Americans because they could tune in anytime, not just at the traditional dinner hour, to get the latest news. Who would be watching this nonstop station? The broadcast experts saw the future of the American media audience, both for newspapers and TV, as an increasingly older population. The trend was under way by the end of the 1970s. The faithful newspaper subscriber as well as the consistent news viewer was well past thirty and could count on living more than three decades longer. Health news and information had a big appeal to such a viewer.

CNN was hard-pressed for cash, but it managed to place sparsely staffed bureaus in nine cities, including Los Angeles and San Francisco. Those areas, of course, were two of the hardest hit by the epidemic. Because the network was based in Ted Turner's hometown of Atlanta—another economizing measure to take advantage of the anti-union laws of Georgia—CNN also had easy access to the Centers for Disease Control. The CDC became a major news source for the network's science and medical teams, and its proximity was probably the prime reason that CNN was the first broadcast outlet to run a story on the epidemic, on July 7, 1981. The brief segment flashed on the screen "Koposi's Sarcoma," a misspelling of the skin disease Kaposi's that had been diagnosed in "forty-one young gay men."

Science and medicine had a privileged position at CNN because many of the segments were sponsored by Bristol-Myers, the pharmaceutical company. When correspondents at the bureaus were not busy covering their regular beats, they all had orders to work on medical stories, according to Schonfeld. CNN had to fill those minutes bought by Bristol-Myers.

By the early 1980s, CNN owner Ted Turner, the heir to a small southern media company, had begun calling his creation "America's most important network." The most ambitious, at any rate. In the early years, the network's audience measured about 1 percent of that watching ABC, CBS, or NBC. Cable TV reached only a little more than a third of the households in America. The medium came into its own later in the decade, when cable reached a majority of households. (By 1988, 55 percent of U.S. homes were wired for cable.)

For the three major broadcast networks, the expansion of cable meant the information oligopoly they had created would be forced to stretch far more. CNN was joined by other new networks. By the mid-1980s, the networks' decades-old dominance of TV was being challenged; the percentage of prime-time viewers tuned into ABC,

NBC, or CBS—an overwhelming 77 percent in the 1984–85 season—started sliding. (By 1988, the audience had sunk to 66 percent.) The rising competition, which cut into ad revenues, along with the cost of doing business in Manhattan, forced programs like CBS's "Evening News" to cut back sharply on staff. CNN's biggest advantage was its newness: "It's not hampered by thirty years of cost escalation and union growth," said ABC's Lord. As the decade passed, news executives increasingly began to watch the newcomer. But during the early years of the AIDS epidemic, CNN certainly was no news leader for the major networks or any other significant media outlet.

AIDS and Diet Pills

The lack of coverage by the print media not only made it easy for the networks to avoid the story, but also seemed to encourage broadcasters to trivialize the epidemic. "The disease called AIDS . . . sounds less than deadly, more like a diet pill," said NBC co-anchor Roger Mudd, in a lead-in for an AIDS story broadcast in mid-1983. At the time, the number of AIDS cases in the United States had risen to 1,500. As abrasively corny and inappropriate as the lead was, veteran broadcaster Mudd obviously had an audience in mind when he delivered those words. The target is usually what the white, late middle-aged male executives envision as "middle America."

"We think of our audience as a family," explained ABC's Bill Lord. "Mom's busy getting dinner ready, pop's home from work having a beer, the kids are running around." Ozzie's in the living room, and in the kitchen is Harriet, the busy midwestern mother who occasionally takes a diet pill, perhaps even the once ambitiously marketed Ayds diet candy. This family would understand Mudd's attempt at a pun, no doubt, but would they pick up on the severity of the new scourge: that AIDS the disease slimmed down its victims, as well, but to deathly skeletons of their former selves?

God, Man, and Dan Rather

Fleeting time, the print media's ignoring AIDS, and smaller news staff all took their toll on the quality of broadcast news. But probably the most important negative influence on AIDS coverage was the conservative attitude at the networks themselves. No one personified that attitude more than the "princes" of the medium, the anchors.

ABC's youngish star, the Canadian Peter Jennings, who was in his early forties when the epidemic began, admitted that network executives, including himself, were generally homophobic in the early years, and that AIDS stories were not of much interest. NBC's Tom Brokaw was hardly more progressive, but he more readily accepted the judgments of medical reporter Robert Bazell, who was consistently covering the story. Whereas Jennings did not have the final say on what would appear on the nightly newscast, Brokaw shared news decisions with co-anchor Roger Mudd in the early eighties. When Brokaw became the sole anchor in December of 1983, and then managing editor as well, news judgments were generally made by consensus.

At CBS, Dan Rather served as both the anchor and the dominating news czar of the evening broadcast. Not only was he involved in writing and sometimes reporting the news, but he also had control of the final product. Vesting that much power in one man makes the network particularly vulnerable. When, for example, in 1988 Rather walked off the set in a huff over his newscast being preempted momentarily by a sports event, he effectively shut down the whole news operation.

Despite the New Right's conviction that Rather is rabidly liberal, those who have worked with the man describe him as conservative and often inflexible. He is extraordinarily sensitive about appearing biased, and he has little interest in promoting causes. If the often caustic newsman has a hidden agenda, it does not include homosexuals. His social conscience certainly was not provoked by an epidemic sweeping their ranks. Getting AIDS stories past Rather in the early years meant doing an end-run around that inflexibility.

More than any other factor, the network's AIDS coverage suffered because almost no one was admitting any personal connection to the people suffering from the disease. At other fairly conservative media organizations like *Newsweek*, which covered the crisis well from early on, there was at least one person who had a strong link to the crisis. Even at Associated Press, where no one who covered AIDS claimed to have a connection, other journalists within the organization who were not reporting on the epidemic did acknowledge such a tie and showed particular interest in how their colleagues were handling the crisis. That kind of feedback, especially with a breaking story filled with such uncertainties as AIDS, is extremely helpful in judging appropriate emphasis and even rounding up sources.

But at CBS, for example, one executive claimed: "There are no gay people at the network." More likely, a business set in the heart of Manhattan is employer to scores of homosexuals, none of whom apparently were willing to admit openly their concern about the epidemic that was swirling around them. Even NBC's Robert Bazell, married and with children and whose strong interest in the disease derived from the science mystery it posed, was rarely approached by gay colleagues commenting on his work. "I do know of gay people within the NBC organization," said Bazell, "and they have been remarkably silent."

The only openly gay broadcast journalist who pushed for early coverage was ABC's Joe Lovett. A producer for the network's news magazine, "20/20," he successfully lobbied to get that show to air a segment on the disease in 1983. Lovett came to the story early in part because he knew people who were getting ill. He was also a friend and neighbor of AIDS activist Larry Kramer. Lovett remembers mentioning Kramer's name to ABC medical correspondent George Strait. Strait eventually was introduced to Kramer by another of the playwright's media acquaintances, Carl Bernstein, the former *Washington Post* reporter of Watergate fame who worked briefly at ABC as Washington bureau chief.

When Strait began covering AIDS as a social issue, he used that contact. Kramer, as he had done before for dozens of other journalists, served as Strait's guide to the fast-lane life of gays in New York City. That connection paid off in some sophisticated reporting.

Strait's inside knowledge and Bob Bazell's expertise, however, were not enough to keep the networks from producing stories with embarrassingly bad emphases, inconsistencies, and downright errors.

By early 1983 scientists studying the disease had a good idea that AIDS could be spread through blood tranfusions. The rise of cases in hemophiliacs proved that, as did a number of otherwise unexplained incidences of the disease. In January the American Red Cross tried to calm rising fears by publicizing its plan to screen donors more carefully. Nonetheless, Dr. Joseph Bove of the American Blood Bank Association seemed reluctant to alarm either those who needed blood or those who might want to donate. Gays, especially in San Francisco and New York, for years had been some of the best donors. So when CBS interviewed Bove on February 26, 1983, he flatly denied that any special screening for blood donations was needed: "We have no medical or scientific evidence that justifies such a course right now," he said. "I think it's an overreaction."

The reaction, of course, continued to heat up as more evidence was uncovered that AIDS really was spreading through blood transfusions. Only five days later, when ABC came calling, Dr. Bove was significantly more alarmed. "Clearly there is some concern . . . that AIDS, whatever it is, is in the blood supply." Blood banks were deciding to use a questionnaire to screen out Haitians, drug users, and gays. It was an obvious contradiction that could have led journalists to a major story. How contaminated was the blood supply? Were the blood banks covering up for what might be turning into a deadly situation? No wonder the viewing audience was confused about AIDS. Not only were journalists who were reporting on the issue befuddled, but they were contradicting each other routinely. What was safe, and unsafe, no one seemed to know, and the networks were not working to straighten it all out.

The Look and Sound of AIDS

Stories about such contradictions in the world of medicine and science do not play well on television, primarily because they are not "visual," they do not lend themselves to fancy graphics or eye-catching scenes. The whole AIDS story suffered from lack of graphic interest. There were only so many shots, or so it seemed, that could be used to illustrate AIDS. There was the typical street scene in the gay community: a shot of men walking hand-in-hand with other men on the sidewalks of San Francisco's Castro District or New York's Greenwich Village. With the networks' fear of shocking their audiences with things homosexual, even that image was not used very often. For a clinical story on how the disease affected the body, or some new finding on AIDS devastation, there were the hospital shots of a patient withering away or closeups of Kaposi's sarcoma spots. The third most used pictorial was that of an individual going through the routine of his or her daily life, used to illustrate the personal consequences of the plague. Many patients were not willing, however, to risk the backlash of bigotry against themselves or their families that often followed going public with the disease, so appropriate visuals for TV were often hard to come by.

Broadcasters tell stories of their executive producers refusing to run breaking AIDS news unless a dramatic shot of a deathly ill patient could be delivered. The TV journalist, especially one who worked for the networks, could often meet this demand by convincing a patient to go public for the sake of educating others. Increasingly, however, the person portrayed didn't represent the groups most affected by the disease. For example, in a survey of TV portrayals of people with AIDS done in 1987 by the Center for Media and Public Affairs, heterosexuals were eight times more likely to be shown than homosexuals, although there are about eight times as many homosexuals with the disease. Similarly, women make up about 14 percent of televised depictions of AIDS patients but represent only 7 percent of the total AIDS cases in the nation. In the early years of the epidemic, middle-class whites with AIDS were much more likely to be photographed than poor minorities.

If the broadcasters' attitudes towards AIDS and the graphics they chose to illustrate the epidemic were misleading, the language they used was dangerously subtle. It was not just the older generation of broadcast journalists like David Brinkley who were bashful about using straightforward language. David Hartmann, former host of ABC's "Good Morning America," in his early fifties at the time, refused to use any terms that had to do with male sexual problems like impotence, according to the network's Bill Lord. ABC's medical and science correspondent, George Strait, who was then in his late thirties, remembered dancing around issues of explicitness with regard to AIDS. "Contact" was the preferred way to describe how AIDS was transmitted, he recalled, which bolstered all the wrong ideas about the epidemic.

No one at the networks was drawing up strict guidelines to prohibit use of explicit, and accurate, language. As one executive put it, "The standards of comfortableness tend to be set fairly informally." But in the back of news executives' minds is the fear that if the language is too bold, people will turn their TVs off. "We go into homes during dinnertime," Lord pointed out. Of course, that did not stop journalists from covering other intricate and unpleasant medical matters, such as the emergency operation on President Reagan after the attempted assassination in 1981, or his colon cancer operation later in the decade. Yet broadcasters seemed wary of offending the public with sexual explicitness. The greater fear, of course, was that advertisers' dollars would vanish, as well. That threat is faced by every news executive, though none would admit being influenced by it. Four years into the AIDS crisis, the network evening news programs were still avoiding clear language on how the disease was being spread. ABC's

George Strait, in 1985, found a way to break the language barrier: he asked Dr. Anthony Fauci of the National Institutes of Health to use the term "anal sex" on the air so the reporter would not have to.

ABC's Lord compared the breakthrough to the network's challenge when covering the Vietnam war protests: "The protesters would shout 'One, two, three, four, we don't want your fucking war,'" he recalled, "and we finally had to run it." Lifesaving plaintalk and college kids' crudity were hardly on the same scale of courageous broadcasting, but that seemed to elude most TV journalists. CNN was the important exception. As early as September 21, 1981, the network described diseases among homosexuals as being transmitted through "anal and oral sex." In June 1983 CNN went inside a bathhouse to report on sexual promiscuity among gays. Only a tiny percentage of Americans was watching CNN at this point in the epidemic. For the most part, the facts of AIDS, as aired on TV, would remain unmentionable mysteries.

Indeed, "mysterious" was one of the broadcasters' favorite modifiers to describe the disease. CBS's Dan Rather seemed to prefer "deadly and mysterious" when he introduced AIDS stories. ABC's Peter Jennings moved from "new and frightening" to "terrible and new" over a year's time. He finally settled on "mystery disease." NBC's Tom Brokaw was a bit more imaginative, moving from "terrifying and mysterious" to "fatal, mysterious" and eventually the punchier "mysterious disease."

None of these phrases were nearly as descriptive as simple and clear language would have been: "anal and oral sex," for starters, and "infection through intravenous injection with a dirty needle." Instead, terms that mystified the disease tended to generate the kind of fear of the unknown that "cancer" traditionally had provoked. Broadcasters were helping to instill and foment the worst anxieties in Americans.

Cats, Monkeys, and the Caribbean

CNN, for example, picked up Randy Shilts's story in the *San Francisco Chronicle* about AIDS being spread by a kiss—between an elderly woman with AIDS and her husband. Despite CNN's strong commitment to science and medicine coverage and AIDS reporting in particular, it did not follow up on the frightening story and never told its viewers that the story had turned out to be false.

ABC turned to the possibility of AIDS transmission by way of contact with pets. It discovered feline leukemia, which had been studied for sixteen years: "It is called FAIDS; it is almost identical to AIDS in humans," correspondent Roger Carras reported. No one had shown that there was a connection between Feline Acquired Immune Deficiency Syndrome and AIDS. But the comparison made a compelling "news bite," a five-second to ten-second quote or phrase designed to grab the attention of viewers and hold it for the rest of the story. The FAIDS report ran for four minutes and twenty seconds, longer than any previous story on the AIDS epidemic.

In March of 1984, CBS focused on a monkey disease, which had been dubbed Simian AIDS. This ailment at least was structurally similar to the human malady. And doctors genuinely believed that by studying SAIDS, they might come up with clues to the origins of human AIDS. It was a carefully worded report, cautioning that no therapy was just around the corner.

If broadcasters were hunting for other ways to cover AIDS, however, they should have followed Robert Bazell's example. In a June 1983 story, he took viewers inside epidemic-wracked Haiti and detailed the transmission of AIDS more clearly than any of the major networks had done up to that point. There was a visit to Chez Denise, a bar that also served as a meeting place for male prostitutes and their clients, many of them Americans. Bazell visited Haitian folk doctors, who with rates of $2 per visit had become the foundation of the poverty-stricken nations' health-care system. In one practitioner's office, used hypodermic needles floated in a bowl of lukewarm water, waiting to be inserted in the next patient. Was AIDS making its way from Haiti to the United States? Bazell asked. Just as likely, he pointed out, the disease was coming from the United States brought by tourists, and passed through sex and the use of dirty needles. As with all groups, Haitians were not predisposed for AIDS. They were being infected in the very same ways as American and Euorpean gays, i.v. drug users, hemophiliacs, and heterosexuals worldwide. Only two years later did the federal government take reports like Bazell's to heart and remove Haitians from the list of groups at high risk for AIDS. However, even in the late 1980s, they remained one of the "four H's," along with homosexuals, heroin (i.v. drug)

users, and hemophiliacs, the groups most closely identified with the
disease.

The AIDS Brightener

Journalists follow the leader—and broadcasters do so more than most. As William Paley, the CBS kingpin, once said, TV is a consensus medium. Broadcasters try "not to threaten the middle," as one top ABC executive put it. What is deemed to be most important by agenda-setting media institutions tends to be picked up and played prominently by other outlets. That was how transmission stories became big news in 1983. ABC had done six minutes of AIDS coverage in 1982 on its nightly news program. The next year the network did twenty-three minutes, most of them devoted to how the disease was or was thought to be spreading. In the same period, NBC's nightly news coverage jumped from five minutes to thirty-two minutes. But no network had a bigger leap in interest than CBS: its scant two minutes and thirty seconds of AIDS news reported in 1982 was dwarfed by almost thirty-five minutes in 1983.

By the end of 1983, many journalists—especially broadcasters—believed they were running out of AIDS news, even though almost no one was looking into the funding problems, the internal struggles in the scientific research establishment, or the scandals that were part of the story of the epidemic. Many in print media were focusing on the personal stories of the epidemic: *Newsweek*'s cover story on AIDS and gays, for example, and the *New York Times*'s groundbreaking series on the epidemic in communities across the country. ABC's Joe Lovett and others were doing similar stories. But nightly news broadcasters were less eager to do features on homosexuals. Increasingly, they began to seek out AIDS brighteners.

It has been said that the American imagination has little room for sadness. Films with tragic endings tend to flop at the nation's box offices, and situation comedies, in which the contrived conflicts are always settled before the final commericals begin to roll, are always popular. The evening news follows the same pattern, almost always ending on an upbeat note. Despite starvation in Ethiopia, bloodshed in the Mideast, and droughts in the heartland, if Dan Rather can sign

off with an amusing brief, all's right with the world. Or so some executive producers seem to think.

Likewise, Peter Jennings broadcast this ray of hope in the late fall
of 1983:

> Doctors may have a new clue about the mysterious disease
> AIDS. . . . Researchers are examining a plant fungus which has
> been found in the blood of three AIDS victims. The fungus seems
> to act like a drug which has been known to lower the body's resis-
> tance to the disease.
>
> Doctors say their research is very preliminary but one re-
> searcher says, "We are very excited about it."

Was this big news, or wasn't it? ABC gave it only twenty seconds, yet
it was the first breakthrough on AIDS that "World News Tonight" had
broadcast. Once again, the story opened a floodgate of questions the
network had no intention of answering.

The *New England Journal of Medicine* was the source of the lead. Researchers at the National Institutes of Allergy and Infectious Diseases,
a part of the National Institutes of Health, had written up their findings in a letter to the publication, which printed it with a dozen other
pieces of correspondence. The Associated Press picked it up and ran
a brief story on the item, couching the news in cautious terms: "the
fungus might turn out to be another opportunistic infection . . . or
even a contaminant of the (AIDS) culture." No one was calling the
work a "breakthrough."

But for the year and a half the nightly news of the major networks
had been covering AIDS, this was the first hint Jennings might have
seen of a discovery that could prompt work toward a cure. If the audience was going to continue listening to the sparse reports on the epidemic, they would have to be given upbeat news now and then, some
broadcasters believed. The ABC staff could not remember how the
story was reported, but clearly it was taken directly from the Associated Press wire, sliced to twenty seconds, and popped into the broadcast. This mouthful of a news bite, about which at least one researcher
was "very excited," was never heard of again on Jennings's news show.

Jennings was not the only one guilty of this. On April 4, 1984, Dan
Rather slid this thirty-second story into the last minutes of the broadcast: "Cornell University Medical College doctors reported they have

discovered a potentially treatable defect in the immune system of people suffering from AIDS. This finding raises hope that gamma interferon will be the first effective medicine for the disease." After frustrating and controversial trials, such as the one Thomas, the brother of *Newsweek* correspondent Vincent Coppola, had been involved in, interferon proved to do little for AIDS patients. Nonetheless, the April 4 story was the first and last mention of gamma interferon as an AIDS treatment on the CBS "Evening News." That night, Rather ended the news with a brief on Bozo the Clown, who was celebrating a birthday.

Researchers whose data did not flower as they might have fancied are not likely to track down once-enthusiastic reporters to correct the matter. That is one important way in which bad research becomes news—and myth. With every mention of a new treatment on the network evening news, hundreds and sometimes thousands of phone calls poured into scientists' and government offices. The calls came from friends, families, lovers of AIDS patients, and from patients themselves. There was an extremely receptive audience on the other side of the screen who deserved to know not only that a drug or treatment trial seemed successful, but also that it had failed. Journalists who had raised such hopes had a responsibility to tell the whole story.

Downscaling the Downbeat Story

With no particularly good news to report, and no indications that AIDS was spreading in some horrible new way and threatening the "average" American or journalist, media coverage throughout the nation began to drop off in early 1984.

The announcement of the discovery of the AIDS virus in late April predictably caused a new spurt in AIDS reporting, in newspapers and magazines as well as on television. CBS claimed to have broken the story about the discovery with its April 19 report: "Researchers in the U.S. and France have new evidence that a type of virus first identified in AIDS victims in France might be the cause of the disease." In fact, NBC's Robert Bazell had reported almost a full year earlier on the American research being done on the virus, although he made no mention then of the French discovery, which preceded the Americans' by more than a year. Bazell did not report on the Pasteur Institute's early success until April 22, 1984. CBS featured the French discovery on April 20: "It was at Paris's Pasteur Institute that the first major breakthrough in the cause of AIDS took place," the network reported. The AIDS culprit had been named, too: "Lymphadenopathy-Associated Virus, or LAV."

On April 23, all the networks started their newscasts with the press conference held by Secretary of Health Margaret Heckler, introducing Dr. Robert Gallo and his findings. Not only was it the first time AIDS gained the esteemed "top of the news" slot, but it was one of the rare occasions when a report on the epidemic wound up in the first half of the news program.

Reporting Dr. Robert Gallo's findings did not make for the best television. CNN had become the trusty news source that almost always covered such announcements at length, and the conference was no exception. ABC summed up the media show by repeating the overly ambitious Heckler claims that a vaccine would be tested in two years. NBC was characteristically much more cautious, saying development of a vaccine might take much longer than two years. CBS, which had touted the French discovery days earlier, was suddenly backing away. After the U.S. government crowned Dr. Gallo the discoverer of the AIDS virus—in what the *New York Times* was calling a "fierce fight for credit"—CBS embraced him. So much for the network's reputation of baiting the Reagan administration, which Rather was supposed to have fostered.

The tough questions about this discovery and the credit-sharing were largely left to the print media to ask. After the Heckler press conference, AIDS disappeared from broadcast news for months. It was as if these journalists had been waiting for the premier story to break so that they could dispense with the epidemic. It would be picked up, some perplexed reporters predicted, when a vaccine had been found, and then once again when the cure was discovered.

Regardless of the reasoning, AIDS news on the three major networks dropped dramatically for the rest of 1984. By year's end, CBS's coverage had been cut in half, NBC's by almost two-thirds, as compared with 1983. ABC spent only slightly more time on AIDS than it had in 1982. "Shouldn't we be doing more on this story?" Strait asked a producer, at the end of 1984, when the AIDS toll had risen to nearly eight thousand. "Why should my life be controlled by eight thousand people?" the producer responded, according to Strait.

The Day the Plague Touched America

For months rumors were flying about Rock Hudson and the Pasteur Institute. Americans with AIDS were trekking to the world-famous research center to be treated with the latest "best hope" for those fighting AIDS: HPA-23. The drug was supposed to attack the virus and, in some cases, kill it outright. The French doctors had had some surprising successes with it.

The husky, handsome actor was seen in the facility, looking disturbingly gaunt. He was hospitalized at another institution and, of course, kept away from the rest of the patients, secluded in a private suite. The doctors were sworn to secrecy. Nonetheless, journalists eventually stumbled onto Hudson's trail. Was he in Paris for treatment with HPA-23? Was America's most easily recognizable macho man dying of "the gay plague"?

Hudson held the inquiring minds at bay, until his public appearance back in California, on July 15, 1985. He had agreed to help Doris Day, a longtime friend and costar in film classics like *Pillow Talk,* at a press conference promoting her new television show. At the podium, the two stars had their arms wrapped around each other, but it looked as though it was as much out of necessity as affection: Hudson seemed on the verge of collapsing. At one moment, Day looked up at her leading man affectionately, as he brushed away a stray hair from her clearly nervous but smiling face. The press conference did not make the nightly news. The medical story dominating television that week was President Reagan's colon cancer operation, reported in extraordinary detail in the media. Just a week and a half later, though, the tenuous scene between Day and Hudson was replayed repeatedly on broadcast outlets across the United States.

At the press conference, Hudson insisted he was suffering from the flu. He'd bounce back in no time, he claimed. In fact, he soon returned to Paris, for more HPA-23 treatments. There, six days later, on July 21, Hudson collapsed in the lobby of the Hotel Ritz and set the paparazzi into action. All journalists can at one time or another be called on to play the role of celebrity hound. Hudson, with the fast and furious rumors of his AIDS infection, was a perfect catalyst for that instinct in American journalists.

United Press International was the first major U.S. media outlet to the news. Filing from Los Angeles on July 23, the wire service ran the following bulletin: "Actor Rock Hudson, last of the traditional square-jawed, romantic leading men, known recently for his TV roles on 'McMillan & Wife' and 'Dynasty,' is suffering from inoperable liver cancer possibly linked to AIDS, it was disclosed."

That evening ABC repeated the UPI assertion that the actor was suffering from "inoperable liver cancer," but no mention was made of a link to AIDS. NBC reported that Hudson was suffering from cancer and added that the actor "may be seeing AIDS specialists." CBS missed the story entirely. None of the networks were willing to go with UPI's AIDS link, because neither Associated Press nor another major media source had yet established the connection. UPI is known for taking greater risks, and making more mistakes. Although Hudson's homosexuality had been Hollywood's worst-kept secret for years, any intimation to the American heartland that the man might be suffering from the "Gay Plague" would have to be broached with the utmost care.

The next night CBS attempted to make up lost ground with a story on the conflicting reports about Rock Hudson. By this time the networks had their own correspondents on the story. Aside from commenting that other Americans were seeking treatment in Paris, CBS gave no clear signs that Hudson might be suffering from AIDS. NBC did not waste time rehashing the unanswered questions. It used the Hudson lead to jump into a story about the San Francisco AIDS ward, a compelling look at the frontlines of the epidemic's battlefield. It was a revealing study of just how thin resources were, and the difference a small cadre of committed doctors, nurses, and other health professionals could make in fighting the disease. This piece was exactly the kind of journalism the broadcast outlets could have focused on long before, and should have used to help give a face to the faceless plague much earlier.

On July 25, President Reagan returned to the White House for the first time following his cancer surgery. Although the operation had dominated the front page and TV for weeks—it was the most reported medical event of 1985—his return did not make the top of any of the networks' nightly news. That spot was reserved for Rock Hudson's AIDS diagnosis. After weeks of intense scrutiny, and with his health deteriorating rapidly, Hudson ordered his spokesperson to come out with the truth.

That night ABC gave AIDS news seven minutes and twenty seconds, unprecedented in the entire four-year history of the epidemic.

CBS devoted five minutes to it. NBC, which had the best perspective of any of the three on exactly what constituted groundbreaking AIDS news, ran a story lasting four-minutes and thirty seconds. All three networks focused on Hudson, of course, but they also included a diverse mix of other news. ABC looked at the need for more AIDS funding, the first time the network broached the critical subject on "World News Tonight." CBS ran a story on Australian women being infected with the disease from a Sydney sperm bank. It was the network's first mention of AIDS outside the United States, Africa, or Haiti. Where had these stories been hiding? There was some important news breaking: a test recently had been developed to screen blood bank supplies for the AIDS virus, and the Defense Department went public with its decision to test recruits for infection. But the funding stories and controversies like that surrounding the Sydney sperm bank had been around and simply went unreported before. It was not until the diagnosis of Hudson, a longtime friend of the Reagans, that the epidemic crept onto the agenda of the national political reporters. AIDS reporting by ABC's Sam Donaldson and his colleagues on Capitol Hill was reminiscent of the Kennedy Administration days, when the president decided what was important and the media dutifully reported it. Reagan had never put the disease on his agenda. Indeed, he did not utter "AIDS" in public until September 1985, months after his friend's illness was revealed. The media hounds had accepted his silence.

After months of scant reporting on AIDS, media coverage across the United States boomed, especially in broadcast. For instance, in 1985 ABC did four AIDS stories before the July 25 Hudson revelation, and twenty-eight after. CBS and NBC had similar leaps in coverage. Nationwide, media coverage tripled. In some cases, publications, including major dailies in the heartland, were writing about the disease for the first time, not merely picking up wire service copy. AIDS reporting in print media increased by 270 percent between Hudson's diagnosis and the end of 1985. By going public with his ailment, Rock Hudson obviously had not set off spontaneous research, nor had he provoked the rash of other issues that were finally being covered.

Some media pundits have tried to explain the explosion in interest about the epidemic in pseudo-scholarly terms of audience-interest reaching a critical mass. The simple fact is, newsmakers, from the executive producer at the major network to the assignment editor on the metropolitan daily in Des Moines, were for the first time touched in a direct, personal way by the epidemic. Although Hudson's homosexuality had been common knowledge in Hollywood, *USA Today* editorialized on the day of his death, October 2, 1985: "Many of us are realizing that AIDS is not a 'gay plague,' but everybody's problem." Ironic that a gay man accomplished that feat.

Hudson's passing made for the perfect TV death. As the eulogies spilled across the screen, featuring the face of the quintessential all-American male, the media across the nation convulsed in one final sigh of belated coverage. "Rock Hudson was the first one [person with AIDS] we all knew and cared about," said Strait. That connection—at once personal and impersonal—turned out to be the most important agenda-setter of all.

"All the News
That's Fit to Print"

The New York Times

Late Edition

Weather: Mostly sunny and warm today; increasing cloudiness tonight. Mostly cloudy, chance of rain tomorrow. Temperatures: today 73-78, tonight 53-58; yesterday 62-77. Details, page B4.

VOL.CXXXII...No. 45,689   Copyright © 1983 The New York Times   NEW YORK, WEDNESDAY, MAY 25, 1983   50 cents beyond 75 miles from New York City, except on Long Island   30 CENTS

An Old Bridge's Birthday Is a Hometown Carnival

By DEIRDRE CARMODY

With an unabashed outpouring of affection, New York celebrated the 100th anniversary of the Brooklyn Bridge yesterday.

It had been billed as a great day in the history of the city, and that is exactly what it turned out to be. In the morning, thousands of pedestrians, horse-drawn carriages and marching bands — filling the air with martial music — paraded across the stately bridge under summerlike skies.

Later there were street fairs, speeches, roof parties, boat rides and a harbor-craft parade. Evening fell gently over the bridge. As darkness came, a luminescent full moon filled the sky while a dramatic sound and light show was played on the bridge and recreated its history.

Then the sky simply exploded with fireworks. Red, white and blue shells, golden comets changing to silver, crackling stars in red and green, appeared to fill the entire sky, while hundreds of thousands of people gasped at the sheer dazzle of it all.

At times both towers were bathed in a golden glitter as a barrage of meteors showered down on the bridge. It was the biggest show ever put on by the Grucci family of Bellport, L.I., and included a total of 9,600 rockets, comets, aerial shell bursts and other pyrotechnics.

Many of the spectators rode a flotilla of fireboats, tugboats, military craft, private yachts and fishing boats that had moved up river under the bridge earlier in the evening. Some of the fireboats shot plumes of water into the air.

It was not the events, however, that made the day. It was the crowds. All day, it was abundantly clear that people were there by the thousands for no other reason except that they wanted to be there. They were there not so much to see as to participate. Enthusiasm and good humor burst from behind the barricades along the parade route.

The police estimated that 2.1 million people watched the evening festivities

Continued on Page B4, Column 1

Part of the parade crossing the Brooklyn Bridge on the way to Manhattan. At left, fireworks exploding over the bridge last night.

High Court Bans Tax Exemptions For Schools With Racial Barriers

Burger Writes Forceful Opinion on Bob Jones and Goldsboro Cases, a Rebuff to Administration

By LINDA GREENHOUSE
Special to The New York Times

WASHINGTON, May 24 — The Supreme Court ruled today, 8 to 1, that racially discriminatory private schools are ineligible for Federal tax exemptions.

In an opinion by Chief Justice Warren E. Burger, the Court said there was no question that the Internal Revenue Service was correct when, in 1970, it stopped granting tax-exempt status to discriminatory schools.

President Reagan sought last year to revoke the 1970 policy because, he said, it had "no basis in law," in that there was no specific law written in the reve-

Excerpts from opinions, page A22.

nue service code. This action came to symbolize his Administration's break with the civil rights policies of the recent past.

The Court's decision today, phrased in unusually unequivocal and forceful language, was a nearly complete repudiation of the Administration's legal position. Associate Justice William H. Rehnquist cast the dissenting vote.

The White House referred questions today to a statement by Attorney General William French Smith. Mr. Smith said the Court's ruling made it "clear that additional legislation is not needed" and that the I.R.S. should now enforce the law.

"There can no longer be any doubt," Chief Justice Burger wrote, "that racial discrimination in education violations

Continued on Page A22, Column 4

William T. Coleman Jr., who argued position upheld by Court.

Mutiny Dismissed by Arafat As a Bit of Qaddafi's Mischief

By JAMES M. MARKHAM
Special to The New York Times

MEJ EL ANJAR, Lebanon, May 24 — Yasir Arafat sat smiling tonight under a photograph of himself surrounded by equally loyal commanders of the Yarmouk brigade.

In a bantering humor, the chairman of the Palestine Liberation Organization dismissed a mutiny among a handful of his commanders down the road — in a place called Ait el Fakha — as a bit of mischief by Col. Muammar el-Qaddafi of Libya and Palestinian radicals gathered around a renegade known as Abu Musa.

"All of them are about 150," said Mr. Arafat in his enthusiastic but imprecise English. "Now the head of this problem is Qaddafi. You can go anywhere in the Bekaa, in Tripoli. All the troubles they are exaggerating."

Since May 7, when Col. Abu Musa, a commander of the Fatah guerrilla group, tried to seize control of the elite Yarmouk brigade, Mr. Arafat has been traveling just about everywhere in the Bekaa region, rallying the 12,000 men he says he has here in eastern Lebanon and checking the contagion of rebellion.

For a group of journalists brought into the Syrian-controlled Bekaa today at dusk in the company of Mr. Arafat, Palestinian hospitality did not include a visit to Ait el Fakha, where the band of mutineers is said to have established itself behind barricades. Less than a mile, and some Syrian troops, separate the group from the Israeli lines.

'Only the Bad Ones Have Stayed'

"All the good people have left them, and only the bad ones have stayed," declared a young green-uniformed Fatah man who said he had deserted Colonel Abu Musa today. Sitting around a bright kerosene lamp, he and his comrades said that Colonel Abu Musa had some heavy guns but that the people with him were mostly gullible Palestinian teen-agers trucked in from Damascus, who had been told they were going to fight the Israelis.

The rebellion in the Bekaa has presented Mr. Arafat with problems with a problem, since it is evident that Colonel Abu Musa could not hold out

Continued on Page A8, Column 1

Continued on Page A22, Column 1

PRESIDENT'S PLAN FOR BASING OF MX APPROVED IN HOUSE

KEY VICTORY FOR REAGAN

Vote Is 239-186 for Resolution to Release $625 Million for Tests and Engineering

By STEVEN V. ROBERTS
Special to The New York Times

WASHINGTON, May 24 — The House of Representatives today approved President Reagan's plan to base 100 MX missiles in existing shelters under the plains of Wyoming and Nebraska. The vote, a major victory for the President, was 239 to 186.

The vote reversed a decision by Congress last year to block funds for the huge weapon, which could deliver 10 warheads to Soviet targets with great accuracy. The key to the switch was an

House roll-call, page A18.

intense lobbying campaign by Mr. Reagan, who played on the inclination of many lawmakers to support the President in matters of foreign policy and national security.

The measure approved today would release $625 million for engineering and flight testing on the missile, funds that had been frozen by the lawmakers last year in disagreement with the Administration's plan for basing the missile in a closely spaced pattern known as "dense pack."

Senate Approval Likely

The Senate is also likely to approve the resolution when it votes on Wednesday. The measure does not need the President's signature.

The MX survived a test vote in the Senate today when the lawmakers, 59 to 35, blocked an attempt to delay consideration of the resolution.

The resolution freeing the $625 million is only the first hurdle facing the MX in coming weeks. The lawmakers must also vote on bills to authorize and appropriate $4.6 billion for the actual procurement of the weapon, a reduction from the original Administration request of $6.2 billion.

Continued on Page A18, Column 1

Reagan Links Lobbying to Arms Talks

In his lobbying efforts, the President portrayed the missile as the essential leverage in his search for an arms control agreement with the Soviet Union. In an article on the Op-Ed Page of The Washington Post this morning, Mr. Reagan described the impending vote by saying, "At stake is the future of arms reductions — balanced, verifiable arms reductions that can make the world a safer place for all the earth's people."

Critics retorted that spending billions on a vulnerable new weapon at a time of

---

Nash Convicted of Killing 4 in Parking Lot on Pier

By SELWYN RAAB

Donald Nash, whom the prosecution described as a hired assassin, was convicted yesterday of murdering a Federal witness and three CBS employees in a Hudson River parking lot last year.

He was also found guilty of conspiracy to murder the witness and another potential witness last year. The second witness disappeared 10 months ago and is presumed by the police to have been slain.

A jury in State Supreme Court in Manhattan deliberated 13 hours before two days before returning with a verdict at 4:30 P.M. To reach the jury box, the nine men and three women had to walk in front of the 47-year-old defendant as he sat at the defense table. None of the jurors looked at him.

Then the jury foreman, Jean Shaw, announced that Mr. Nash was guilty of all charges — four counts of second-degree murder and one count of conspiracy to commit second-degree murder.

Mr. Nash, a husky, dark-haired man who wears thick tinted glasses, raised the same composure he had during the seven-week trial. After hearing the five guilty verdicts, he vigorously shook the hand of his lawyer, Lawrence Hochheiser. Later, Mr. Hochheiser said Mr. Nash had told him, "You did the best you could, don't worry."

As Mr. Nash was escorted out of the courtroom by guards, he smiled and nodded at the prosecutor, Gregory L. Waples.

Mr. Hochheiser said he would appeal. Each murder count carries a minimum sentence of 15 years to life or a maximum sentence of 25 years to life. The conspiracy conviction provides for

Continued on Page B2, Column 1

Donald Nash listening as the verdict was read in State Supreme Court.

April Consumer Prices Up 0.6%; Jump Is Tied to Gasoline Tax Rise

By ROBERT D. HERSHEY Jr.
Special to The New York Times

WASHINGTON, May 24 — Higher prices for gasoline, housing and food helped raise the Consumer Price Index six-tenths of 1 percent in April, the biggest increase since last July, the Labor Department reported today.

However, most analysts said the rise, which was twice the average monthly advance for the period from September 1981 through March, did not signify any worrisome revival of inflation that some have feared could erupt as the economic recovery gathers strength. Rather, it was regarded as an aberration resulting in part from the 5-cent-a-gallon increase in the Federal gasoline tax on April 1.

"This figure does not provide cause for alarm and does not indicate a long-term upward shift in the inflation rate," Martin S. Feldstein, the chairman of the President's Council of Economic Advisers, said in a statement.

The rise in the New York-northeastern New Jersey area was even greater, 1.1 percent, and was the sharpest increase since last October, with higher shelter costs, airline fares and gasoline prices the main factors. [Page D6.]

The national increase in April amounted to an annual inflation rate of 7.2 percent, but Mr. Feldstein noted that, if energy was excluded, the annual rate of increase for the month would drop to 4.7 percent.

"Statistical distortions, whether on the up side or the down side, do not change the fact that, when transitory effects are excluded, the rate of inflation is now somewhere in the 4 to 5 percent range," Mr. Feldstein said.

Private analysts generally agreed. "It's a one-month blip, not anything to

Continued on Page D4, Column 3

INSIDE

Satellite Sale Questions
The Justice Department has data that may contradict a former Administration aide on his role in a plan to sell Government satellites. Page A17.

Margiotta Clemency Drive
Nassau County Republicans are seeking Presidential clemency for Joseph M. Margiotta, whose two-year prison term is to start next week. Page B1.

Health Chief Calls AIDS Battle 'No. 1 Priority'

By ROBERT PEAR
Special to The New York Times

WASHINGTON, May 24 — The Government's top health official said today that the investigation of acquired immune deficiency syndrome had become "the No. 1 priority" of the United States Public Health Service.

Dr. Edward N. Brandt Jr., an Assistant Secretary of Health and Human Services, said the Government was taking steps in an effort to identify the cause and find a cure for the mysterious illness, known as AIDS, which leads to a breakdown of the body's immune system against disease. Dr. Brandt announced six new research grants for study of the ailment and the approval of a new heat treatment for blood products, through which some scientists believe the infectious agent might be transmitted.

At a news conference, Dr. Brandt said he was urging state and local health officers to report all cases of AIDS. He said the Federal Centers for Disease Control had stepped up surveillance of the disease. Since June 1981, they have received reports of 1,450 AIDS cases, of which 558, or 38.5 percent, resulted in death. Among the 76 cases diagnosed at least two years ago, the fatality rate was 82 percent.

In the last three weeks medical journals have carried reports suggesting that the disease could be sexually transmitted from men to women and could

Continued on Page A18, Column 1

---

1   THE *NEW YORK TIMES*'S FIRST FRONT-PAGE ARTICLE ON AIDS, MAY 25, 1983. THE SCOURGE RATED ONLY A BOTTOM PLACEMENT. COPYRIGHT © 1983 BY THE NEW YORK TIMES COMPANY, REPRINTED BY PERMISSION.

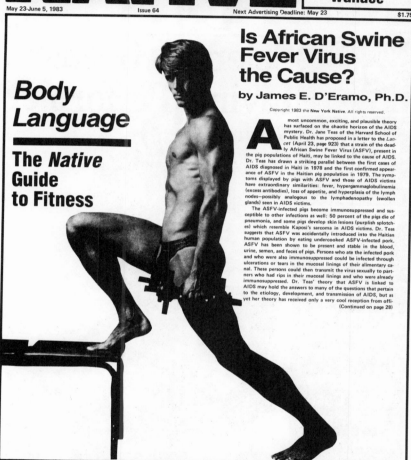

N E W · Y O R K

NATIVE

A Night at the Circus

Holleran & Wallace

May 23-June 5, 1983   Issue 64   Next Advertising Deadline: May 23 $1.75

Is African Swine Fever Virus the Cause?

by James E. D'Eramo, Ph.D.

A most uncommon, exciting, and plausible theory has surfaced on the chaotic horizon of the AIDS mystery. Dr. Jane Teas of the Harvard School of Public Health has proposed in a letter to the *Lancet* (April 23, page 923) that a strain of the deadly African Swine Fever Virus (ASFV), present in the pig populations of Haiti, may be linked to the cause of AIDS. Dr. Teas has drawn a striking parallel between the first cases of AIDS diagnosed in Haiti in 1978 and the first confirmed appearance of ASFV in the Haitian pig population in 1979. The symptoms displayed by pigs with ASFV and those of AIDS victims have extraordinary similarities: fever, hypergammaglobulinemia (excess antibodies), loss of appetite, and hyperplasia of the lymph nodes—possibly analogous to the lymphadenopathy (swollen glands) seen in AIDS victims.

The ASFV-infected pigs become immunosuppressed and susceptible to other infections as well: 50 percent of the pigs die of pneumonia, and some pigs develop skin lesions (purplish splotches) which resemble Kaposi's sarcoma in AIDS victims. Dr. Teas suggests that ASFV was accidentally introduced into the Haitian human population by eating undercooked ASFV-infected pork. ASFV has been shown to be present and stable in the blood, urine, semen, and feces of pigs. Persons who ate the infected pork and who were also immunosuppressed could be infected through ulcerations or tears in the mucosal linings of their alimentary canal. These persons could then transmit the virus sexually to partners who had rips in their mucosal linings and who were already immunosuppressed. Dr. Teas' theory that ASFV is linked to AIDS may hold the answers to many of the questions that pertain to the etiology, development, and transmission of AIDS, but as yet her theory has received only a very cool reception from offi-

(Continued on page 28)

Body Language

The *Native* Guide to Fitness

2   *NEW YORK NATIVE* FEATURES SEX AND DEATH ON THE COVER OF THE GAY BIWEEKLY, MAY 23, 1983. REPRINTED BY PERMISSION OF CHARLES ORTLEB.

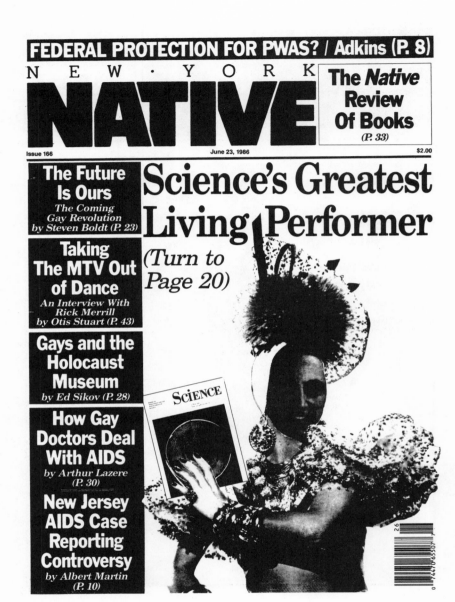

FEDERAL PROTECTION FOR PWAS? / Adkins (P. 8)

N E W · Y O R K
NATIVE

The *Native*
Review
Of Books
(P. 33)

Issue 166   June 23, 1986 $2.00

The Future Is Ours
The Coming Gay Revolution by Steven Boldt (P. 23)

Taking The MTV Out of Dance
An Interview With Rick Merrill by Otis Stuart (P. 43)

Gays and the Holocaust Museum
by Ed Sikov (P. 28)

How Gay Doctors Deal With AIDS
by Arthur Lazere (P. 30)

New Jersey AIDS Case Reporting Controversy
by Albert Martin (P. 10)

Science's Greatest Living Performer

(Turn to Page 20)

SCIENCE

3   PREMIER AIDS RESEARCHER DR. ROBERT GALLO IS PARODIED IN CAR-
MEN MIRANDA DRAG ON THE COVER OF THE *NEW YORK NATIVE,* JUNE
23, 1986. REPRINTED BY PERMISSION OF CHARLES ORTLEB.

LIFE

July 1985/$2.50

**A Race To Save
America's Great Movies**

**Koko (the Gorilla) Is
Captivated by Kittens**

**That Fabulous Night:
Teen Proms '85**

NOW NO ONE IS SAFE FROM
AIDS

4   *LIFE* SENDS OUT AN ALARM TO HETEROSEXUALS, JULY 1985. RE-
PRINTED BY PERMISSION OF LIFE PICTURE SERVICE.

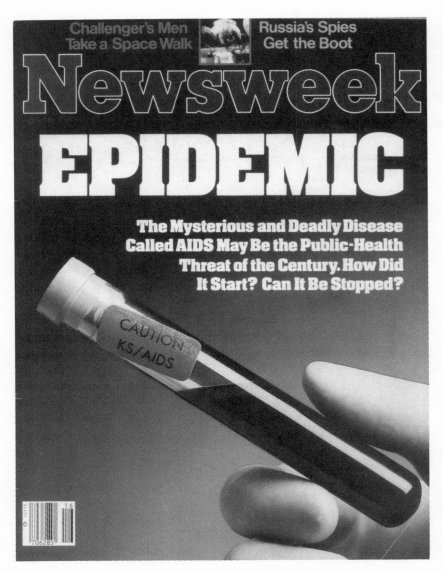

5   *NEWSWEEK*'S "EPIDEMIC," THE FIRST TIME AIDS GRABBED THE COVER
OF A NATIONAL MAGAZINE, ON APRIL 18, 1983. PHOTO BY ROGERS/
GAHAN—PRISM PHOTOGRAPHY. COPYRIGHT © 1983 BY NEWSWEEK,
INC., REPRINTED BY PERMISSION.

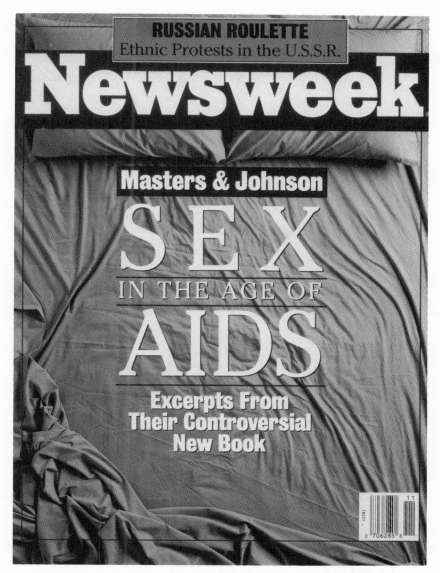

RUSSIAN ROULETTE
Ethnic Protests in the U.S.S.R.

Newsweek

Masters & Johnson

SEX
IN THE AGE OF
AIDS

Excerpts From
Their Controversial
New Book

0 706285 8

6   *NEWSWEEK* USES A SEDUCTIVE LAYOUT FOR ITS "SEX IN THE AGE OF
AIDS" COVER, MARCH 14, 1988. PHOTO BY GEORGE HAUSMAN AND
ARTY BEAL. COPYRIGHT © 1988 BY NEWSWEEK, INC., REPRINTED BY
PERMISSION.

Original Contributions

Immune Deficiency Syndrome in Children

James Oleske, MD, MPH; Anthony Minnefor, MD; Roger Cooper, Jr, MD; Kathleen Thomas, MD; Antonio dela Cruz, MD; Houman Ahdieh; Isabel Guerrero, MD; Vijay V. Joshi, MD; Franklin Desposito, MD

• The present epidemic of acquired immune deficiency syndrome (AIDS) was originally described in homosexual men and subsequently in intravenous drug abusers, Haitians, and hemophiliacs. Profound defects in cell-mediated immunity (CMI) are associated with Kaposi's sarcoma and a variety of serious opportunistic infections. Recently, we and others have encountered a group of children with an otherwise unexplained immune deficiency syndrome and infections of the type found in adults with AIDS. In this report, we describe eight children from the Newark, NJ, metropolitan area born into families with recognized risks for AIDS. These patients have had recurrent febrile illnesses, failure to thrive, hypergammaglobulinemia, and depressed CMI. Four of these children have died. Our experience suggests that children living in high-risk households are susceptible to AIDS and that sexual contact, drug abuse, or exposure to blood products is not necessary for disease transmission.
(*JAMA* 1983;249:2345-2349)

mal" infants and children as additional victims."

In this article, we report our experience with eight children with unexplained immunodeficiencies, some of whom had the opportunistic infections and fit the working definition of AIDS developed by the Centers for Disease Control (CDC).

PATIENTS AND METHODS

Since 1979, eight children from the Newark, NJ, metropolitan area have been found to have a disease complex compatible with AIDS. Laboratory and epidemiologic studies were done on these eight children and their family members, and hospital records and biopsy and autopsy reports were reviewed. The four surviving

THE ACQUIRED immune deficiency ... an increased risk for the development

---

editorials

JOURNAL OF THE AMERICAN MEDICAL ASSOCIATION MAY 6, 1983

The Acquired Immune Deficiency Syndrome
The Ever-Broadening Clinical Spectrum

The acquired ...

is true, then AIDS takes on an entirely new dimension. Given the fact that the incubation period for adults is believed to be longer than one year, the full impact of the syndrome among sexual contacts and recipients of potentially infective transfusions is uncertain at present. If we add to this the possibility that nonsexual, non-blood-borne transmission is possible, the scope of the syndrome may be enormous. Again, I must reiterate the fact that we must be cautious in our acceptance of these infant cases as being truly AIDS. However, the

donation but who subsequent ... blown AIDS. Other uncon ... stusion-related AIDS have ... ters for Disease Control (C ... ence for a transmissible ag ... t as strong as it can be, d ... no agent has been iden ... se been able to be transmit ... he current issue of THE J ... hat are of potentially grea ... g saga of AIDS (p 2345 ... n with syndromes of sev ... ere born into families v ... The similarity to AIDS va ... and the authors thems ... of the eight are strongly s ... Nevertheless, they believe with s

... pp 2345, 2350, and 2370.

---

7 THE *JOURNAL OF THE AMERICAN MEDICAL ASSOCIATION*'S "ROUTINE HOUSEHOLD CONTACT" ARTICLE OF MAY 6, 1983, ALONG WITH AN EDITORIAL BY A WELL-RESPECTED PHYSICIAN SEEMINGLY BACKING UP THE CLAIM, HELPED SET OFF A FIRESTORM OF MEDIA COVERAGE. COPYRIGHT © 1983 BY THE AMERICAN MEDICAL ASSOCIATION, REPRINTED BY PERMISSION.

8   THE *NEW YORK POST*'S INFLAMMATORY STYLE MADE FOR SHOCKING HEADLINES, SUCH AS "AIDS MONSTER" ON OCTOBER 12, 1987. REPRINTED BY PERMISSION.

9   ROCK HUDSON AND DORIS DAY HELD A JOINT PRESS CONFERENCE AN-
NOUNCING THE ACTRESS'S NEW TV SHOW, IN JULY 1985. TEN DAYS
LATER HUDSON'S AIDS DIAGNOSIS WAS MADE PUBLIC. PHOTO BY
MONTEREY HERALD/ORVILLE MYERS, REPRINTED BY PERMISSION.

EPIDEMIA SIN FRONTERAS

10   "AIDS, EPIDEMIC WITHOUT BOUNDARIES" WAS ONE OF THE FEW
MAJOR REPORTING PROJECTS DONE ON THE DISEASE BY A MINORITY
MEDIA OUTLET. THIS SUPPLEMENT APPEARED IN THE JULY 8, 1987,
EDITION OF *LA OPINION* (LOS ANGELES). REPRINTED BY PERMISSION.

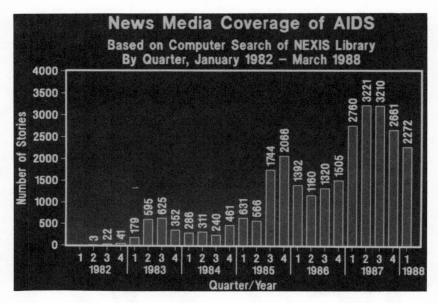

News Media Coverage of AIDS

Based on Computer Search of NEXIS Library
By Quarter, January 1982 – March 1988

11 THE RISE AND FALL OF U.S. MEDIA COVERAGE, TIED NOT TO SCIENTIFIC DEVELOPMENTS OR NUMBERS OF DEAD, BUT TO THE EXTENT TO WHICH THE THREAT TO MAINSTREAM AMERICANS SEEMED TO BE INCREASING. GRAPH PREPARED BY THE CENTERS FOR DISEASE CONTROL.

Chapter 8
Chronicler
of the Castro

During a routine phone conversation in March 1985, the source had told *San Francisco Chronicle* reporter Randy Shilts, "No matter what you ask, I won't tell you anything about Mary Agnes Bauer." Shilts, of course, had never even heard the name before. The coy tactic is frequently used by sources who want to lead a reporter to a story, but do not want the reporter's trail to lead back to them. The tip on Mrs. Bauer came from a health agency contact Shilts worked with on other articles.

Shilts scrambled through his network in the health community to find out why this Bauer woman was important enough to require "official" confidentiality, but he came up empty-handed. He thought a clue might be found at the upcoming farewell party for San Francisco's public health director, Dr. Mervyn Silverman. The doctor had been a key figure in the fight against the epidemic in Northern California, and Shilts knew that many of those who were privy to the AIDS bureaucracy's secrets would be on hand at the fete.

Nearly everyone there got drunk, except Shilts, a recovering alcoholic. From a tipsy public health official he discovered that the elderly Mary Agnes Bauer had got AIDS from a blood transfusion during a heart-bypass operation at a local hospital. By the spring of 1985, transfusion cases were not all that rare, though the blood banks were hesitant to discuss just how widespread the incidents were. Why was Mrs. Bauer so special? From another loose-lipped official Shilts discovered that her husband was suspected of having AIDS, too. If he did have the disease, that would make the Bauers one of the first, clearcut cases of female-to-male sexual transmission in the United States.

Shilts jotted down the name of the couple's doctor, Robert Illa, whose practice was located in a suburban San Francisco town. When Shilts phoned him, the physician confirmed that the seventy-two-year-old Donald Bauer was suspected of getting AIDS from his wife. But not through sexual transmission. "They stopped having sex years ago," Shilts recalled the doctor telling him. "It was saliva transmission."

That was a scoop worthy of the front page, which is where it ran.

"New AIDS Puzzle in Bay Area—Victim's Husband Is Ailing," the headline blared. The story elaborated on Dr. Illa's claims. Donald Bauer contracted the deadly disease from a kiss, or worse, perhaps from routine household contact. Had Dr. James Oleske, who wrongly identified what he claimed was household-contact transmission in 1983, finally been vindicated?

Any reader breezing through the *Chronicle* that day had good rea- son·to be alarmed. Only the rare reader, the one who actually follows a story past the front page to the jump, which happened to be on page sixteen, learned that Dr. Illa was being contradicted by experts in the field of AIDS research. Officials at the Centers for Disease Control said they had tested Donald Bauer's blood and found he did not even have antibodies to the AIDS virus, much less the full-blown disease.

Despite the CDC's heavy-hitting denial, Shilts went on to describe the fear among Bauer family members about catching AIDS from their grandmother or grandfather. "My sixteen-year-old daughter worries that her life will end at twenty-one," said Bauer's daughter, Terry Owen.

And for Donald's part: "I don't have that much time to go," he said. "As long as it leaves the children alone, I'll feel all right." San Fran- ciscans were not very calmed by Mr. Bauer's mellow demeanor. The San Francisco AIDS Foundation was flooded with a 30 percent in- crease in phone calls, most from people worried about getting the dis- ease this new way.

As it turned out, AIDS was not "catching" in the Bauer family. The CDC was right after all: Donald's blood did not show that he had come in contact with the virus. In fact, his illness, lung cancer exacer- bated by pneumonia, was not related to AIDS. The Southern Califor- nia lab that had declared him infected used a faulty test that had not been approved by the government for AIDS-virus testing.

Another *Chronicle* reporter followed up Shilts's story the next day with quotes from yet another leading researcher refuting the AIDS diagnosis. Still, the article, which was wedged into a corner on the bottom of page three, maintained that "Donald Bauer of San Bruno may be the first person known to have contracted acquired immune deficiency syndrome through contact with saliva." More than two weeks passed before the *Chronicle* would print that Donald Bauer was AIDS-free.

The incident highlights the contradictory nature of America's best- known AIDS reporter. Shilts is an openly gay man whose strong con-

CHRONICLER OF THE CASTRO

nection to the story prompted him to cover it from early on. He had
better sources to many of the people engaged in the fight against the
epidemic than almost any other journalist. He is also known by many
of his colleagues as the reporter who most wanted to make his career
with the AIDS story. Shilts was driven by the scoops the epidemic
offered. So driven, in fact, that he sometime played too fast and loose
with the facts or overdramatized the news. The Bauers from San
Bruno are just one example. *And the Band Played On,* the book he
wrote about the first years of the epidemic, offers others.

For example, one of the intriguing stories he and his publishers
pushed to sell the book—airline attendant Gaetan Dugas's travels
throughout North America, during which he spread AIDS to his sexual partners—was at best misleading. Shilts suggested that Dugas was
the man who brought the disease to North America. In 1984 the public health officials tracking the handsome French Canadian steward
did link him to forty cases of the disease in New York and Los Angeles, and thus dubbed him "Patient Zero" in that study. Associated
Press reported the story back then, and the *New York Times* ran it, buried deep inside the paper. Shilts's dramatic play of the story was excerpted for the cover of *California* magazine: "Patient Zero: The Man
Who Brought AIDS to California," the October 1987 cover blared. His
book was a best-seller, but the story itself was sensational—and wrong.
Targeting a single culprit in the AIDS epidemic simply can not be
done with any accuracy, since there were so many ports of entry for
the disease, and so many carriers early on. Researchers have identified the virus in the United States in blood samples as early as 1969.

What Shilts did best in his reportage of the AIDS epidemic—better
than his work on Dugas or the Bauers—was to tell the gay community's tale, a story of how one group was radically changed by a health
crisis. None of his work, not even his resourceful reporting on the
government intrigue behind the gross lack of federal funding for
AIDS research, was more powerful or more controversial than that
coverage.

The Chronicler of the Castro

"I've never separated my life from my job," Shilts said. Since he came
out of the closet during college at the University of Oregon in 1972,

both his political and journalistic interests have reflected his sexuality. Shilts was born in 1951, the third of six sons. He grew up in Aurora, Illinois, a suburb of Chicago. The former Eagle Scout says he was first politicized as a teenager during the Goldwater campaign. In high school he considered himself a Libertarian, founded a chapter of the Young Americans for Freedom, and even attended meetings of the John Birch Society, which he could not join because he was too young. His politics changed substantially when he left home at eighteen.

He was close to his family, especially his mother, but after finishing high school he decided to leave the Midwest in search of the counterculture. Shilts ended up in Oregon. He had not been a particularly good student, but decided to matriculate to ward off the draft board. At Portland Community College he earned straight A's, and he went from there to the University of Oregon, where he got involved in student government, left-wing politics, and heterosexual flings.

A philosophy class jolted Shilts into acknowledging his homosexuality. The professor had invited a group of homosexuals to speak to her class, and Shilts was enthralled. Not only did he recognize what he had been trying to deny all those years, but he also understood the reason to be politically outspoken about one's homosexuality. Shortly after, Shilts came out of the closet in a similarly abrupt fashion: in a single day he told virtually all his friends. He was part of the first rush of gay liberation sweeping the United States, and he, like many others, assumed all gays would come out within three or four years. Homophobia, Shilts believed, would simply fade as a result of the increased knowledge about gays and their life-style.

Wanting to help that change along was one reason he gave up politics and got involved in journalism. "I felt you could do more outside of the political system," he said. During his undergraduate years he worked on the university's daily paper, serving a stint in the coveted managing editor slot. He won two of the prestigious William Randolph Hearst awards, both for stories dealing with gays.

He was always attracted to San Francisco, the center of America's counterculture, and dreamed of working on the *Chronicle*, partly for its location and partly because of its eccentric tradition. The paper has never quite evolved away from its origins in 1865 as "The Daily Dramatic *Chronicle*," a scandal sheet for the rough and tumble frontier. There was a concentrated effort in the 1940s, and again in the 1970s, to gain for the *Chronicle* greater respectability. Nonetheless, the imprint of the original publishers, Gustavus and Charles Young, remains in inflammatory headlines and front page stories featuring gruesome details of murders from around the world. The *Chronicle* was "A place I thought I'd fit in," said Shilts. He graduated in the midst of the Watergate scandal, when the two "boys" at the *Washington Post,* Carl Bernstein and Bob Woodward, were busy bringing down the Nixon administration. It seemed almost every aspiring reporter wanted to do Woodstein-style investigative journalism.

Despite an impressive academic record—Shilts was ranked in the top 10 percent of his class and had award-winning feature articles to back up his grades—he found it tough getting a job in any major city. He was particularly puzzled when some of his classmates landed jobs on the Portland *Oregonian,* the state's biggest daily. He finally had to face the fact that the most notable clips in his prizewinning portfolio were gay-related. Rather than force him to hide his sexuality, the setback convinced him that the homophobic public was simply suffering from a lack of information. He began free-lancing for the *Advocate,* a national gay-oriented magazine, and for other publications. After five months, Shilts realized Oregon's cities were not big enough media towns for him to make a living. He packed his bags and headed for San Francisco. He arrived in the fall of 1975, only weeks after George Moscone was elected mayor.

True to his first instincts, Shilts reported on what he lived. He came down with hepatitis, a common sexually transmitted disease among gays, and so he did an article on it for the *Advocate.* As an active gay man, he wrote a feature on risky sex. He produced a piece on alcoholism among homosexuals, even before admitting he had a dependency problem.

Shilts's work was not going unnoticed. In April 1976 he wrote a tongue-in-cheek piece on a gay conference at San Francisco State University. He was amused by the painfully politically correct gay men and women who had gathered to argue the issues of the day; many of his readers were not similarly tickled. The magazine received scathing letters, and Shilts was lambasted by some gay activitists.

He also got the attention of a local television station. From the moment he arrived in San Francisco, Shilts kept applying for jobs at the *Chronicle* and the other local newspapers, as well as at TV and radio outlets. He never wanted to work for the gay press full-time. "It was tough writing for newspapers you couldn't send home to mom because they were full of sleazy advertising," he said. Finally, in 1977 he was asked to write free-lance features about gays for KQED-TV, the city's public broadcasting channel. He jumped at the chance. His first story was about an iconoclastic gay politician named Harvey Milk, who was running for a seat on San Francisco's Board of Supervisors.

Since the 1960s gays had been a power in the city, a group hetero-sexual politicians courted for support. In the ten years that followed, the city's international reputation for tolerance swelled the gay com-munity's ranks and made it an even more potentially powerful elec-toral force. Harvey Milk wanted to represent that community. Shilts had told his story before in the pages of the *Advocate:* about how Milk traded in his high school teaching job in New York for a place on Wall Street; how when he finally moved to California in the early 1970s, he found his calling in politics; how he made a career out of campaign-ing; how he built a grass-roots political organization that undercut the gay establishment's support of straight, liberal politicians in municipal elections. He was the brash pretender to the throne of gay leadership.

The back-slapping, Machiavellian Milk made good copy, even more so when he finally won a seat on the Board of Supervisors in the 1977 race. The middle-aged perpetual candidate became not only the first openly gay city official in America, but also the leader of a new gay movement. Milk's politics dominated it: pragmatic, street-smart, highly vocal, and very visible. That was the kind of antiestablishment ap-proach that young gay San Franciscans could relate to, including the twenty-six-year-old Shilts. There were other gay political associations in San Francisco, of which the Alice B. Toklas Club was the most influ-ential. However, they were "Pre-Beatles," as Shilts describes them, not particularly influenced by the Vietnam war protests or the counter-culture. The Toklas crowd was middle-aged and establishment.

It was a halcyon time for a reporter who could explain to the general public this cutting edge of gay politics, which had suddenly become mainstream. Later, when Anita Bryant began her drive to criminalize homosexuality in Florida, and then aimed at gays in California, Shilts was an obvious choice to cover the story. In 1978, when State Senator John Briggs proposed an initiative that would prohibit gays from teaching, Shilts was at the center of the action again. He began free-lancing for the local KSAN radio station and did feature articles for *New West* magazine.

Many gays were not pleased with his reporting. They claimed he gave Senator Briggs too much play in his stories, or that he mocked gay political activists. The gay establishment also was nervous when

Shilts aired its issues in the mainstream media. "If he had stayed in the gay papers," says a longtime San Francisco activitist, "Shilts would have avoided much of the criticism." Instead, Shilts occasionally was verbally assaulted by angry gays on Castro Street, the center of San Francisco's gay community. Shilts's high energy and brashness would suit him for the city desk of the "Front Page." Despite his bravado in the face of politicians' criticisms, he agonized over the critical remarks from apolitical gays, his friends and neighbors, his community. In that regard, Shilts was like a small-town reporter who immediately feels the impact of his stories from the people he meets on the sidewalk every day.

At the same time, Shilts was ambitious, and he understood that he could capitalize on his intimacy with the gay community by covering the aftermath of San Francisco's City Hall nightmare.

The Slaughter at City Hall

Despite his lack of political experience, Harvey Milk proved to be a pro as an elected official. As a left-leaning liberal on a generally liberal to conservative board, he made common cause with Mayor George Moscone, a longtime progressive. Some conservative supervisors felt their power increasingly threatened, especially Dan White, a young former policeman who represented a bygone San Francisco, a city that had been mostly white, Roman Catholic, working-class.

Finally, in a fit of pique over a lost vote, White resigned from the board. The mayor initially had said he would give the ex-cop his job back, but days later Moscone reneged. On November 27, 1978, Dan White strapped a .38 Smith and Wesson to his waist and went to see the mayor himself. After crawling through a basement window to avoid City Hall's metal detector, the former supervisor made his way to the mayor's office. Face-to-face with Moscone, White pumped two bullets into the mayor's body, then knelt and drilled another through his head. After walking to Milk's office down the hall, he opened fire on San Francisco's first gay supervisor. Five bullets ripped through Milk's body before he expired.

The trial of Dan White was speedy, and shocking. His attorney argued what became known as the "Twinkie defense," that White had been rendered temporarily insane by an excessive intake of sweets before the shooting. Coupled with the understandable perception that he and his constituents were losing control over the city, the lawyer said, he cracked. For the murder of two of San Francisco's most prominent citizens, Dan White was sentenced on May 21, 1979, to five years in prison. That night the gay community erupted. An angry wave of men and women poured out of the Castro district and surged down Market Street to City Hall. There they smashed windows and overturned police cars, setting some afire.

The next day, Oakland's KTVU-TV put Shilts on the story. From that reporting he wove together *The Mayor of Castro Street,* a highly readable account of the life and times of Harvey Milk. Far from glorifying the man, which became a popular pastime after his death, Shilts's book described him as a political animal in the center of social upheaval. The work was received enthusiastically nationwide. In the gay community, Shilts went through what he calls his first "rehabilitation" into respectability.

Covering a Gay Plague

By 1981, Shilts was a nationally known gay writer. However, even that reputation probably would not have won him his treasured spot on the *Chronicle* news staff. He was offered a position that August only after another gay reporter, who was covering gay politics reluctantly, suffered a heart attack.

The *Chronicle* was the only major metropolitan daily in America with a reporter assigned to a "gay beat." The paper is not a particularly progressive force in San Francisco. Its editorial page offers up a conservative Republican perspective on most issues. However, the *Chronicle* also reflects its city. Local politics was big news in San Francisco, and gays were an important part of it, especially after the election of Harvey Milk. The city is also the most sexually tolerant, and unblushing, metropolis in the country.

By the time Shilts arrived at the *Chronicle,* the paper already was covering the epidemic. The news about homosexuals dying from a fatal pneumonia in Los Angeles, as first reported in the Centers for Disease Control's June 5 *Morbidity and Mortality Weekly Report,* caught the interest of *Chronicle* science editor David Perlman. If the disease was spreading in Los Angeles, he said, undoubtedly it was in San Francisco, too. Perlman localized the story and it ran on page four, titled "A Pneumonia That Strikes Gay Males." No flood of coverage followed, but Perlman and others kept the story alive.

Perlman is self-effacing and congenial, two qualities that have made him a popular mentor for generations of journalists. In the newsroom, crammed full of reporters' desks overflowing with notebooks and files, he has a private office. Even reporters, who often loathe being supervised by editors, admit that the paper does not have enough editors. That is due mostly to publisher Richard Thieriot, who carries on the paper's notorious tradition of being tightfisted. The editors on hand often oversee ill-defined territories. In the midst of this chaos, a decisive and reputable voice is a particularly strong force.

The sixty-seven-year-old Perlman came to the paper in 1940, after graduating from Columbia University's Journalism school. He was in the corps of bright young men that the youthful editor Paul Smith recruited to make the *Chronicle* a more serious daily. His long tenure at the paper—he's served in almost every position, from reporter to city editor—combined with his professionalism give Perlman clout. His recognizing the importance of the epidemic paved the way for the paper's reporting on all aspects of the crisis.

Perlman, however, was calling only for science coverage of the disease. He was missing the social and political stories. The gay community was hardly a beat he felt comfortable with. His first encounter with vocal gays came while he was reporting on a medical convention in New York in 1969, and he stumbled into the first protest-parade after the famous Stonewall riots. The clash between cops and homosexuals during a raid of a drag-queen nightclub had set off the modern gay movement just days before. Perlman, unaware and uninterested in such historical milestones, joined a crowd of bystanders that was attempting to shout down the gays. Only years later, serving as city editor when Milk and Moscone were killed, did Perlman gain a sense of why gays had organized themselves politically.

That understanding meant that Perlman, unlike many editors and reporters at other major dailies, did not shy away from the epidemic because of its gay angle. He was among the small group of pioneering journalists who attended the first meetings hosted by Dr. Marcus Conant, a University of California dermatologist and organizer of the first AIDS Clinic in San Francisco.

Nonetheless, Shilts did not immediately cover the crisis when he first arrived. He had heard about the disease that summer. At a cocktail party a guest mentioned the "gay cancer," and Shilts was miffed. "Great, now they're trying to pin that on us, too," he said. Otherwise he dismissed the crisis altogether. He left the *Chronicle* for six months, to promote his book, *The Mayor of Castro Street.* During that cross-country tour, he repeatedly was asked about GRID, Gay Related Infectious Disease. If the small number of cases already had touched the public's imagination, he knew, the malady would become an even hotter story as the death toll rose.

The first thing Shilts did when he returned to the *Chronicle* was phone Jim Geary, head of the Bay Area Shanti Project, which had organized some AIDS victims into a support group. Most of the stories up to that point had not humanized the plight of these patients. Telling the personal side of the news was always Shilts's strength. His boss approved the feature and sent a photographer to accompany Shilts. Facing the Shanti Project gathering, made up of men Shilts's age or younger, shrinking to their death like malnourished Biafrans, was a frightening challenge. But that was not the only obstacle the reporter had to overcome.

On the trip to the meeting, the photographer began arguing that they should call it off, that the topic was not worth covering. "We're doing a story because they're gay and have cancer?" Shilts remembers him saying sarcastically. When they arrived at the house, the photographer at first refused to go into the same room with the men. He wanted to stay outside and shoot the pictures through the window. Shilts insisted that he come inside. Back at the *Chronicle,* he finished the story quickly, then waited. A week went by, and the piece still had not run. Another passed, and Shilts heard rumors that some editors had made rude jokes about the story at the daily conference where they discussed what would go into the paper. Finally, Shilts went to the paper's library and began gathering the clips of stories that the *Chronicle* had run recently on other diseases that had not happened to affect a socially ostracized group like gays. There was a thick pile on Legionnaire's disease, the mysterious microbe that had killed twenty-nine members of the American Legion in Philadelphia in 1976. Reporting on Toxic Shock Syndrome, the disease first recognized in 1980 that had killed ninety-three young women, amounted to half as many articles. Next to those two stacks lay the four articles that made up the total coverage of the nearly year-old epidemic, which already had claimed 136 lives. After the third week drifted by, Shilts was livid, and intended to present this indictment of *Chronicle* coverage to city editor Jerry Burns. Before he had a chance, the story ran.

The piece appeared on May 13, 1982, titled "The Strange Deadly Diseases That Strike Gay Men." The headline was vintage *Chronicle*, but in this instance it seemed to fit. Some 335 Americans had been diagnosed as having GRID, almost all of them homosexuals. The story that followed was pure Shilts: "A 45-year-old San Francisco man looked at the purple spots covering his arms, face and chest and contemplated the death sentence they might foreshadow," it began. "'Every time I see a new spot, I think I'm a step closer to death,' said Jerry, a former waiter. 'I don't even look in the mirror any more.'"

Shilts was clearly intrigued by the malady. If it had not yet affected him or his friends, it was hitting people he knew about. People like Jerry, articulate about their disease, were hard to forget. And Shilts could not overlook the regular column by GRID patient Bobbi Campbell that ran in a local gay weekly. This epidemic was no longer just a story best left to Perlman and the other science writers; it was an issue with serious implications for the gay community.

Months went by, however, before Shilts wrote another piece. He had taken a leave of absence to write a screenplay of *The Mayor of Castro Street*. (Shilts's script eventually was abandoned, though an Oscar-winning documentary on Milk's life was later produced by other writers.) The GRID story did not disappear from the *Chronicle*, but it became open game for staff reporters, and the quality of coverage was hit or miss.

Reporter-cum-Politico

When Shilts returned to the *Chronicle* in October of 1982, he was in no shape to track the story as he claimed it should have been followed. He was drinking a lot, as well as snorting coke regularly. His romantic relationship with a local TV weatherman was on the skids. Finally, in late 1982, he moved out of his lover's apartment. As Shilts stepped out the door, his lover shouted, "Go out and be single and you'll be just another gay cancer statistic." The warning haunted him. Throughout that fall he would wake up startled in the middle of the night and begin searching for the telltale Kaposi's sarcoma lesions.

While Shilts floundered, the *Chronicle*'s competition produced some important pieces. On October 24, 1982, the *Examiner* ran the first front-page story to appear in San Francisco's daily press. "New Worry about Gay Disease" outlined the threat of AIDS with a comprehensive analysis of the current medical knowledge. The *Chronicle*'s Shilts was not covering the crisis then. Although he harshly criticized reporters across the country for disregarding the epidemic, he was guilty of the same sin early on.

In early 1983, Shilts began to understand the scope of AIDS: not just its potential deadliness, but the political turmoil it was causing in the gay community. For years, sexual liberation had been the corner-stone of the gay movement. Now, the Harvey Milk Democratic Club, which embraced the slain supervisor's pragmatic politics, was calling for gays to put a halt to promiscuous, unsafe sex. No one was better connected than Shilts to describe the new drive. The main forces behind it—the charismatic Bill Kraus; former street protestor-cum-political aide Cleve Jones; Supervisor Harry Britt, the political successor to Harvey Milk; and Britt's aide, Dick Pabich—had all been sources for Shilts in the past. He had also grown close to them while he wrote *The Mayor of Castro Street*. So intimate was he with that part of the gay political apparatus that, according to one Milk Club activist, though Shilts was never actually a member of the group, he nonetheless made his views known at the meetings.

These activists provoked Shilts into once again writing about the AIDS crisis. First, in March 1983, Bill Kraus had Shilts read Larry Kramer's "1,112 and Counting," which excoriated the government and gays for not taking the epidemic seriously. Then Shilts picked up the weekly gay newspaper, *Bay Area Reporter*, and happened upon a news story about a candlelight march being planned by a local therapist and AIDS patient named Gary Walsh. The protest was an attempt to push for more federal funds to fight the epidemic, the same thing Kraus and Kramer were calling for. Finally, when Kraus leaked to Shilts a study done by epidemiologists at the University of California at San Francisco, the reporter knew he had to take on the epidemic again.

Marked "CONFIDENTIAL," the report revealed the stunning statistic that one in every 350 single men in the city's gay neighborhoods had been diagnosed with AIDS. If the rate of increase continued, by the year's end one of every 175 single men in the gay neighborhoods would have AIDS. Not included in this bleak summary was the number of people who had been infected with the virus, but were not showing any signs of the illness. No one knew that total, which was the population most likely to be passing on the disease. Shilts thought back on his life and realized the odds of his having come in contact with the disease were frighteningly high.

When Shilts began doing the reporting on the study, he was hit with a strong chorus of opposition. Pat Norman, a gay activist in the Public Health Department, warned that the Shilts piece might cause hysteria: "We don't want people thinking they can't eat in Castro restaurants," she said. The president of the Alice B. Toklas Democratic Club claimed it would result in the authorities putting up barbed wire around the Castro. At the time, there was a bill in front of the Texas Legislature to repeal the state's prohibition against sodomy; Shilts got phone calls from Texans who said the law would not pass if he went ahead with the piece. Even the epidemiologists who did the study wanted to stop Shilts from publishing it. They said they had been warned that if they released the information, the gay community would no longer cooperate with their efforts to track the disease. Gays' assistance in the past had been crucial to understanding how the potentially deadly hepatitis B was spread and to developing a vaccine.

Shilts hesitated and then got angry. "I thought there was incredible denial in the gay community," a denial he had grappled with during those sleepless nights when he inspected his body for KS lesions. Shilts went to ask David Perlman's advice. It was an important story, a good scoop. When he got the nod, Shilts produced the "Startling Finding on 'Gay Disease'," on March 23, 1983, which ran on page two of the newspaper. That breaking news marked a turning point: it was picked up by the wire services, published in a handful of papers across the country, and helped establish the national perception that San Francisco was the center of AIDS. It also represented Shilts's reentry into the story, which would take up increasingly more of his time.

The response from the gay community was quick and harsh. Shunned for his critical reporting in the late seventies, Shilts had received an award from gay community leaders for *The Mayor of Castro Street* in February of 1983. (That year, the same group honored David Perlman for his reporting on AIDS.) Now Shilts could not walk down Castro Street without being shouted at: "gay Uncle Tom," they'd holler, or "sexual fascist."

He was astounded. Shilts had been out of the closet for years, in

fact had been a bathhouse regular. He had even worked in a Eugene
170 bathhouse during college.

A City under Siege

On May 2, 1983, San Francisco Mayor Dianne Feinstein announced a
citywide AIDS awareness week, the first of its kind in the country.
That evening Gary Walsh's candlelight march drew six thousand participants to the mile-long trek from Castro Street to City Hall that the
gay community had walked so many times before. That morning's
Chronicle featured Randy Shilts's "How AIDS Is Changing Gay Life-
styles" on the front page.

"Most socially active gay men in San Francisco now know somebody
who has contracted, if not died, from AIDS—a grisly reality that is
causing a revolution in gay social habits," Shilts wrote. "'Illness and
death have now come to a group of people who have lived in a sub-
culture of youth and beauty,'" said one gay man. Shilts went on to
document the discrimination against AIDS patients: people lost their
jobs, their homes, even their friends when they were diagnosed with
the disease. He uncovered a small group of gays who were not exactly
embracing the life-style changes the majority of their brothers had
adopted. "Sometimes I get so frustrated about AIDS that I go out
and have sex I know I shouldn't be having," said one man quoted by
Shilts, typical of a minority of gays who were actually found to have
increased their high-risk behavior since learning of the epidemic.

Such an open discussion of changing sexual mores did not shock
San Francisco. Since its founding, the *Chronicle* had featured sexual
explicitness uncommon in American media. In the 1950s, for example, the newspaper ran a column called "Beauty and the Beast," a
vulgar precursor to Dr. Ruth Westheimer's "Sexually Speaking," in
which author Marco Spinelli gave advice on perking up marriages
with erotic games.

Shilts's reporting, however, did further goad the gay community,
which was sensitive about its privacy. Some feared publicizing the minority of gays who continued to play the game of high-risk sex with
many partners might be just what homophobes could use to quaran-
tine gays or bring back other punitive measures left behind in a not-
so-distant past. Some gays also believed publicity about AIDS could

taint them and reduce their political power in San Francisco. Shilts included a friend from college as a source for the life-style story. The man was so angry about the piece that he did not talk to Shilts for two years afterward. That reaction to the reporter and his work became more common in the gay community as his coverage grew more controversial. And it soon did with the eruption of the bathhouse debate.

Sex, Politics, and the Reporter

The *Chronicle*'s coverage of the bathhouse issue was spurred in May 1983 with a lead item in the local column by Herb Caen. The pun-filled prose of this San Francisco media fixture draws many of the *Chronicle*'s 500,000 readers. During the more than half century that he has produced the daily column, he has established connections to almost every corner of the diverse city, and he has provided a wealth of tips to local reporters. From an unnamed source came the claim that an AIDS patient was frequenting the baths.

One of Shilts's editors saw the piece and wanted to know precisely what went on in the city's twenty or so bathhouses. So began the education of the *Chronicle*'s editors and readers about the realities of the city's sex establishments. The interest in San Francisco's bathhouses and backrooms was piqued in part by the fact that the annual Gay Freedom Day Parade, only weeks away, regularly attracted hundreds of thousands of out-of-town gay visitors to the city. The streets, bars, and baths would be filled with gays from across America, and from cities that might not yet be affected by the disease. Would some take the AIDS virus home after a tryst in the "tubs," as they were known?

That was the theme of Shilts's May 27, 1983, piece, "Gay Freedom Day Raises AIDS Worries": "'There's the potential that AIDS will be spread from here around the country,' said Dr. Mervyn Silverman, director of San Francisco's Department of Public Health. 'There has been some pressure on me to close the bathhouses. . . . Certainly, promiscuous and anonymous sex appears to be linked with AIDS in the gay male community.'" But the most Silverman said he would do was bet on the better judgment of gay visitors: "I hope that people coming here will realize they can't do the kinds of things they might do at home."

To some gays, including the Milk crowd, Silverman was shirking his duty. Shilts quoted one vocal doctor involved in the AIDS effort: "I'd love to have a reason to close them [the bathhouses] down," but at the very least the bars and baths should be forced to post health warnings about the dangers of unsafe sex. Not surprisingly, Shilts was sure the Milk Club's battle plan was the right tack, and he hinted at this in a June 11 analysis titled "The Politics of AIDS."

"'They're going to destroy gay businesses,' snarled one Toklas leader," who was opposed to any actions taken against bathhouses or other sex establishments. A Milk leader got the last words in the article: "Business isn't the point. Gay people are dying and the Toklas people are only concerned about keeping their political power." In the piece Shilts speculated that the Toklas Club was having a far greater effect on city policy. The San Francisco Health Department had no plans to mail education pamphlets about AIDS. Could it be, Shilts suggested, that Mayor Dianne Feinstein was listening more closely to the Toklas Club because it had endorsed her in the last election, and the Milk Club had not? With this piece, many in the gay community thought Shilts had stepped over the line. Not only had he aired the gay debate in the straight press, but now he was editorializing in the news pages.

Political analysis often seems to cross the line into editorializing. The distinction is much more obscure when the writer is as closely involved in the organizations he or she is analyzing as Shilts was to the Milk Club and the gay community. The *Chronicle* editors might have recognized the problems this connection was raising had Shilts been covering almost any other brand of politics. Despite the paper's interest in reporting on gays, the editors did not pretend to understand, or to *want* to understand, gay politics. They kept hands off.

Shilts made his point of view clear in a bombastic article in *California* magazine. "Whitewash," the June 1983 cover screamed. Inside, two free-lance journalists, Peter Collier and David Horowitz, detailed the trouble Shilts had run into in attempting to put together his "Startling Finding on 'Gay Disease'." The piece indicted Pat Norman, the gay Public Health Department worker Shilts had quoted, along with some other gay leaders and the public health establishment. Nearly everyone, it seemed—at least everyone in power—was trying to downplay the epidemic for political reasons, according to Shilts.

To the supporters of Norman, who was challenging Milk's successor, Supervisor Harry Britt, for his seat on the Board and his place at the head of the gay community, the politics were being played by

Shilts. After all, they said, it was clear Shilts supported Britt, the Milk Club candidate. The tempest drew the attention of a local TV station, which produced a documentary. The result was a TV story on a magazine story on a newspaper story, "media done with mirrors," Shilts said. He had chosen to be the most prominent image reflected in the glass. To defend himself, Shilts agreed to participate in a televised debate with Jerry Falwell, as well as with San Francisco's Public Health Director Dr. Silverman and psychotherapist Gary Walsh, who had become an AIDS activist. The broadcast devolved into a verbal wrestling match between Falwell and Walsh, with the preacher claiming AIDS was simply the wrath of God.

This was not the first time, nor would it be the last, that Shilts left himself open to accusations from politicos. That summer he was particularly vulnerable to criticism. On June 29, his mother was killed by a stroke. It was completely unexpected, and devastating for Shilts.

One night Shilts's lover, whom he had moved back in with, looked at the beleaguered reporter and asked, "Why do you continue writing this stuff?" Shilts thought about his reasons. His editors were not particularly thrilled about the broadsides he was taking. AIDS was an interesting beat, but there were many other aspects of the epidemic he could be covering besides San Francisco gay politics. At the bottom of it all was the fact that he had personalized the story. There were results he wanted, conclusions for which he was willing to weather some nasty storms. The desire to change things had directed him toward journalism in the first place. Now, he wanted to frighten his fellow gays into avoiding unsafe sexual behavior. He tried throughout 1983 and 1984 to get his stories on the dire consequences of promiscuous sex run on Friday, before men would hit the bars or baths. "I wanted everyone to have the fear of God in them."

One of the best examples of this was his reporting on AIDS just before the gay parade in late June of 1983. In one story Shilts reported the CDC's prediction that the current number of AIDS cases was a small fraction of the cases to come: "Because the incubation period gives victims a long time to transmit AIDS to sexual partners, . . . the 1,642 known AIDS victims in the country may be only 5 percent of the people who have been exposed to the still unknown element behind the illness." Embedded in the story was a sidebar announcing "Gay Parade, Celebration Tomorrow."

Shilts's articles, along with the work of other *Chronicle* and *Examiner* reporters and broadcast media like KPIX-TV, undoubtedly helped

tame the voracious sexual appetites of many gay men in San Francisco.
In mid-1983 three local psychotherapists found significant changes
in sexual habits among six hundred gay men they polled. The Bay
Area's media share much of the credit, with the San Francisco AIDS
Foundation, for influencing behavioral change.

The Bathhouse Debacle

Ambitious reporter that he was, Shilts also covered AIDS because it
was a beat he knew had epic proportions: death, sex, changing social
mores. That was Pulitzer Prize material, he thought. He was not going
to give up the beat, even if he was facing friendly fire. Anger played a
role in keeping Shilts on the local AIDS story, as well. The value of
anger was something he was reminded of by Gary Walsh. Shilts had
followed Walsh from the time he first read about him in the *Bay Area
Reporter* to the AIDS effort he fought and, finally, to his sick bed. On
August 13, 1983, Shilts detailed Walsh's struggle in "When the Diagnosis Is AIDS":

> "I'm not afraid of death," says the 38-year-old psychothera-
> pist, "but I'm afraid of dying, of all the pain." The question of
> when death comes is problematical. It may come, Walsh knows,
> from any one of the dozen known—and, perhaps, unknown—
> maladies that now afflict what just last year was a handsome,
> gym-toned body. His arms are marked by the purplish lesion of
> Kaposi's sarcoma and he has a hard time eating because these
> lesions probably have spread to his insides, coating his stomach.
> . . . [Walsh] found a great source of energy in anger. "I
> stopped being an AIDS victim and became a fighter—victims
> are helpless, and I decided to fight."

That fighting spirit pushed Shilts to go back to the bathhouse debate. He was alarmed at the news that after a summer decline in the
number of anal gonorrhea cases—the marker for high-risk sex—the
incidence of the disease was on the rise again six months later. Business at the baths was still brisk.

At this point, almost no one involved in the bathhouse debate was
ignorant of what exactly went on in these sex establishments. The
secrets of the bathhouses' raunchiest features—"sling rooms," for

example, where one man would strap himself into a device that suspended him in midair while another, or several others, performed anal sex on him or slowly pushed a fist up his anus—were now being described in some mainstream media. Shilts took *Chronicle* readers on a tour of one facility; the *Examiner* regularly described "unsafe sex practices": anal sex, oral sex, "fisting."

The baths were wildly popular, all together drawing an estimated twelve thousand customers per week, according to the owner of a medium-sized bathhouse, which grossed about a half-million in a good year. And many of the patrons were "straight" men from the suburbs, married, perhaps with children, whose only contact with the gay community was through anonymous sex at the "tubs." These were not the only places men congregated for anonymous sex: backrooms in bars, in bookstores, porno theaters, and public parks presented endless opportunities for quick, and sometimes dangerous, rendezvous. Because the bathhouses offered so much more privacy and security, they were better suited to accommodate a smorgasbord of risky sex.

"You don't open a candy store to show people how to have a diet," thought Shilts. He contacted the CDC's Dr. James Curran, head of the agency's AIDS Task Force, who said the bathhouses "should all go out of business." To drive home the link between the rising death toll and the baths, Shilts corralled some local big guns for his February 3 article, "AIDS Expert Says Bathhouses Should Close": Dr. Donald Abrams, assistant director of the AIDS Clinic and a well-known gay man; Supervisor Harry Britt; Dr. Selma Dritz, a down-to-earth epidemiologist who had been tracking the spread of AIDS. They all supported the move against the bathhouses. Only Public Health Director Dr. Mervyn Silverman was opposed to it.

"Closing the baths is not the answer, even though it might make me look good to a lot of people in the straight community," Silverman was quoted in the article. "History shows that government generally has not been very influential in changing people's sexual habits."

Contrary to Shilts's first suspicion that Feinstein was the force behind the city's hesitation to move against unsafe sexual practices and venues that seemed to promote them, Silverman actually was the deadweight. He could have requested that the facilities post warning signs about unsafe sex; he could, in fact, have closed them down. Unable or unwilling to pull the sides together, Silverman concentrated on holding the middle, and did nothing. "Any action on this," he said, "will have to come from the gay community, not my office."

Most of the gay leaders did not have the foggiest notion about what their community wanted. A survey by the *San Francisco Examiner*— one of the few, if imprecise, weathervanes for the time—indicated that a majority of gays polled favored some public-health action against the baths. Some 34 percent wanted the establishments closed altogether, a stunning referendum from a community spawned largely by the movement for sexual freedom.

Nonetheless, the criticism directed at Shilts was not dying out. After the Curran article ran, the Toklas Club voted to condemn him as homophobic, the gay community's equivalent to shunning. The insults on the street became so bad that some of his friends wouldn't be seen on Castro with him. The cruelest blow that February came when AIDS activist Gary Walsh died.

Shilts was working the night shift, 2:00 p.m. to 10:00 p.m., the evening the news broke. A reporter from the *Advocate*, which was putting together an obituary on Walsh, phoned Shilts. Randy felt the reporter was asking particularly hostile questions, and he was sure he was going to be slammed in the gay press. Depressed and anxious, he cut the interview short and went to dinner. Memories of Walsh marching, arguing, organizing, struggling for his life came rushing back. Shilts had several stiff drinks before returning to work. The *Advocate* reported phoned again, and Shilts managed to finish the interview in a drunken stupor but was in no shape to complete his shift. He finally left when an editor suggested that he go home. He knew his drinking was getting out of control, that he was losing control. His alcoholism threatened the most important thing to him: his career. That night he took his last drink.

Legislating Morality

San Francisco had established itself as a leader in dealing with the AIDS crisis. Although it had only the third largest number of AIDS cases in the United States, behind New York and Los Angeles, San Francisco was the first municipality to appropriate funds for education. By 1984 it had devoted millions to the AIDS fight, surpassing all other cities and even *states* except for California. It was also the first city to establish an AIDS clinic, and one of the first to pass an anti-AIDS discrimination ordinance. Now it was becoming a political laboratory for civil liberties in the age of AIDS.

In March 1984, into the fray stepped Larry Littlejohn, an activist who had pioneered the gay movement in the sixties and seventies. Shilts announced Littlejohn's drive to get a measure on the ballot prohibiting sexual activity in the city's bathhouses, a move Littlejohn thought was necessary to save his community from more deaths. It was not a much beloved initiative. If gays were split on how to approach the bathhouse conundrum, most were certain that a ballot measure, which would allow the mainstream community "to legislate morality" for gays, as one local gay newspaper put it, was not the answer. Instead, a growing contingent of gay businesspeople, doctors, and politicos wanted Silverman simply to act and close the establishments.

Said one local gay spokesperson: "When the Democratic Convention comes to town [in July of that year] with 10,000 reporters, we don't want the big local issue to center on gays' rights to commit suicide in bathhouses." The entire issue was fast evolving into little more than a debate over how the media would play it.

For the next week, Silverman suffered a powerful bout of health-policy schizophrenia, at first supporting the closure of the baths, then reneging. Finally, Silverman did neither and instead ordered a ban on high-risk sex in the city's gay bathhouses and sex clubs as an emergency measure to stop the spread of AIDS. In a *Chronicle* article about Silverman's decision, Shilts pointed out that 500 people in the Bay Area, and some 3,900 nationwide, had been diagnosed with AIDS.

Silverman's order called for inspectors from the health department to make periodic tours, "similar to restaurant inspections," as the *Chronicle* described it, to make sure dangerous sex—oral and anal sex, fisting, etc.—was not going on in the bathhouses. Those facilities that did not conform to the new guidelines would be closed down. However, investigating the sex habits of the homosexual male was going to be a bit tougher than tracking roaches and mice droppings; it required nothing short of sex police. The whole plan quickly ran into trouble on the Board of Supervisors. Because ensuing controversy might tarnish San Francisco's image, the supervisors decided to postpone any decision on the matter until after the Democrats' national convention, which was to begin on July 16. They thought they could delay any embarrassing protests that might spring up as the out-of-town press hit the city. In fact, by pushing back the decision date, San Francisco guaranteed that the bathhouse controversy would be an oft-repeated feature in the reportage during the Democrats' convention. That was partly because the major media from the Northeast were on the lookout for the most offbeat stories, which were supposed to typ-

ify California.

For the reader who cared to follow the tortuous trail of accusations and denials, pronouncements and refutations, the *Chronicle* was little help. As the debate dribbled on into late 1984, other reporters were filling in for Shilts, who was tackling other stories, and the relevance of the bathhouse news was becoming increasingly vague. In the fall of 1984, Silverman finally got around to ordering investigators into the bathhouses and sex clubs. They found risky business as usual: fisting, the more prosaic forms of anal sex, and even intravenous drug use.

Some media outlets, including the *New York Times* and CBS "Evening News," followed up on the story. It fit the criterion of offbeat news that New York-based journalists focused on when they covered California: gay-controlled San Francisco mired in sexual politics. Except for National Public Radio, which had a science correspondent located in California, most East Coast outlets disregarded the major medical and scientific work on AIDS being done on the West Coast. When reporters looked for sources from the research community, they usually chose from institutions in Boston, New York, Philadelphia, or Washington, D.C., even though doctors at UCLA, University of California at San Francisco, and Stanford had made early and major breakthroughs on AIDS. This oversight on the part of the Northeastern media establishment was typical of the way America's major magazines, networks, and the nation's "paper of record" viewed most news beyond the Hudson River: it was odd or curious, but not particularly significant to the rest of the nation. As a result, the zany or bizarre was much more likely to be covered than the important or the critical development that would shape national policies or issues. So the bathhouse debate was covered, rather than the extraordinary coordination of public services that San Francisco had developed for people with AIDS or even the internecine battles for funding in California between care providers.

Media Coverage Is out of Focus

When, in early October of 1984, Silverman finally closed the bathhouses, it was anticlimactic. There was little protest against a decision that had plagued Silverman for a year. San Francisco's sophisticated and caring response to the AIDS crisis served throughout the world as the model for dealing with the epidemic. Yet the bathhouse mess was nothing but an embarrassment. In light of the hundreds of other pressing AIDS issues, the local and national media's concentration on the sex establishments was a troubling example of inappropriate focus.

The bathhouse issue could not, and should not, have been avoided by Shilts or any other journalist. His play of the news, however, and his politicization of it, made progress in preventing AIDS much more difficult. By focusing on the bathhouses as though they were the primary sources of infection, he tended to discount the more basic problem: changing individuals' sexual behavior. Although anonymous sex at the baths undoubtedly contributed to the epidemic, the most important factor was an overriding sexual more of the gay culture, a consequence of oppression and denial, that encouraged promiscuity and unsafe sex. Closing the bathhouses simply bred a false sense of security for those gay men who had never visited or would not visit the establishments.

Shilts got what he called "my scalp": the three-foot-by-three-foot price board from the Hothouse Baths, detailing the cost of a locker and a room. It now hangs in Shilts's bathroom. With the bathhouse stories, the *Chronicle* engendered more suspicion about its ethics. And Shilts became a pariah for many vocal, and nonvocal, gays.

His role as flamboyant media personality did not help calm the critics. Along with his appearance in *California* magazine, he was featured on the cover of a city magazine as one of San Francisco's new gay power elites. He happened to pen the piece that ran on the inside. Far from being the congenial town he had emigrated to a decade before, San Francisco had become a hostile place to live.

Following the Paper Trail

One gay who remained friendly with Shilts was Bill Kraus, the aide to Phil Burton and one of the key Capitol Hill insiders who had been pushing for increased federal money to fight the epidemic. Along with Tim Westmoreland, an aide to Southern California Representative Henry Waxman and another Shilts source, Kraus had informants in almost every area of federal government involved in AIDS research, education, or funding.

In the spring of 1983, Secretary of Health Margaret Heckler testified in front of a congressional committee investigating whether the government was devoting adequate resources to the epidemic. "I really don't think there is another dollar that would make a difference [in the AIDS fight]," she said. Kraus knew that was not true. Some labs at the CDC could not get test tubes, let alone afford the scientists who were needed to keep on top of the AIDS epidemic. Facilities like the San Francisco General AIDS Clinic, which relied on federal funds for a good chunk of their budgets, could not care for all the sick and dying. Nearly every department in the budget-crunched Reagan administration, except for the Pentagon, had been told to cut back. Even the frantic redistributing of resources from other poorly funded branches of the CDC or Public Health Service was not providing a fraction of the money required.

Shilts followed up on the story. High-profile public health officials like Dr. James Curran, and even lower-level researchers pinched by the government's frugality, would not talk. However, Kraus and other aides, including Waxman's assistant, Tim Westmoreland, knew internal memos had been written. Shilts did not admit that these sources led him to the revealing documents that provided background for groundbreaking articles, but clearly these Capitol Hill operatives were helpful in directing him to the right vaults in the government catacombs. There were thousands of pages of confidential interdepartment correspondence. Under the Freedom of Information Act, Americans are supposed to have access to those records that are not central to protecting the government's national security. Shilts used that law to uncover the April 23, 1983, memo written by Dr. Donald Francis, director of AIDS research at the CDC, to the bureau's director. The tone was angry and adamant: "The inadequate funding to date has seriously restricted our work and has presumably deepened the invasion of this disease into the American population. . . . It is time to do more. It is time to do what is right."

The document pointed to a trail of other urgent memos, ending at the pen of Assistant Secretary of Health Edward Brandt. On July 25, 1984, Shilts published key parts of the Brandt document in "U.S. Health Service Chief Asks [For] More AIDS Research Money": "In order to seize the opportunities which the recent breakthroughs have provided us, we will need additional funds for both the remainder of this fiscal year and for next year." Brandt had written that memo months earlier to his superiors at Health and Human Services. It was a clear refutation of Secretary of Health Margaret Heckler's testimony before Congress that no increased funding was needed. Shilts uncovered a stack of evidence indicating that the government officials responsible for the health and welfare of the nation had been lying.

The story was picked up by the Associated Press, but it quickly disappeared. If it had been run in the *New York Times*, or if a *Washington Post* reported had uncovered the trail, the media reaction undoubtedly would have been much different. But because the *Chronicle* is perennially discounted by the Northeastern press establishment, and has long been considered a sensationalistic rag, the news fell through the cracks.

The fact that no journalists in the mainstream media were aggressively pursuing the AIDS funding scandal is a perfect example of the dangers of a disinterested media. Shilts was anything but disinterested. With each diagnosis of a friend, he became more committed, and angrier. In October of 1984, when Bill Kraus was told he had AIDS, Shilts was certain that the government, the media, the establishment did not care that gay men were dying. "I was convinced they were going to let us all die," he said. That paranoia was shared by gay men across the country, including Larry Kramer and the *New York Native*'s Chuck Ortleb.

A Death in the Neighborhood

Although Shilts's national reporting proved largely ineffective, he could still personalize the news powerfully, communicating the increasing despair of San Francisco gays. Near the end of 1984, he teamed up with two other *Chronicle* reporters, Katy Butler and L. A. Chung, to produce a series of articles describing the impact of the AIDS crisis on the gay community. Chung pieced together a yearbook of fallen young gay men—including an artist, a cop, a law professor— producing a powerful montage.

One main character in the series was a Latino lawyer, a working-class kid who had worked his way to a law degree in the East and had returned to California to practice law. Shilts and Butler described his life and death amid the web of human relationships he had built with both gays and heterosexuals.

"A week before Felix Velarde-Munoz died of AIDS, his doctor came into room 657 of Presbyterian Medical Center and put it bluntly: his brain was deteriorating." The article began with the personal and immediately gripping lead that is Shilts's hallmark. For the next sixty inches the reporter wove a story that seemed to encompass the whole of the gay community, and the heart of it, including Felix's initiation into the nightlife of discos and the political life of gay marches and protests.

"The summer of 1980 was to gay people what the summer of love had been to hippies—we had finally found our gay Camelot," Shilts quoted Cleve Jones, a prominent gay activist and a friend of Felix. "We had been through all the turmoil—the assassinations of Moscone and Milk, the riot, Anita Bryant. And we had survived."

That era of unbridled optimism seemed to disappear overnight. Suddenly the carnival of sex and the Castro's round-the-clock party seemed to come from a different, more innocent, time. One of Felix's closest friends, Jim Stacy, heard of his buddy's diagnosis and began changing his own life: no more visits to the baths, and nights in the bars were replaced with quiet evenings of gin rummy with friends.

He did not abandon Felix. "Every afternoon," Shilts wrote, "Stacy lifted his dying friend to watch the sunset from the hospital on Pacific Heights. They watched the blue bay turn a dark silver, watched the yellow car lights tracing their way across the Golden Gate Bridge, watched Alta Plaza's emerald grass darken, watched the light leave Felix's favorite city. Pink clouds streaked the sky, and a dull red glow remained against the hills after the sun dropped below the horizon.

"An hour after the sunset of November 8, Felix Velarde-Munoz took three long breaths and died." It was the kind of journalism Shilts did best: highly personal, community-based, dramatic. Nonetheless, some of his reporting tactics continued to get him in trouble.

Convenient Villains

The *Chronicle* newsroom got a phone call January 3, 1985, from an angry nurse at San Francisco General Hospital. The day before police had picked up Silvana Strangis, a thirty-four-year-old prostitute. Before bringing her to headquarters, they tried to force her to get an AIDS antibody test at the hospital's clinic. They had been told her boyfriend had AIDS, and they wanted to make sure she was not spreading the disease on the street. It was an understandable, if illegal, move on the officers' part. But the AIDS clinic was closed.

The next day, Shilts's editor sent him out after Silvana for an interview. He found her at the Algonquin Hotel, a flophouse in the Tenderloin section of San Francisco, home to hookers, drug dealers, and two-bit criminals of all varieties. Her boyfriend warned her not to go with the reporter. But she wanted to go back to the AIDS Clinic, to get a note from the doctors saying she did not have the disease. The reporter said he would give her a ride. Shilts and Silvana arrived at the hospital shortly after 1:00 P.M., closing time for the clinic on Fridays, and they were told to return Monday. The prostitute had swollen lymph nodes and complained of night sweats and chronic fatigue, clear signs of AIDS. If she was infected, she would have all weekend to spread the disease, Shilts thought. The next day, the *Chronicle's* front page shouted "A 'Monster' Dilemma on AIDS: Working Prostitute Waits for Test": "A prostitute who believes she has AIDS was turned away from San Francisco General Hospital's AIDS Clinic yesterday after she was sent there by police officers to determine whether she has AIDS." By that afternoon, camera crews from local TV stations were combing the Tenderloin in search of Silvana.

Dr. Paul Volberding, head of San Francisco General's AIDS Clinic, believes it was a staged performance. Later, Shilts admitted he was embarrassed by the sensationalistic way the story had been handled: "I knew the clinic had closed. My point was that this was a working prostitute." Nonetheless, "I shouldn't have let the city editor do the lead saying she was turned away," he said. "It wasn't fair."

Shilts infuriated AIDS-care workers, especially the San Francisco AIDS Foundation, with his handling of other incidents: for example, revealing the names of individuals who had asked for confidentiality. No matter how Shilts reported the AIDS beat, he could not have avoided all such criticism. Often he had to make new rules as he went along, because he was covering territory uncharted by journalists. For instance, should the name of a working prostitute with AIDS be published to save her future johns from infection? Other questions are as old as the journalism craft, but given new urgency in a health crisis: Can a reporter who intimately knows the issues and players not become politically involved in the story? How sacred is, or should be, objectivity in the midst of death and dying?

These are questions reporters like Shilts have not successfully answered, but will continue to face. Thousands of San Franciscans will soon follow the thousands who have already been buried. Most of them will be gay. Some 97 percent of the city's AIDS victims are homosexual.

Already, the epidemic's impact could be seen in the tightly drawn faces of workers at San Francisco General's AIDS clinic, and at the local AIDS Foundation. People in their late twenties, early and mid-thirties who had made their way to the dream that was San Francisco now ministered to its casualties with the fortitude of war veterans. They all lost friends, and leaders like Bill Kraus.

In 1988, nowhere was the effect of this coverage more evident than in the Castro. There, on the same street corner where flocks of men used to strip to the waist in a macho mating ritual, the passing conversation was no longer just about discos and parties. It was about wakes and funerals, and about surviving. Studies show that gay men have drastically cut their risk for AIDS, and the incidence of other less deadly sexually transmitted illnesses has been sharply reduced. The same community that made sexual excess into a way of life seemed to have grown up, and set a noble example with its care for the dying.

Shilts noted that more gays were getting involved in local causes than ever before. More than ever, San Francisco's homosexual leadership seemed out of step with its constituency. In the 1987 mayoral election, in which the majority of gay politicians supported a longtime local ally, 80 percent of the city's gays voted for his opponent, who won.

Home Is the Hunter

Since the release of *And the Band Played On*, in 1987, Shilts has been swamped with positive press about the book. He claimed he was offered jobs by newspapers across the country, though he said he'd rather stay at the *Chronicle*. At this point, he could afford to do just about anything he'd like. His $40,000 *Chronicle* salary has been supplemented by royalties from brisk sales of the book, and the movie rights brought in an additional six-figure sum.

Probably the most important payback for Shilts was what he calls his "second rehabilitation." While he walked near Castro Street recently, he was stopped by an admirer who recognized Shilts from one of the hundreds of TV interviews and newspaper photos his book spurred. The man gushed his approval of both the tome and Shilts. The reporter treasured this warm recognition from the gay-on-the-street. In his idealized version of himself, he is the dragon slayer confronting the establishment, including the government, the media, and the gay powers that be.

Chapter 9
A plague in the villages, by Robin Nagle

When the nation first met Ryan White on network evening news in mid-1985, it saw an energetic teen zipping from house to house on his bike, chucking the *Kokomo Tribune* onto front lawns. He looked like an average junior-high schooler. But Ryan was far from average. His story polarized the town of Kokomo, Indiana, drastically changed at least one reporter's life, and brought national condemnation to the formerly quiet community.

In Arcadia, Florida, the three Ray boys, all infected with the AIDS virus, had the same impact on their small town. The effect of the networks' TV cameras is still being felt there. And the decisions local journalists made about how to cover the story still influence their lives.

In Mesquite, Texas, how local journalists reported the case of pediatrician Dr. Robert John Huse irrevocably changed his life, too.

Coverage of AIDS has provided a particularly good example of how the media work. The power, responsibility, and character of journalism were never more evident than when the disease came to small-town America.

KOKOMO, INDIANA: A TOWN DIVIDED

Kokomo is the heart of the heartland. It sits in the midst of Howard County's seemingly endless and perfectly flat fields of corn and soybeans, about fifty-five miles north of Indianapolis. The town's forty-eight thousand residents are proud, mostly white, working-class people. Fundamentalist Christianity thrives in most of the county's three hundred churches. The politics of the farmtown, which used to be the national headquarters of the Ku Klux Klan, are staunchly conservative, with tinges of the reactionary. In the mid-1980s, it became a difficult place for Ryan White to call home.

Ryan has hemophilia, a blood-clotting disorder. Like most hemophiliacs, he has relied on the blood of others for transfusions and treatments all his life. In December 1984, when he was hospitalized with *Pneumocystis* pneumonia, it was discovered that Ryan had received blood product factor VIII that included more than the vital clotting substances he needed. Along with half of the twenty thousand hemophiliacs in the country, Ryan had been infected with the AIDS virus by receiving tainted blood.

Choosing Sides

While Ryan was a *Kokomo Tribune* paperboy, Christopher MacNeil was a *Tribune* reporter. MacNeil, thirty years old at the time and a Kokomo resident since early childhood, first heard about the AIDS-infected boy almost by accident. In early March 1985 the local Red Cross asked the newspaper to publish an appeal for blood donors. AIDS-tainted blood was making the news in San Francisco and Los Angeles, and had been a major story on the network news for more than a year. The networks still described AIDS in ambiguous, ominous language. CBS usually called it "a deadly, mysterious disease"; at ABC, it was "new and frightening"; at NBC, "terrifying." In part because of the widespread publicity, a large percentage of Americans believed they would somehow be at risk of *getting* AIDS by giving blood. The fear was severely affecting blood banks across the nation. MacNeil was assigned to report on the problem in Kokomo. The Red Cross officials told him about the winsome thirteen-year-old, one of the local residents desperately dependent on the kindness of donors.

Later in March, MacNeil wrote an article about the Whites, revealing that Ryan was infected with the AIDS virus. The story drew no public reaction. It wasn't news to officials at Western School Corporation, the district that included Ryan's junior high. Jeanne White had told the school months before, to explain her son's frequent absences from class. Ryan missed almost his entire seventh-grade year because of his illnesses. He was destined to miss more. In the early summer, when Jeanne White went to reenroll him for the fall of 1985, she was told he would not be allowed to return to the classroom. Homebound tutoring, the school board had decided, would be an acceptable alternative. Ryan was not the first child with AIDS to be shut out of school. Youngsters in Miami, Florida; Queens, New York; New Haven, Connecticut; and Santa Ana, California had also been prevented from enrolling. Parents around the country were understandably skittish about allowing their children to share a classroom with a carrier of a fatal and contagious malady, even if the disease was hard to get and nearly impossible to spread in a typical school setting. Ryan's protest was the first to be heard in court and the first to gain the national spotlight.

However, one mother's struggle with a recalcitrant school board was not the stuff of network newscasts, even when the debate was AIDS-related. That changed dramatically in late July 1985, when Rock Hudson was diagnosed with AIDS. Newspapers and networks, which had not done a dozen stories on the disease in the previous seven months, now did a dozen in seven days. Overnight, AIDS was transformed from an obscure threat to gay men to a disease it seemed anyone could get. Suddenly, reporters throughout the nation were scrambling for leads on stories about the epidemic. Ryan's story—that is, how the disease was affecting a small town—drew an Indianapolis TV reporter to Kokomo. She had read about the infected boy in the *Tribune*.

Ryan first appeared on television July 30, 1985. The Indianapolis reporter had talked to School Superintendent James O. Smith and the Whites. Ryan told her he did not want to be barred from school, that he would miss his friends.

CBS "Evening News," hungry for a way to put a sympathetic face on the epidemic, picked up the story the next night. Superintendent Smith was quoted as admitting that he had made his decision to ban the boy before he had "all the facts." The CDC's Dr. James Curran underscored the locals' ignorance and called Ryan's exclusion from the classroom "baseless." ABC "World News Tonight" followed up on August 3 with a nearly identical story. NBC was slower, covering Ryan only after the first round of court battles.

Tribune publisher Arden Draeger, a longtime Kokomo resident, knew his town. He also understood that the story, especially as it was being played on the national news, could divide Kokomo into two camps: defenders of Ryan White and those siding with the frightened parents. Draeger and his managing editor, John Wiles, spent long hours debating how Kokomo's single daily newspaper, the only locally produced news source for the town, should play the story.

No one had yet investigated what official guidelines might exist for handling the situation. Draeger contacted the Indianapolis Board of Health. If anyone in Indiana had wrestled with the issue yet, it would be the health officials in the state's largest city. As it turned out, no one in Indiana had experienced this kind of case before, but Draeger was told that Indianapolis—and the State Health Department, as well—would follow the Centers for Disease Control's guidelines: the only children infected with the AIDS virus who should not be admitted to school were those with open sores, or who could not control their bodily functions. Ryan fit neither category.

On August 2, the *Tribune* published its first editorial on the issue, called "Every Right." Written by Wiles and approved by Draeger, it quoted from the State Health Board's recommendation that children with AIDS be allowed in the classroom and listed the precautions a school could take to minimize risk of exposure. Draeger thought Superintendent Smith's call to bar Ryan from the local school was wrong. But he wanted to press that point as diplomatically as possible. Small-town papers do not stay in business by attacking the establishment.

"The decision made by Smith is understandable," the editorial allowed. "An untreatable disease causes fear. Before more was known, those with handicaps, epilepsy and cancer received similar treatment. But the decision to ban Ryan from school should be reconsidered. He has every right to attend. . . . Any other decision just further punishes the child for a situation over which he has no control."

The only response was a spate of letters from angry readers.

Caught in the Media Lights

In August, when the Whites filed suit against Western School Corporation in the Indianapolis federal court, Kokomo residents hoped the judge would make a ruling quickly, one way or the other. Judge James Noland was not so cooperative.

"Noland ruled that AIDS children barred from attending school must go through local and state education channels before a court can intervene," reported MacNeil in a story on August 17, 1985. The issue now promised to be a protracted battle, and the nation's attention remained focused on the town. In the last two weeks of August, the networks ran six stories about Ryan: three on CBS, two on NBC, one on ABC. This was equal to the coverage each network had given the

1984 announcement of the global breakthrough of the discovery of the AIDS virus.

Kokomo was beginning to feel self-conscious, for very good reason. On August 25, MacNeil reported on the national coverage. "Western School Board President Daniel Carter has observed the Ryan White AIDS case had all the makings of 'sensational' news," wrote MacNeil. "Some [local residents] said the press reported the case as accurately and objectively as it could, considering what isn't known about the disease. Many others said the media entered the case convinced of who was right and wrong, and 'refused to be moved by the facts.'" Indeed, the consensus was that Kokomo was not getting a fair shake.

Carter, the School Board president, believed the electronic media were not as thorough or objective as print media, and that the national media at large were irresponsible. "The national [media have] gone into this with a preconceived notion," he told MacNeil. "The [school] corporation has been painted as ignorant . . . a country bumpkin type of hick school." He had a point.

On August 26, all three networks did a story on Ryan White, using the same format. Ryan was still banned from school, they reported, and school officials had suggested installing a phone hookup between Ryan's home and his classroom. The networks each duly noted that Ryan said the connection was not clear enough for him to hear what was going on. Each reported that Jeanne and Ryan, predictably, resented the ban and this latest solution. None of the network reporters talked to school officials. But then each network produced a slightly different picture of sentiment at the school. ABC said Ryan's fellow students disagreed with the ban; CBS quoted a student whose parents said to stay away from Ryan. NBC claimed the students supported the ban. There were students who reflected each of these views, of course, but the networks distorted that complexity. The broadcasters were searching for a dramatic consensus, and molded their own. What were viewers to believe? That would probably depend on which newscast they had tuned in that night.

Personal Cost of the Story

At the *Tribune*, MacNeil was given a free hand in covering the story. His approach mirrored Draeger's. Both thought the newspaper's role was partly that of educator. They reasoned that if people were presented with enough clearly explained facts, they would reach a well-informed intelligent decision, and let Ryan back in school. That mission, to bring clarity to the day's issues, draws many individuals to the journalism profession. The limits and failures they face in doing just that drive many away.

MacNeil had that righteous ideal of "reporter as educator" in mind when he began covering Ryan White. Although he was a product of the white, conservative Midwest, the civil rights movement and Martin Luther King, Jr.'s assassination had made a profound impact on him, and he grew sensitive to bias. When Ryan was first locked out of school, MacNeil bristled at what he thought was outright discrimination. AIDS victims, and their civil rights, should become a central issue in the United States, he thought. He could help eradicate the problem of discrimination by writing about AIDS, he decided. An accurate and thorough presentation of the facts would ease opposition to Ryan. More than that, he wanted to refute the notion that AIDS was a gay disease, that homosexuality itself was a viable basis for discrimination, and that anyone who supported the boy was either gay or sympathetic to gays. MacNeil's was an extraordinary challenge.

He was a good reporter and an adept writer. Draeger and Wiles gave him freedom to report. He began by doing stories on the Whites: who they were, why they decided to fight the school board, what they felt about the town's reaction to them. Then he branched out, writing on AIDS patients beyond Kokomo who had experienced discrimination, and on AIDS outreach and education efforts in Indianapolis. He filed stories on insurance company concerns, AIDS-virus testing programs and their problems. He even began covering heightened homophobia in Indiana and elsewhere. He interviewed Indianapolis bathhouse owners and gay activists about safe sex (there were no bathhouses and certainly no gay activists in Kokomo). He interviewed teachers around the country who wanted to show support for Ryan, but who feared backlash from parents. He spoke with people in Swansea, Massachusetts, where another young hemophiliac, also injected with the AIDS virus, had found warmth and encouragement from his school and town.

MacNeil's readers hardly shared his enthusiasm. He had not considered the conservative nature of his audience and the anger his articles might provoke. Oddly enough, neither had *Tribune* Publisher Draeger. MacNeil became a regular target of death threats. His father accused him of being a homosexual, and during one heated argument the elder MacNeil slashed his son across the arm with a broken soda bottle. Friends, many of whom he had known since his own school days in Kokomo, seemed to disappear. He was so fearful for his safety that he stopped buying groceries in town and instead drove an hour to Fort Wayne or Indianapolis. At one point, he needed police protection and was advised not to frequent Kokomo proper unless it was absolutely necessary, hard advice to follow for a reporter covering Kokomo. There were several attempts to burglarize his home, and his car was vandalized more than once. He was routinely accused by townspeople of sleeping with Jeanne White, and with gay activists in Indianapolis.

The community's reaction was not surprising. Kokomo is an insulated, Bible-belt town. The neighboring county is still a stronghold for the Ku Klux Klan. Most of the *Tribune*'s thirty-four thousand readers have no more than a high school education. However, MacNeil did not stop writing. In the sixteen months he covered the story, he wrote more than three hundred articles.

The reporter could continue his crusade only because Managing Editor Wiles and Publisher Draeger continued to back him. In fact, Wiles and Draeger persisted in running editorials in support of the Whites. Ryan and AIDS became the issue on which they staked their independence as news people. Fortunately for them, their resolve was not met with the ultimate challenge. No businesses pulled their ads from the *Tribune*, probably because the newspaper is a monopoly in its market and thus one of the few advertising outlets available in Kokomo. However, Draeger did not go unscathed. His house was pelted with eggs, and he received numerous threatening phone calls, often late at night. "If I ran a story today that attacked something, I'd get phone calls," he said. "But the frequency then scared me."

Not everyone opposed the Whites. Only one customer on Ryan's paper route asked that he not deliver their paper. A *Tribune*-sponsored charity, the Goodfellows Fund, collected close to $100,000 for the beleaguered family. Draeger claimed the anti-Ryan furor that came to typify the national image of Kokomo was started and maintained by a small but zealous group of parents. Some parents of Ryan's classmates supported the Whites' fight. Others were quietly concerned about the potential of their children becoming infected in the classroom. Those subtleties were lost on network TV.

In almost every one of the nearly forty national television stories that ran between July 1985 and December 1986, Ryan and Jeanne appeared first, reaffirming that they wanted Ryan back in school and that the school board was unjust, that ignorance prevailed in Kokomo. Then the reporter would talk to parents, students, school officials, and national experts, not always in that order. The students' comments were often mixed, some in support of and others opposed to Ryan's return. Almost all of the parents, on the other hand, were portrayed as on the defensive, often angry and shouting, "defending their paranoia," as one broadcaster described it.

Parents who opposed Ryan's admission to school believed they were acting in the best interests of their children. Although they had been told countless times that there were no cases of AIDS transmitted by the kind of casual contact between students in a classroom, as long as public health officials could not categorically guarantee their children's safety, the risk from this new horror was too high for them. The nature of television—and of print media, to a lesser extent—is to amplify these loudest voices. They are the ones that draw the most attention from journalists, and hence from viewers.

The outside media's portrayal of Kokomo intensified the local crisis, first polarizing and then humiliating residents. An issue that would have drawn scant attention from most in Kokomo became a defining controversy in which every citizen was forced to participate. Much of the harassment of reporter MacNeil sprang not from his stories, but from the national media's ridicule. He just happened to be the closest journalist-target. Publisher Draeger said he published every letter to the editor he could fit into the *Tribune,* and they fell into two groups. Correspondence from people in Kokomo mostly criticized the paper and the Whites for the crisis. People outside the community condemned Kokomo residents and the school.

The Kokomo Goliath

After months of court maneuverings and appeals, the Western School Corporation was ordered in April of 1986 to admit Ryan. The town was still opposed to his presence in the classroom and bitter about the outside media's fixation on the story. The Whites' victory was hollow. They endured one long year of hostility and loneliness in their hometown and then left Kokomo in the summer of 1987. The networks pulled their cameras out, too, though they did not forget Ryan. He occasionally showed up when the AIDS story turned to civil rights, as in ABC's "Nightline" broadcast in 1987. His cute and impish manner

made him a highly photogenic victim. A *People* magazine follow-up in
the spring of 1988 showed a cheerful, scruffy Ryan playing with
friends in his new home in Arcadia, Indiana. *People* reporter Jack
Friedman wrote of the Whites' last days in Kokomo: "If responding to
AIDS has become one of the litmus tests of human decency, Kokomo
failed it badly." In the same story, Ryan is described as "purified of the
petty distractions that plague and mess up most lives." He was the
child of "serenity" battling the town were "fear and hatred were rank
in the air." Such simplistic caricatures of the people involved in the
Ryan White story are typical of outlets like the networks—and *People*
magazine, which is a print equivalent of the TV medium—quick images, and little time to explain the subtleties.

Christopher MacNeil was eventually pulled from the Ryan White
story when a local television station showed him greeting the Whites
at an airport and putting an arm around one of them (no one remembers if it was Jeanne or Ryan). His editors said *Tribune* readers who
saw that would no longer believe MacNeil was objective, if, in fact,
there were any who still thought that. He was assigned to cover the
local courts.

Months after the Whites had left town, MacNeil still traveled an
hour one way for groceries. Friends who deserted him still had not
returned. He did not receive death threats any more, but his father
still would not speak to him. Life in Kokomo was isolated and lonely
for him. He wanted to move on, but other papers in Indiana told him
his name was too volatile. If he wanted to work for another publication, it would have to be far from Kokomo.

In the end MacNeil left both Kokomo and small-town journalism
for law school at Purdue University, in Indiana.

ARCADIA, FLORIDA: TOWN WITHOUT PITY

"Fifty miles and fifty years from Sarasota" is how one Arcadian describes his home of six thousand, the seat of Florida's west-central
DeSoto County. The town is proud of its high school, its history, and
especially its southern neighborliness. That neighborliness was sorely
challenged in the summer of 1987, when the story of the Ray family
caught the attention of the locals, and of the nation.

The plight of the Rays took most of the town by surprise. Tim

194 Adamson, editor of the *Arcadian,* a local weekly paper, first heard about it on his way to church on Sunday, April 12, 1987. A fellow parishioner asked him if he had seen the front page of the *Tampa Tribune,* the largest daily paper in the region: "Fear, Ignorance Force Family to Flee," read the headline. A fifty-nine-inch article told how an Arcadian family had been barred from church and school because three of its four children had antibodies to the AIDS virus. "I'd never heard of these people," said Adamson. "The story was going on a year and I'd never heard a thing." Neither had many others, apparently. "Church that morning was just abuzz," he said.

Adamson's competition in town was the *DeSoto County Times,* Arcadia's other weekly paper. *Times* editor John Edmondson also first stumbled onto the Rays in the Sunday *Tampa Tribune.*

The *Arcadian* has a circulation of three thousand and a sixty-five-year history. Adamson, in his thirties, is a fifth-generation Arcadia native and has been at the paper's helm since 1985. The *DeSoto County Times* was not established until 1983, but it has three times the *Arcadian's* circulation. Editor Edmondson, in his forties, has worked in newspapers all his professional life; he moved from Virginia to take the *Times's* helm only four months before the Rays' story broke. On that April morning, when Edmondson and Adamson read the story in the paper that scooped them both, they sensed the news would have a profound impact on their community. That is the extent of their agreement on the news and how to cover it. Adamson saw himself as the hard-pressed reporter who would retain his objectivity, no matter how unlikely a role that would be for the Arcadia native son. Edmonson, the outsider, knew his paper had to report the news objectively, but he believed he had to take a stand. In the end, they both took sides in the conflict.

As in Kokomo, the national press played a decisive role in inciting Arcadia's local passions and distorting a complex and volatile situation.

The Battle Begins

For the Rays, the nightmare had started months before the story first broke in the *Tampa Tribune.* In August of 1986, Clifford and Louise Ray discovered that their three hemophiliac sons, Richard, Robert, and Randy—ages ten, nine, and seven, respectively—tested positive for HIV, the AIDS virus, though they did not have the disease. The family sought guidance and solace from their church. The minister told a fellow preacher at the church. No one is exactly sure how the news traveled from there, but soon the entire congregation knew about the Ray boys. The minister asked the family not to return.

A new school year was about to begin. Despite the Rays' wish to keep their sons' HIV status a secret, word was already out among some in Arcadia, and Louise Ray decided to tell school officials. "The last thing I wanted was some enraged mother running into the classroom where my young'uns were and yelling at them and causing problems," she told the *Tampa Tribune* reporter. When school started at the end of August, the Ray family was told their children could not attend. Candy, the youngest Ray child, tested negative, and she was readmitted to school two weeks later. The boys were promised tutoring at home until the school board could decide how best to fit them into a regular classroom. The homebound program provided about three hours of schooling a week for each boy. Their parents thought that was inadequate; children in a regular classroom get about twenty-five hours a week. The school board seemed unwilling to compromise or find a way to incorporate the boys back into the classroom, despite repeated promises to "study" the problem. After struggling with school officials for the first half of the school year, the Rays gave up.

In late winter 1987, the family decided to move. They headed north to Bay Minette, Alabama, where no one knew them or the boys' HIV status. The children attended school and began to make new friends. The peace lasted about three weeks, until the medical records arrived at the Rays' new school. On March 31, the boys were removed from the classroom until the principal had time to review the situation. The scenario was all too familiar to the Rays by this time.

Dr. Jerry Barbosa, a pediatric hematologist and oncologist from All Children's Hospital in Sarasota, was treating the boys. He had already offered to meet with the Arcadia school board when they were deliberating about the children, but the board turned him down. When the Rays faced the same trouble in Bay Minette, it occurred to Barbosa that they might benefit from having their story aired. After all, the guidelines for handling HIV positive kids in schools already had been established. Even the Surgeon General, C. Everett Koop, said HIV-positive and AIDS children should be in school except in rare circumstances. When the story hit the press, Barbosa told the Rays, people would be informed and therefore not afraid. The doctor echoed the same faith in the media that *Kokomo Tribune* reporter Chris MacNeil had before he began AIDS reporting. It was as misguided in small-town Florida as it was in small-town Indiana.

Barbosa contacted the *Tampa Tribune*'s metro reporter Bettinita Harris. Her beat included areas outside Tampa, including Arcadia. The Rays did not want to talk to Harris until after they left town, but once they had settled in Alabama, she was invited up for an interview. Harris's detailed retelling of their odyssey ran on the front page of the *Tampa Tribune* on April 12, when it first caught the attention of Arcadia's own media. Harris's story also was seen by a reporter at the Associated Press.

How did such major news in a small, tight-knit community like Arcadia get overlooked in the local papers until an out-of-town paper got the story? The Rays are not the kind of people who make it into the papers anywhere, small towns or big cities. They lived in a poverty-ridden neighborhood on the outskirts of town: if Arcadia had been larger, their neighborhood would have been called a "slum." Clifford Ray was born and raised in the town. He had little education and was not very articulate. As in many other towns and cities across the country, AIDS was invisible when it struck people who were invisible to the power-brokers or agenda-setters. That's why the epidemic was so slow to be covered in the first place.

The *Times*'s John Edmondson later speculated that if the Rays had been among the town's prominent families—in this largely lower middle-class community, that would mean that Mrs. Ray belonged to the PTA and Mr. Ray coached Little League—their story would have unfolded quite differently.

The *Arcadian* Plays It Safe

The *Arcadian*'s staff of nine includes the publisher, the receptionist, and everyone in between. Page two is always devoted to a lengthy column called "To DeSoto With Love, Donna," a chatty round-up of weekly events by publisher Donna Latimer. "All members, past and present of the Mt. Ephraim Baptist Church are reminded of the 51st Annual Homecoming this Sunday," Donna wrote in one column. "Our DeSoto Bulldogs did it again last Friday night with a 53-0 victory over Ft. Meade" was another item. The paper's headlines reflect issues of local concern: "Flood insurance is topic of special meeting" and "Motel gets ripped off." The paper runs about sixteen pages most weeks, split into two parts. Tim Adamson oversaw the news of the publication, served as chief reporter, and occasionally wrote editorials.

On April 23, 1987, he commented on the Rays: "How sad it is that Arcadia must live with the notoriety of being a town of ignorant and frightened people who would persecute a family already burdened with illness." That initial strident tone would be reined in substantially in future editorials. "At first it was hard keeping any personal opinion to myself," he later wrote in a trade journal for reporters. "But I am only a newspaper editor. . . . I realized that if I took one side— regardless of which side—I would be viewed as biased. People would believe I could not fairly report the story."

Yet Adamson had a decidedly personal stake in the coverage. No one born and raised in Arcadia who intended, as Adamson did, to spend the rest of his life in the community can afford to alienate its citizenry. And neither could the paper, with aggressive competition from another local newspaper, take the chance of angering its readers or advertisers. The *Arcadian* had to play the comfortable middle ground. That meant that Adamson was not going to judge the actions of his townsfolk. In the interest of his and the paper's future, he had to keep his original opinion about the Ray crisis out of his paper. He stopped writing editorials.

Adamson did print dozens of letters to the editor, representing every stand on the issue. He did not attempt to keep up with the *Tampa Tribune*'s scoops on the story, because he realized early on that he could not compete with the daily newspaper. This was driven home to him when he interviewed the Ray family by phone while they were still in Alabama. Louise Ray said they were not returning to Arcadia. Adamson gave the story front-page play on April 23, the day they moved back. But it didn't remain a prominent topic; there were other issues that deserved attention. DeSoto County celebrated its centennial in May 1987; the Watermelon Festival started in early June; in July a citrus processing plant announced it was canceling plans to reopen.

On June 18, the front page focused again on the Rays, who had filed suit against the DeSoto County School Board. Adamson devoted two other pages to the story and to AIDS in general. He consulted AIDS experts at the Centers for Disease Control, at the National Institutes of Health, at various universities. The doctors from the CDC,

NIH, and most of the universities said the Ray children posed no significant threat. Adamson's other sources, which included a physician who hadn't treated AIDS patients, claimed the boys were a health menace.

On July 16, when the Rays went before a hearing in U.S. District Court in Tampa, Adamson ran a kind of debate on the front page of the *Arcadian*. On one side ran a photo of the Rays' physician, Dr. Jerry Barbosa, who had handled both hemophiliacs and AIDS cases. The caption below his picture read, "There is no reason at all why the Ray children should not attend a regular classroom. They do not pose any significant health risk to other students or to the teachers." On the other side was a picture of Dr. Steven Armentrout: "I believe that placing the Rays in a classroom poses a significant risk of transmission of the AIDS virus to other children." Armentrout was described as an "AIDS expert," though he had not specialized in epidemiology, virology, immunology, or pediatrics. He shared a hematology practice with another doctor. That colleague happened to have worked with AIDS patients.

Adamson, in his drive to be "fair," stretched to include all voices almost equally, including "experts" without any experience in AIDS research or treatment. Using "objectivity," a guise journalists hide behind frequently, Adamson distorted the news.

Small Town, Big News

Since Ryan White's story gained national attention, schoolchildren and AIDS had been a big news item for the mainstream media. The *New York Times* covered its own local controversy, when parents in Queens fought to keep a child infected with the virus out of the local schools. Other cases were making the front page in California and now in Florida. If Rock Hudson's diagnosis touched the heart of Americans—or at least piqued the interest of American journalists—kids hit by the plague touched the nation's soul. And unlike most AIDS stories, small-town scenarios provided backdrops and images to frame the drama. In short, it allowed television to do what it does best.

A few days after the Rays filed suit in June, NBC and ABC appeared in Arcadia. On June 22, NBC ran a story that included an interview with the assistant pastor of the church that had shunned the Rays, who said anyone unafraid of AIDS was either ignorant or a liar.

A school board official defended its action against the Rays. A parent concurred.

ABC's story on 24 June was similar. After talking to the Ray children, the reporter interviewed randomly chosen Arcadians. One said he would move away if the family came to the local fishing tournament. Another said he would remove his child from school if the Ray boys attended. Robert Ray said the local barber would no longer cut his hair.

Adamson bristled at the picture of his town as a redneck backwater. Other Arcadians were up in arms. The town image would look much worse before the story was over.

Taking a Stand at the *Times*

The *DeSoto County Times*'s John Edmondson thought there was an obvious right and wrong side to the Ray story. His paper ran its first story on 16 April. Like the *Arcadian*'s article, "it was basically a rewrite of the *Tampa Tribune* story," said Edmondson. The following Thursday, Edmondson published the first in a series of strong editorials.

He briefly explained hemophilia and how the boys had been exposed to the AIDS virus. "The boys do not have AIDS," he explained, "nor can what they have be spread by casual contact. . . . As a caring community, we have an obligation to allow [the Rays] a chance." The next editorial, on May 28, appealed to Arcadians' pocketbooks. The Rays, back in town, had yet to file suit against the school board, but they were discussing it. "If the Rays were to win a lawsuit—a very strong possibility—it could cost DeSoto County taxpayers dearly," wrote Edmondson. "Not the school board, but the taxpayers," upwards of $250,000, a fortune for a small town.

Edmondson proposed a solution: "Put the Ray boys back in the regular classroom next week. . . . The youngsters will need to go to summer school. . . . Let them continue in a normal classroom setting through the summer. Publicity and attention would die down. Things could genuinely get back to normal in DeSoto County."

In August 1987, the court ruled that the DeSoto County School Board would have to admit the Ray boys when school started later that month. Edmondson was overjoyed. The day after the ruling he wrote, "The ignorant and the stubborn were defeated yesterday." The DeSoto County School Board had acted like "imbeciles," he wrote, and had given the Ray family "despicable treatment." Many Arcadians did not see the decision in the same light. To calm local tensions, the school planned several community meetings on AIDS and the precautions the school would take with the Ray children. At one such gathering, Edmondson recalled, he overheard a man say, "This ain't nothing a shotgun can't fix." Edmondson was incensed.

In a terse editorial on 20 August, he allowed that Arcadia residents "have reacted in predictable fashion. There has been anger, frustration, anxiety and resolve." But some, he wrote, "have reacted with the breeding of animals and the intelligence of our native alligators." He offered the shotgun remark as one example, and death threats against the Rays as another. "There is no room in our community for this kind of behavior," Edmondson wrote. "We condemn such savage thinking, and only hope that the very good, hard-working people of DeSoto County will speak out against these threats." Some readers reacted by canceling their subscriptions, and a smattering of merchants pulled their advertising.

The Cameras Return

On August 23, NBC reported the Rays' victory in court. The story also recorded Arcadia's reaction. A spokesman for a group called Citizens Against AIDS in Schools was outraged. So were a school board spokesman and local parents. The story ended with a plaintive ten-year-old Ricky Ray, saying he expected trouble from his fellow students when school started.

ABC and CBS filed stories the following evening. Both showed the Ray boys during their first day back at school and reported relentless resistance from the community. CBS noted that a private school had been hastily formed, with a burgeoning enrollment. Citizens Against AIDS in Schools threatened to bring a suit against the Rays to get the boys out of the public school again. The school superintendent said he thought that was a good idea.

The Final Solution

If anyone in the community was speaking out in favor of the Ray boys, they did not speak very loudly. The chronic threats against the family grew louder and more frequent. The Ray boys, in keeping with the court order, started on Monday, August 24. On Friday, the Rays went to visit friends. Their small, single-story house on Illinois Street was doused with gasoline and torched.

The fire brought a new onslaught of TV cameras and tape recorders. On the network nightly news, Arcadia was labeled "the town without pity"—the Citizens Against AIDS in Schools were calling for "new tactics" to keep their school safe. On ABC, the mayor of Arcadia defended the discrimination against the Rays. On CBS, a few days after the fire, when the Rays finally moved away, the school principal said he hoped the town would return to normal now that the family was gone.

The fire inspired a total of eleven network stories between the end of August and the end of September. TV crews followed the Rays to their new home in Sarasota. The boys were compared to Ryan White in one story. In another, the reporter was inspired to detail Senate deliberations on measures against AIDS discrimination. The last story, about antibias legislation, is the kind of perspective the networks should provide in incidents like the Arcadia tragedy. All too often, in telling their dramatic tales, they leave it out.

Other media came to the story. An Indianapolis newspaper accused Arcadia of "brutal inhumanity." A Lakeland, Florida paper called the burned house "silent testimony to the ruthlessness of the tiny community's most notorious residents: fear and ignorance." The story caught the attention of the *Los Angeles Times*. Cartoonist Paul Conrad pointed his angry wit at the small town: beneath a rendering of the burned house ran the caption "Arcadia, Florida finds cure for AIDS."

Nothing better crystallizes the difference between the editors of Arcadia's two weekly papers than the tone of their response to the fire. In Adamson's editorial—the only other editorial he wrote since the story broke in April—he decided Arcadians had heard enough about how barbaric they were, and he decried the harsh judgment of the outside world: "Does anyone care to remember a year ago this past week when the town of Arcadia opened its arms to shelter the victims of Hurricane Elena? It would be interesting to talk to those people and ask them if they agree with the portrait being painted by the . . . network newspeople. . . . It's too bad the rest of the world will never know the good things that happen here. I'm sorry to report that for most people, good news just isn't news."

John Edmondson did not recollect for his readers Arcadia's past kindnesses in his front-page editorial of September 3. "What this community has been is not necessarily a 'town without pity,'" taking exception to the network's description, "but a town without leadership." The editorial ran in the upper-left corner. Next to it was a photo of Mr. and Mrs. Ray under the headline "Rays Leave Arcadia." In the lower-right corner was the start of a story called "The Death of Mr. Monkey."

> "Mr. Monkey is dead. He died on Friday, August 28, minutes after 10 p.m. He was well known to just a few but he was loved by those who knew him. He was most loved by an eight-year-old second-grader at Memorial Elementary School.
>
> For a small-town resident, Mr. Monkey had traveled extensively. He had witnessed many a medical procedure in his short years in Arcadia, Florida. He had spent several days in a hospital as a companion to members of a local family. It is therefore fitting that tribute be paid to this unselfish and caring citizen of DeSoto County. His life was one of innocence. His death was a tragic one. . . . Mr. Ray the father had to break the news about Mr. Monkey the friend.
>
> "I told [Randy] Mr. Monkey was gone," [Clifford] Ray said. "He just cried. He just cried."
>
> Don't cry for Clifford or Louise Ray. Don't cry for their house. But you could shed a tear for a tow-headed Randy Ray. He's lost the closest friend he may ever have. Mr. Monkey is dead."

The tribute to the little boy's stuffed animal affected Arcadians in a way that none of his editorials had. "I lost all my major advertisers except one," he said. For three days, the phone rang incessantly with people canceling subscriptions and demanding the *Times*'s delivery tube be removed from their lawns. "This man had lived here less than six months," said the *Arcadian*'s Adamson. "How could he evaluate the town's leadership?"

"Mr. Monkey," conceded Edmondson, "was just too much for a lot of people in Arcadia. We were getting bashed by the nation, and they said, 'You're kicking us, too.'"

The town's reaction reveals a lot about what a small town, perhaps any town, expects from its newspaper: an affirmation of the people's virtues, a light touch when handling their weaknesses. That expectation has always made honest and hard-hitting journalism dangerous.

Adamson and Edmondson generally do not criticize each other for the way the story was handled. "I don't want to get in a shooting match with another paper, but we did it differently," Edmondson said guardedly. Adamson, for the most part, refused to comment on the *Times* at all. He wished the national media, particularly the television networks, would apologize for their stilted portrayal of his town. He was glad to see the story ended and hoped Arcadia could someday recover its good name.

That probably will not happen soon. From their new home in Sarasota, the Rays sued the DeSoto County School Board. In the fall of 1988 an out-of-court settlement awarded them $1 million for breach of civil rights. Some town residents say they think the Rays set fire to their own home, to collect insurance and elicit pity. The burned house still stands, an empty shell in the middle of an overgrown lawn. "It's a rat-infested mess," one neighbor told a *New York Times* reporter shortly after the settlement. "The Rays should be made to clean it up."

MESQUITE, TEXAS:
SUBURBAN SCANDAL

In mid-September 1987, Jeff Kerber, a reporter for the three-times-a-week *Mesquite News*, received an anonymous phone call about an impending court case. A local pediatrician was seeking an injunction against a man spreading rumors that he had AIDS. Kerber's editors sent him to investigate. Journalists often receive anonymous court tips, but they are rarely pursued. Kerber could not remember why he was told to follow up on this particular tip. Perhaps because it had to do with AIDS, a hot topic at the time, or maybe because the doctor was fairly well-known. He did recall how surprised he was to discover the lead was for real.

Mesquite is a conservative Dallas suburb, home to mostly upper-middle-class young families, and the former residence of Dr. Robert John Huse, a highly regarded pediatrician. Huse had worked in Mesquite for ten years and had a thriving practice when he took a test for the AIDS virus in 1985. It was positive. He did not tell his patients' parents, but he did tell his lover, Tyrone Wesley Sims. When the romance later turned sour, Sims began spreading the rumor that the doctor had AIDS, Huse told local reporters. Sims allegedly threatened blackmail and made good on the threat, Huse claims, by telling the physician's patients and employees about Huse's positive HIV test.

Huse sought a restraining order against his former lover. In the court documents, he identified himself by name. He was granted the order on September 1, with a hearing set for ten days later to allow Sims to argue against a continuance. The anonymous caller who phoned the *Mesquite News*—perhaps it was Sims, perhaps not—tipped Kerber about the legal action.

Dave Barton, publisher of the *Mesquite News*, was equally surprised the lead was legitimate. He was also concerned. He knew that news of the story could ruin Huse's career. "We got copies of the court order," he said, "and called our attorneys for legal advice. We were on the phone until we went to press." Jeff Kerber, then twenty-six, had a good reason to argue for running with the story. The *Mesquite News*, with a circulation of ten thousand, is a starter paper, a place where new reporters can cut their teeth before moving on to bigger media outlets. Kerber had been at the paper only four months when the Huse story broke, and he was on the lookout for other opportunities. The case had the marks of a great opportunity for greater visibility.

In reporting the story, Kerber called Huse's attorney, William Nelson, for comment. Nelson immediately sought a restraining order against the *Mesquite News*. Nelson argued that Huse's "reputation and medical practice will potentially be destroyed if the court does not recognize the emergency situation which exists and restrain the *News* from running a story." Nelson also asserted, "This threatened story will unjustly feed the general public's paranoia regarding AIDS and homosexuality."

The court ruled against Nelson, in a basic First Amendment decision upholding the paper's right to report. The story broke on Friday, September 11, the morning of the Sims/Huse hearing, with the banner headline "Doctor Requests Order to Stop AIDS Rumors."

"A Mesquite pediatrician is attempting to have a district court judge issue an injunction against a former roommate, forbidding the man from spreading rumors that that physician has AIDS," wrote Kerber. Huse was identified by name at the end of the second paragraph. Suddenly, the staid suburb of Mesquite had a big problem. One of its most trusted pediatricians turned out to be not just gay, but also positive for the AIDS virus.

The story was compelling for major media outlets because, like the Kokomo and Arcadia tales, it involved the implicit threat of infection of children. If Huse had been a general practitioner rather than a baby doctor, it's likely even the dramatic way his HIV status was revealed would not have resulted in much interest from journalists outside the community. The Huse story appeared on the network evening news a few days after the story appeared in the *Mesquite News,* and it was a topic on "Good Morning America" early the following week.

"I'd Like to . . . Crucify Him"

Some people in Mesquite were aware that Huse was gay, including many of his colleagues in the medical community. Jeff Kerber's father, a local physician who worked with Huse at Charter Suburban Hospital, was one of those who knew. "My father didn't want me to write the story," Kerber recalled. The day the story broke, he said, "my father walked into the hospital cafeteria and other doctors pointed him out as the guy whose son ruined a doctor's career." The medical community believed the reporter was guilty of gross invasion of privacy. Most of the parents of Huse's young patients, on the other hand, felt Kerber had done them a tremendous service.

Kerber did not have to go far to interview a source for the second Huse story. Jennifer Skinner, Kerber remembered, "walked into our office yelling and screaming." The September 13 story, headlined "Parents React to AIDS News with Concern," quoted Skinner at length. "'He's been taking care of my sons since birth,'" she told Kerber. "'I'd like to know how to crucify him and stop him from taking care of anyone else's. . . . Anybody in that circumstance who takes care of people's children—my babies—should let people know where he stands and give them the right to decide if they want him for a pediatrician or not.'" Skinner said Huse had given her the impression he was married.

By September 16, it was clear that Huse's practice was in ruins. Kerber wrote, "Huse said he saw 10 patients Monday and five yesterday compared to his normal 25-patient average." Kerber had had an interview with Huse, the first and only one the physician granted him. "It took him five days before he'd talk to me," says Kerber, "because I broke the story. He didn't talk to me until after he'd spoken with other reporters" in the Dallas area. After that first round of interviews, Huse declined to give any more, except to an AIDS reporter at the *Dallas Morning News* the following February.

Not all parents wanted to crucify Huse. Many were supportive.

The *Mesquite News* reported their reaction on September 18, a week after the story first broke. "The number of the opposition may far outweigh the supporters, but Dr. Robert John Huse is not alone in his battle against the AIDS virus and the professional downfall that has accompanied the public disclosure of his condition," wrote Kerber. "[Tracy] Chamberlain said she was never concerned for her daughter's health, the result of her being familiar enough with the virus and how it is spread." A father told Kerber, "'When it comes right down to it, unless he is going to have sex with kids or give them a transfusion or trade needles with them, there just doesn't seem to be that much to be worried about.'" Another parent was starting a petition drive to show support for Huse.

But the damage had been done. Huse's practice was destroyed. Even his medical partner of five years felt the fallout. Many parents did not want their children in the same office space where a man infected with the AIDS virus had spent time. Even in late 1987, in the suburb of a large city, people worried AIDS could be spread through air ducts, toilet seats, and doctor's offices.

Sensitivity or Sensationalism?

The *Mesquite News* was not the only paper tipped by the anonymous caller. The man was thorough. He also phoned the two Dallas papers: the *Morning News* and the *Times Herald*.

In 1987 the Dallas papers were caught in one of the most hotly contested battles for market dominance in America. Silly contests and provocative columnists were part of the armaments, but scoops were the big guns. Nonetheless, the two papers were very different fighters. The smaller *Times Herald* was considered scrappier and more outrageous, with bigger headlines and more sensationalist coverage. The staid Times-Mirror company, which owned the *Los Angeles Times,* reportedly abandoned the battle-weary newspaper in June of 1986 in part because it felt the *Times Herald* had sullied its reputation. The *Morning News,* on the other hand, had a long and conservative history. It considered itself the sensible, moderate voice of Texas, and often read like a comfortable southern gentleman. The two papers covered AIDS differently as well.

The *Times Herald* had no consistent approach to the epidemic, but tackled stories as they arose. The *Morning News* prided itself on its sensitive AIDS reporting, and its staff included a reporter and editor who spent almost full-time on the story, as well as a medical reporter who sometimes covered the epidemic. The paper has a policy of withholding names of HIV carriers or people with AIDS unless granted permission to print them.

The first *Times Herald* story, on September 11, used Huse's name. In fact, the paper played the story big on the front page with the banner headline "AIDS Scare Dooms Doctor's Practice." It knocked Pope John Paul II's Dallas visit off the front page. The Huse story continued to grab the same front-page spot for three days in a row.

The *Morning News* pursued the tip as well, but after verifying it, reporter David Jackson and his editors decided not to run the story immediately. They wanted to see if the continuance Huse had filed would be granted. But the *Times Herald*'s story forced the *Morning News*'s hand. The *News*'s first story appeared September 12, without Huse being named.

The *Times Herald*'s approach influenced the *Morning News* throughout this breaking story. After the first article, the *Morning News* printed Huse's name. Assistant city editor Terry Box later said he wished the paper had handled the court case like any other civil suit and printed only one story. They ran more, he said, because the paper felt pressure from the *Times Herald*.

The *Morning News* went to great lengths, however, to portray Huse sympathetically and concentrate on the larger issues of the story. One article discussed the problems of confidentiality in AIDS testing; another examined the issue of health-care workers who are HIV positive. In January of 1988, William Nelson, Huse's lawyer, lost his lover to AIDS. A story about his death ran on the front page of the *Morning News*. William Wayburn, president of the Dallas Gay Alliance, remembered it brought a great outpouring of sympathy.

However, Wayburn also recalled the coverage of the Huse story with some bitterness. He did not argue with the newspapers' printing Huse's name, but he criticized the *Mesquite News* and the *Times Herald* for not attempting any AIDS education efforts before they broke the Huse story. He was not surprised that Huse's patients reacted the way they did: they knew so little about AIDS. The story about Huse, said Wayburn, "was like yelling 'fire' in a crowded theater."

"When you stampede the people," Wayburn said, "they're going to run some place, and they'll trample another person's rights." All of

208 this is true, but exactly what should be the role of the media, then? Kerber at the *Mesquite News* and the reporters at the *Times Herald* were undoubtedly driven more by the sensational aspects of the story than those who covered AIDS at the *Morning News*. But in a private business, which a newspaper usually is, should the journalist be required to be an educator? Isn't that the public health official's role?

In Mesquite reporters had the power to end a man's career, but Huse himself might have avoided the entire disaster by simply using a John Doe on the complaint he filed. That legal maneuver might have made it impossible for the physician to be uncovered, even with a determined tipster trying to spread the news. Journalists will and should use public records in getting the story. Huse's tragedy may or not have been inevitable, but as it evolved, it was almost predictable.

Such a story might have boosted a young journalist's career. Instead, Jeff Kerber has since left the *Mesquite News* for another small, suburban Dallas newspaper.

THE NAKED REPORTER

Small-town journalism is glorified in the American media tradition. That's where the lone reporter or editor-owner takes a stand, then takes the heat, and eventually makes a difference. Such confrontational drama does not happen often, however. In many towns, perhaps most, the journalist is as much a part of the establishment as the mayor, the school board chief, and the minister. Such cozy company rarely causes a fuss. And in communities where there is more than one newspaper competing for the same advertising dollar, angering the local powers that be is not sensible business practice. The *Arcadian's* Tim Adamson knew that. John Edmondson of the *DeSoto County Times*, and *Kokomo Tribune's* Chris MacNeil and Arden Draeger should have known it, too.

These three men are the exceptions. The journalist who can most afford to be noble is the one who is backed by a cadre of editors, highly paid attorneys, and the clout of a major news organization, and who can walk the street freely after writing a searing article. The journalist who has to face angry readers on every trip to the grocery store is downright heroic. Edmondson, MacNeil, and Draeger were all driven by the same force: a sense that part of their jobs was to educate. Commendable as that mandate is, it is also grounded in a certain arrogance. It assumes the journalist somehow knows more or has greater insight than the reader, who ideally should be able to draw his or her own conclusions from an objective story. Often, these three men did know more, something their readers seemed rarely to accept. The effective educator-reporter may be a laudable paradigm, but it's not really what journalism is about. The basis of the craft is telling a story you happened to hear, and that somehow touched your own life so significantly that you want to share it with another. That is the spirit that drives the reporter.

Almost no one in these three scenarios would have played their towns' AIDS story differently, even Jeff Kerber, who said he never wants anything to do with the story again. He knew news when he saw it, performed exactly as a beat reporter should, doing no more and clearly no less. Should anything more have been expected of him?

Undoubtedly, all these journalists would have had an easier time covering their respective controversies if the glare and distortion of national TV had not affected the stories. Once the news broke, the local reporters had to deal with heightened sensitivity and outright hostility from townsfolk who thought they were being unfairly judged.

Of all the players in these stories, Tim Adamson probably came out least scathed. Holding the banner of Arcadia's sanctity high above the real trauma of the Rays, he doubtless kept his long-range goal intact: he will be able to live peacefully in Arcadia for the rest of his life, though he is still waiting for the networks to apologize to his beloved town. That paradigm, of the journalist who knows his or her place in the comfortable scheme of things, is the role most of the media plays.

Chapter 10
The AIDS channel

Fabian Bridges was America's AIDS nightmare. The wiry, thirty-year-old black man looked frail and vulnerable when he appeared on WCCO-TV in Minneapolis on March 20, 1986. He was nervous and occasionally cracked a scared child's smile. There was something very frightening about his innocence. Bridges was broke and hungry, and dying of AIDS. To survive, he was plying the trade he knew best: prostitution. "I'm just to the point where I just don't give a damn," he told the reporter.

During the five years since the disease was first publicized, Americans had watched AIDS move from gays and intravenous drug users to mothers and their babies and then to schoolchildren. The epidemic was always covered when it seemed to pose a threat to "the general population," a vague term that most journalists used to mean themselves and the people they knew personally. Since Rock Hudson's diagnosis, the fear of widespread infection had dissipated. Although the AIDS epidemic was growing, it had seemed safe to assume no one was spreading the disease consciously. Public policy was rooted in that assumption: laws in California and New York, the states with the largest number of cases, protected the confidentiality of those with the disease and those who tested positive for HIV, believing that the informed carrier was the best protection against the spread of AIDS. Now, a desperate man roaming the streets was shaking that trust.

WCCO and the Public Broadcasting System teamed up to produce "AIDS: A Story," but they hadn't originally intended to tell this tale. The crew was looking to illustrate the toll the epidemic took on individual lives when it ran across Bridges. Living in Cleveland at the time, he was homeless and willing to talk. A reporter went to interview him. When Bridges openly admitted that he was continuing to have sex with other men, WCCO informed the Cleveland Health Department. The story exploded in the local press, and Bridges fled town. He went to Houston. There, the crew picked up the story again. While tracking and taping him, the broadcasters picked up his bills as well, including hotel and food expenses. Suddenly, WCCO was not just covering a story, but paying for its own scoops. That's standard practice at the checkout-counter tabloids but something most journalists frown on because it encourages a "manufacturing" of news. Perhaps the worst consequence of all was the perception that the WCCO crew was abetting the spread of the disease by covering Bridge's necessities, including bus fare for travel.

The station argued that it spent a mere $112 on Bridges. The crew also informed his doctor, as well as the health departments in Cleveland and Houston, that he was on the prowl. The broadcasters did their duty. Or did they? Fabian Bridges provided a compelling story to show America the ugly face of the epidemic's spread. But this case study was a slipshod way to make sense of the disease. Just how many such AIDS-stricken prostitutes were traveling across the nation seeking out new customers? How bad a public health problem was it? These questions went unanswered, and interest in that sad character, Fabian Bridges, quickly faded. He died in the fall of 1986.

WCCO-TV, a farm team for CBS News, is nationally known as the station most dedicated to quality investigative reporting. PBS's "Frontline," which aired a slightly different version of the story on stations across the United States, is also a renowned production. Two of the best broadcast organizations produced one of the more questionable pieces of reportage. For even the most surefooted media institutions, AIDS confused the issues. Ironically, the most impressive coverage of the epidemic by local broadcasters occurred at a station in San Francisco, long considered one of the most sensationalistic TV markets in America. At KPIX, two men gripped by the epidemic forged an approach to AIDS coverage that helped set a model for broadcasting. However, even that stellar performance presented serious ethical problems.

Blood and Guts News

San Francisco's biggest daily, the *Chronicle,* was infamous for its front-page play of gory deaths. Likewise, San Francisco broadcasters gave big play to gruesome accidents: "Male genital organ found on the railroad track," an actual promotion on the local KGO's 11:00 p.m. broad-

212 cast, became the archetypal headline to describe San Francisco TV's "blood and guts news." The metropolitan area, with more than five million viewers, is the fifth largest local market in the United States. But some broadcasters feared an assignment in the City by the Bay could damage their careers. That was the climate Art Kern, then thirty-four, walked into when he joined KPIX-TV as general manager in 1980.

He had grown up professionally in the Westinghouse corporation, a company known for fairly high-quality local stations in Pittsburgh, Baltimore, and other cities. San Francisco posed a real quandary. The area had one of the best educated and most affluent audiences in America, far more upscale than the rust-belt cities he had been in. Yet what the local Bay Area audience was being served on the evening news was reminiscent of articles in the *National Enquirer*, geared to appeal to lower-middle-class, poorly educated audiences. The "experts" had debated the reasons for this odd combination, and some concluded it had to do with San Francisco's rapidly changing demographics. After all, it was not so long ago that the town was a patchwork of ethnic, working-class communities. Kern wanted to find out if KPIX could capitalize on the change by offering something different.

The stakes were high. The local evening news is a big moneymaker for many stations, a half hour which they can fill up with lucrative local ads. Broadcasters have long fought drives by the networks—most notably, CBS—to expand their own news half hours to a full hour, because the local stations fear losing the highly profitable audience for their homegrown evening news. At the same time, some stations are pushing to expand their local news shows beyond the half hour, because it saves a huge amount of money that would otherwise pay for syndicated shows like sitcoms, the price of which has accelerated rapidly in recent years. Combined with the greater variety of news choices that cable TV offers, the local news shows have lured away about 25 percent of the evening news audience for ABC, CBS, and NBC since 1980.

The usual approach to buttressing the local news product has been to take advantage of the last decade's boom in technology to make the broadcast look more "network." High-tech graphics that even small stations are now capable of producing can be as striking as those developed by the tech-wizards at NBC headquarters in New York. The wide use of minicameras and satellites, which have allowed CBS's Dan Rather to broadcast live from Moscow, and at drastically reduced expense, also permits local stations to send their own teams to major political and sports gatherings as well as to breaking news events. Conus, a consortium of some eighty local stations that share a satellite, allows these outlets to bypass the networks altogether. By sharing footage from around the country, local broadcasters can piece together national roundups and use their own anchors to focus on the major national news story of the day from anywhere in the world.

But just because the local "talking heads" have access to the most advanced equipment does not mean they know how to report the news once they stumble onto it. On the AIDS story, the gaffes that the networks were making seemed to be amplified by many local broadcasters. In 1985 more than one local TV journalist declared that the disease was being transmitted "through contact," just as ABC's David Brinkley had wrongly reported years earlier, even though it was well established that AIDS was passed only through "intimate sexual contact" and intravenously. The kinds of "breakthroughs" that had so excited Peter Jennings and network correspondents in the early 1980s provoked story after story by local broadcasters in 1986. The single-source stories that the networks too often ran became a staple on many local newscasts as well. For instance, a piece on stormtrooper-type protection that police were demanding to deal with people they suspected might have come in contact with the virus was aired by one San Francisco station without reaction from doctors or public health officials. Was it necessary to wear the astronaut-style garments some had called for? The TV reporter didn't help answer that question.

Even as print media in some medium-sized and smaller towns were becoming more sophisticated about AIDS, following the leads of the wire services and the *New York Times,* many local stations still had not gotten a grip on the facts. Centers for Disease Control scientist Dr. Donald Francis called these broadcast outlets "the weakest link" in the media chain. Sometimes they caused the information process to fall apart completely.

The epidemic had become a curiosity worth covering. For some stations, it was a tailor-made topic for "sweeps month," the four-times-a-year period during which television stations measure their audiences. Because a station's advertising rates are based on how many viewers it can draw during that time period, many broadcasters attempt to air the most dramatic, and sometimes sensational, series. Sex plays big during "the sweeps," as do celebrities and scandal.

Among the journalistic gems produced during these periods was

"Deadly Error?" a two-part series by WSVN-TV in Miami, promoting the theory put forth by *New York Native* publisher Chuck Ortleb that syphilis was the cause of AIDS.

The Stranded Reporter

The network journalists have always had a problem putting dramatic news into context: the visuals often override the story. However, on the local level, those images sometimes are hard to come by, not because of the nature of the news event but because of the fears of those behind the camera. As a result, getting the story told can be a major challenge. Reporter Gloria Rojas's nightmare is a particularly vivid example.

When the AIDS epidemic was first found to be striking American youngsters back in 1983, the news made headlines across the country. Since then, whenever there was a new twist in the story—how kids contracted the disease, how long they lived, how much of a threat they were to other children—it often hit the headlines again. The latest turn in this spiraling tale in the fall of 1985 was children with AIDS in schools. In Kokomo, Indiana, and Queens, New York, frightened parents were fighting to keep infected kids out of the classroom and thus presumably out of reach of their own children. Rojas, then a reporter for New York City's WABC-TV, wanted to tell the other side of the story. Doris Williams of Plainfield, New Jersey, was willing to cooperate.

Williams was a foster mother to two children, one a four-year-old boy with AIDS. Trying to enroll him in a New Jersey public school had become a horror. Rojas drove out to Plainfield to interview her at her home. The camera crew was supposed to follow Rojas, and a short time later the camera operator and the technician arrived. But they refused to come into the house. Rojas went out to talk with them. This was an assignment, this was their job, she said. The crew was not budging. She raised her voice, lost her temper. They still were not going into a house "with AIDS." They would tape her interviewing Williams on the front lawn, they said, using a long lens on the camera and an extra-long microphone. They were not getting any closer.

Embarrassed, Rojas asked if Williams would mind coming outside. The camera crew had set up, on the other side of the street. When the interview was over, the crew disconnected the cord to the microphone

Rojas was holding, threw it on the lawn—they would not let her near the van—and drove off.

In Focus, Out of Context

Even when a station had no trouble getting footage, the news often was out of context, as with the Fabian Bridges story. The lack of perspective was due in part to the lack of expertise in AIDS. Unlike major metropolitan dailies across the country, local stations rarely had full-time science or medical reporters. By the mid-1980s, many outlets did feature doctors who would prepare medical stories and act as hosts on short news segments that often were supported by advertising from hospitals or manufacturers of medical products. None of these physicians, however, were focusing on AIDS, probably because most of them—in cities like St. Louis and Cincinnati—had yet to see an AIDS patient. And for the on-staff reporter, time spent researching the epidemic meant time away from covering a breaking story like a fire, a controversial trial, or a hurricane raging through town.

TV journalism's biggest advantage over newspapers, of course, is its speed. Broadcast technology has shrunk the time from event to reported story. When the news is covered live, there is no time lapse at all. The ability to go live, however, often leaves broadcasters ill-prepared. And because speed is their biggest asset, TV journalists are less likely to spend large amounts of time researching subjects. Poring through the *New England Journal of Medicine* to brush up on the latest findings in the AIDS epidemic is not likely to gain for a reporter more of that all-important air time.

The more a broadcaster is seen, the more he or she is identified with a particular station. That, at the very least, builds job security. Greater visibility also increases a broadcaster's chances of being noticed by larger stations, or even the networks. Not everyone in local television wants to join the networks, where many journalists are forced to travel almost constantly. These days, the pay at some stations in major markets like Los Angeles and Chicago equals or betters network salaries. Nonetheless, the allure of the evening broadcast on ABC, CBS, or NBC, with its audience in the tens of millions, remains very strong. Sometimes an impressive young reporter from a station in the Midwest gets the call from the networks to try for a slot there. But for most of the handful who make it, the climb is a gradual one up through the markets, from small to larger towns, until eventually, with persistence and luck, to a city in the top 20—the score of American metropolitan areas that include the largest TV audiences. (New York City is number one; Sacramento is number 20.) In the pursuit of the top jobs, it is not surprising that the local broadcasters would try to emulate the network stars. Those role models, of course, were not covering AIDS very closely.

Serving It Up Straight

KPIX's general manager, Art Kern, was the initial inspiration behind that station's decision to cover AIDS in a more sophisticated fashion. He first read about the epidemic in an article in the *San Francisco Examiner* on October 24, 1982. One of the facts that piqued Kern's interest was that the disease was spread sexually. He wasn't gay, but he was single and understood that sexually transmitted diseases rarely stayed confined to one social group, especially in a sexually promiscuous population like San Francisco's. At the moment, gays were being struck by AIDS, but single, straight men were also at risk. This was the same motivation that got the story told at most media outlets. Kern just happened to be affected by it sooner than most.

"He kept telling us to get on the AIDS story," remembers KPIX's former news director, Bruno Cohen. General managers usually focus on the business side of the operation, as most publishers do at large newspapers. Most of the time, they do not get involved in lobbying for a particular news story. Kern felt driven, however, in part because his hunch that AIDS was going to be a major story was being backed up by the local print media, the *Examiner* and the *Chronicle,* and by City Hall. The San Francisco Board of supervisors had been discussing the disease for months, and Mayor Dianne Feinstein was the first leader of a major metropolitan area to devote public funds to the epidemic. Throughout the ranks at KPIX, from Art Kern to Bruno Cohen and among some reporters on the staff, AIDS was considered a serious problem worth covering. If the station could develop a solid track record reporting on the disease, Kern thought, San Franciscans would know to turn to KPIX for AIDS information, as the epidemic developed.

It was a progressive mandate, certainly, but to do it right meant making a financial commitment. Cohen was not prepared to assign a reporter to cover AIDS full-time, or even to set aside a part of each week for one journalist to become familiar with the complex epidemic. By mid-1983, the story was being covered by whoever was available. Then Jim Bunn arrived. The thirty-two-year-old from Connecticut was KPIX's newest reporter, an aggressive and experienced broadcaster who came to San Francisco only because he had lost his job back East in a shakeup at his station.

News director Cohen assigned Bunn a story on the Irwin Memorial Blood Bank, San Francisco's depository whose chief was assuring people that the blood supply was safe. Bunn was in unfamiliar territory. He had hardly heard of AIDS at the suburban station he had left, and he certainly did not know anyone with the disease. Suddenly, the talk around him was of epidemics and contaminated blood supplies.

A month later, as the fall sweeps period approached, Bunn was asked to look at the AIDS story again. Kern and Cohen had decided KPIX would do a series on the spread of the disease in San Francisco. Bunn started his research by reading everything he could get hold of on the disease, including *Chronicle* reporter Randy Shilts's coverage. The more he read, the more convinced he was that he couldn't tell the story just from San Francisco. He wanted to go to the CDC, he told Cohen, to Washington, D.C., to New York. "If you want to show the audience you're making a commitment to the story," said Bunn, "I have to travel." By the time he returned to San Francisco, with bags of tape from across the country, he had been struck with the fervor of reporters like Shilts. "This is the health crisis of the century," Bunn announced to Cohen and producer Nancy Saslow.

The four-part series produced from that material included interviews with experts like the CDC's Dr. James Curran, a look at the spread of the epidemic in New York City, reports on the streets of San Francisco and on the work of researchers across the country. That November 1983 primer was the most extensive coverage of AIDS any TV medium had done to date.

Attention, Joe Sixpack

In late 1983, AIDS was seen primarily as a gay plague. A story about how the disease was creeping out of that risk group, and possibly infecting the blood supply, was easy enough to play. But what about a series of features on the rising toll the plague was going to take on health services, or the government's questionable handling of the epidemic? Would viewers stay tuned, or would they tune in at all?

Kern had assumed the epidemic was so important that everyone in the Bay Area would be interested. For most local viewers, the disease was only of fleeting interest. To them, AIDS was a problem confined in the boundaries of San Francisco proper, where the region's largest concentration of gays live. The city makes up only about 15 percent of the area's total audience. Most of the population lives in suburban communities, and many are conservative, blue-collar workers. How do you reach Joe Sixpack in those towns?

Making the average viewer in the hugely diverse television audience care about AIDS, and stay tuned to KPIX, became Bunn's biggest challenge. He is a married man with a family. Tall, blond, and with a coif carefully combed in place, he appears to be the ubiquitous TV personality, with corn-fed American good looks. He has a medium-range voice and a reassuring, relaxed style. Yet Bunn has an edge to him, an obsessiveness that does not show up on the air. The threat of AIDS making its way into the heterosexual population was his current obsession. Bunn had stumbled onto what he believed very well might be the story of his lifetime. That realization is probably the most powerful inspiration for any journalist.

Since his college days at Oklahoma State University, Jim Bunn knew he had a desire "to save the world," as he put it. It started when he organized a candlelight vigil following the Kent State shootings in 1970 in order to defuse the student anger and avoid violence on campus. Some thirteen years later, he still had a good supply of that idealism left, and it would manifest itself in his commitment to do more than just report the AIDS story.

In one of his first jobs in journalism, working for a radio station in Oklahoma, Bunn got a phone call close to Memorial Day from a man who said he had a lifetime of war stories to tell. The young reporter went out and interviewed the old soldier, who detailed among other incidents the horror of witnessing a small boy stepping on a landmine and having his legs blown off. It was a powerful segment, as well as a lesson for Bunn: the most effective journalism is simply stories about individuals. Bunn admittedly brings a certain flair to his storytelling, a style he perhaps learned subconsciously from his father, the former "Jimmie Blane," host of the popular "Ruff and Reddy" TV show during the late fifties.

Bunn used that talent to grab the attention of Joe Sixpack. Tom

Wicker became one of those tales. In late 1983 the gay man called Bunn complaining that he could not get disability from the federal government. He had lost his job, was losing his insurance. And the last safety net, disability, Uncle Sam was pulling away because of red tape. Bunn interviewed him in his hospital room. It was a traditional two-shot: the camera focused on Wicker and then on Bunn as they spoke. Many broadcasters consider that setup dull and outdated. Bunn used it because he wanted to show the audience there was no reason to be frightened of AIDS patients, despite the explosive rumors that the disease could be spread by routine household contact.

"If I was seen having casual contact with someone with AIDS, people would be getting the right message," he said. Bunn was not just reporting, but very consciously trying to educate.

In San Francisco, when KPIX did these personal stories, it almost always focused on gay men. That was not surprising: gays made up the huge majority of AIDS cases in the city, and still do. But Nancy Saslow was predicting problems with the focus of these features: "You can say AIDS is going to affect everyone," which had become the station's coda. "But you can't show a gay on screen to illustrate that."

So Bunn and his crew traveled the country in search of people like Mary Thurman, whose husband was a junkie and had recently died of AIDS. The white, middle-class woman went on camera in heavy makeup and a wig, and her voice was artificially deepened so as to mask her identity. In a lengthy interview with Bunn, she told the story of her husband's death: after months of excruciating pain, he finally began to expire. On that day, Thurman said, "I stayed in bed with him for twenty-four hours, until he died." She now hoped to survive long enough to care for her young children.

Kids became a centerpiece for Bunn's reporting, too. There was Dwight Burke, a baby from Crescent, Pennsylvania, who was dying from the disease. The camera behind Bunn focused on the small child, held in his mother's arms. The woman's husband was a hemophiliac and apparently had been infected through a blood transfusion. Now his wife had the virus, and she had passed it on to their baby while he was in the womb. Would the family survive? "I'm afraid of being alone," she said, tears welling up.

Bunn also reported the case of Ryan White, the teenager with AIDS from Kokomo, Indiana. The fight that erupted over the boy's demand to stay in school after he had been diagnosed gained national attention, and alongside the networks, KPIX was there.

Like WNBC's Gloria Rojas, Bunn knew that showing children with

AIDS on the screen was a compelling way to tell the story of the epidemic, even while recognizing that overuse of children's images was distorting the facts of who was getting the disease.

According to the Center for Media and Public Affairs, in recent TV depictions across the country of those with the disease, heterosexuals were ten times more likely to be shown than homosexuals, although in the mid-1980s, more than eight times as many homosexuals had AIDS than heterosexuals. In San Francisco, those numbers were even more striking. While gays in 1988 made up about 70 percent of the total number of AIDS cases in the United States, they accounted for about 97 percent in San Francisco. What's more, those shown on TV affected by the disease were almost always white and middle-class. Like Dwight Burke's mother and Mary Thurman. In fact, most of the heterosexuals for whom AIDS was becoming a scourge were black or Hispanic and poor. For Bunn, who felt driven to warn his viewers about the coming onslaught and prevent a hysterical backlash, such distortions hardly seemed worth quibbling over. He was acting the role of both public-health educator and reporter, and he was intent on institutionalizing KPIX's AIDS coverage.

By mid-1984, Bunn was covering AIDS almost full-time, the only TV reporter in the country with such a beat. The station had created an entire AIDS unit: reporter Bunn, a camera operator, and producer. KPIX ran more stories on the epidemic than any other broadcast or cable outlet, including the networks: some one thousand from 1983 to 1987. There was plenty of news to cover on a weekly basis, especially for a station set in San Francisco, both a center of the epidemic and of the research to understand and fight it. KPIX did more than cover the heartrending scenarios of babies dying in their mothers' arms. It broke some news stories, including one on a breach of confidentiality in the HIV tests being given to soldiers at the Oak Knoll Navy Hospital. It provided a look into the problems prostitutes faced both with the disease and with avoiding infection. For instance, San Francisco police would often arrest hookers on suspicion of prostitution if they had in their purses condoms, the very protective devices city outreach workers had distributed to the women. These kinds of stories often lacked the visuals that make for "good" TV news. They were complex and sometimes in-depth, a far cry from the "Male genital organ found on the railroad track." However, they were not hurting KPIX's business. During the early to mid-1980s, the station was pulling in record profits and ratings, which is one of the reasons KPIX could afford to experiment.

Although Bunn had no personal connection to the story when he began looking into the epidemic, after a year of crafting what he hoped would be compelling features on the people struck by the disease, he himself could not help but be emotionally involved. After all, some of the people he interviewed maintained contact, calling up Bunn with other stories or just to check in with progress reports. Tom Wicker, the man who could not get disability payments from the government, was one of those people.

Wicker and Bunn chatted off and on for months. In the summer of 1984, right before the Democratic convention was to open in San Francisco, Wicker called the reporter. Bunn was too busy to return the phone call. When the convention ended, Bunn phoned him back. Wicker's phone was disconnected. Bunn never got a chance to say good-bye. "The only time you deal with death so directly is in a war," said Bunn, echoing what dozens of other journalists had said about covering the dying in the AIDS epidemic.

Bunn was surprised to realize what pain he felt after Wicker's death. He asked doctors who dealt with AIDS patients daily how they handled the sorrow. "You have to distance yourself," one of them told him. That's a challenge reporters and doctors failed throughout the epidemic.

Bunn, Art Kern, and others at KPIX believed a consistent information source could become a kind of lifeline for the general public. The idea was honed at a lunch between KPIX producer Nancy Saslow and a spokeswoman at the San Francisco AIDS Foundation. The station called its public information program "AIDS Lifeline" when it was officially kicked off in 1985.

Lobbying the Corporate Types

With the creation of a team to report the crisis consistently, the station also created lobbyists for the story within the organization. Bunn, Saslow, even Kern scrambled to justify why they had concentrated sparse reporting resources on news that had yet to touch the American consciousness. KPIX then went even further and requested extra funds from its parent company in New York, Westinghouse's Group W, to expand its AIDS coverage and produce programs for broadcast nationwide. The company has a tradition of doing top-notch, special programming, such as "Second Chance," a project to publicize the need for donated organs. The seriousness with which Westinghouse approached its public service responsibility was one reason Kern felt justified in pushing the AIDS story. By 1985, however, that public service tradition was waning across the nation.

A half century earlier, the federal government had decided that when it allowed individual companies to use the airwaves, which it considered to be public property, they should have to give something back to the public. Thus licenses were granted to those individuals operating in "the public interest, convenience and necessity"—as the 1934 Federal Communications Act states—not offering only radio comedies or endless commercials. The act was the early impetus for the creation of news shows and the kind of documentaries that groundbreaking broadcasters like Edward R. Murrow made famous.

But in 1981, the law was seen as just the kind of business regulation President Ronald Reagan's supporters in the media believed hindered their operations. After all, cable, which does not use the airwaves but is sent across lines similar to phone wires, was emerging as a real challenge to broadcast's supremacy, and it did not have to comply with many of the government's requirements. With the appointment of laissez-faire advocate Mark Fowler as chairman of the Federal Communications Commission, the chief supposedly in charge of making sure the Communications Act was enforced, the public service obligation began to be loosened.

By the mid-1980s, Group W still seemed to have a strong commitment to the old idea. Nonetheless, the corporate executives in New York weren't buying KPIX's suggestion of expanding AIDS coverage and going national with its programs. It was hard to sell the idea, in part because the networks weren't "doing AIDS yet," one KPIX executive said. Without the prestige of one of the major networks behind coverage of the epidemic, it would not become a concern for broadcasters beyond the local level, and not much beyond local San Francisco. That attitude changed, of course, with Rock Hudson's AIDS diagnosis.

The "AIDS Lifeline"

Ironically, KPIX missed the story on Hudson. Bunn and the others at the station for so long had taken the epidemic seriously, and covered it substantially, that they thought an actor coming down with the disease hardly warranted extensive coverage. They quickly realized that the event was finally focusing broad media attention on AIDS, and KPIX pulled together a one-hour documentary on the disease. "Our Worst Fears: The AIDS Epidemic" ran September 8, 1985, and had the largest audience any public affairs show had ever drawn on KPIX, and the biggest share of viewers of any program in San Francisco that evening. Finally, Kern's hunch was paying off: San Franciscans were turning to KPIX for AIDS information. The program also generated a record number of phone calls to the San Francisco AIDS Foundation, the station's partner in the "AIDS Lifeline" TV project. More than one hundred organizations, from Australia to Canada, requested copies of the documentary. And Group W decided to carry "Our Worst Fears" on all of its stations.

By the following fall, KPIX had expanded its "AIDS Lifeline," with professionally done public service announcements featuring famous personalities like Joe Namath and Dionne Warwick delivering straightforward messages about how AIDS is transmitted. "Fight the fear of AIDS with the facts" was the commercials' refrain. The impact "AIDS Lifeline" had on changing viewers' attitudes, or even on preventing the disease, is difficult to measure. Certainly, San Francisco's media, including the *Examiner, Chronicle,* the gay papers, the other TV stations, and the long list of AIDS agencies, all served to make San Francisco the most AIDS-aware city anywhere in the world. The tone of that information tended to be far more explicit than most AIDS news and public service announcements, primarily because San Francisco has almost always been less prudish than most American metropolises.

Yet despite the various media campaigns, some forms of sexually transmitted diseases are on the rise among heterosexuals in the Bay Area. Gays seem to have taken the message more seriously.

In 1986, Jim Bunn and the other KPIX staffers won the Peabody Award—the Pulitzer of broadcasting—for "AIDS Lifeline." But they have more to be concerned with these days than good journalism. Now that KPIX has gotten itself into the business of health education, should its efforts continue to be aimed at the general heterosexual population? Or should the target be the heterosexual minority population, the largest group after gays to be struck by the disease? And shouldn't the majority of resources continue to go toward encouraging gays to maintain their safe-sex behavior, since homosexual men are still the largest risk group in San Francisco? Those are questions

KPIX has to consider, now that it has gotten itself into the business of health education. Such issues put constraints on journalists, whose primary responsibility is to report what is new rather than target the reporting to specific ends.

The AIDS Crusader

Bunn once described the journalist's job, his job, as "disseminating the truth." It is a disturbing notion, suggesting that there is such a thing as truth to be found in the ever-changing world of news. Jim Bunn, a gifted and extremely conscientious reporter, comes as close to it as, say, Dr. Luc Montagnier does when he describes what he thinks his team of scientists have discovered in the laboratory. Both perceptions are full of "wishing it were so" and "expecting it is the answer."

Even more dangerous, of course, is the suggestion that the reporter has discovered "the truth" and is bent on sharing it with his or her audience. That is the breeding ground of falsehoods, and of dangerous obsessions like the African Swine Fever Virus theory that dominated Chuck Ortleb's *New York Native*. Now that it is known that AIDS is far less of a threat to the nondrug-using population than first believed, do some viewers feel KPIX misled them when it focused on white heterosexuals?

In 1987 Jim Bunn was asked by the director of the World Health Organization in Geneva to continue his anti-AIDS crusade as a public information officer there. He returned to KPIX in 1989, and later started his own company, which disseminates health information. He still sees himself as a journalist.

Six years since that first press conference he attended at the San Francisco Irwin Memorial Blood Bank, Bunn is still loyal to his cause, and believes that journalists can do much more to educate the audience about AIDS and prevent the disease. "We [journalists] have to recognize that we are players in public policy and health policy issues," he said. But can he reconcile that calling with the limits and responsibility of the journalist? Just as former KPIX General Manager Art Kern helped change the face of San Francisco TV journalism with the AIDS story, Bunn helped change the role of the reporter. The future of that crusader bears watching.

Chapter 11
Third World
correspondent

Bukoba, a small village in the northwest corner of Tanzania, has a population of about ten thousand, including the surrounding area. It sits on the shores of Lake Victoria, near the Ugandan border. In a more prosperous era it might serve as a resort town. In August of 1986, when National Public Radio's Laurie Garrett reported on AIDS in Africa from Bukoba, one in three villagers were believed to be infected with the virus.

Since 1983, when the first reports were released about the disease being widespread in parts of Africa, a trickle of news stories made their way into the American media. The *Philadelphia Inquirer* had done a piece that year, and the *New York Times*'s Dr. Larry Altman filed an extensive series from Africa in November of 1985. But Garrett had the most impressive insight into the devastation that AIDS wrought there.

Did the virus spring from that continent? That was the question journalists had been asking. It infuriated Africans wary of Westerners pinning the blame for this horror on them. By the time Garrett began planning her trip there, reports like Altman's had provoked government authorities, especially in Central Africa, to block access to reporters.

Garrett and her producer, John McChesney, and a black African journalist-guide set off in a private plane from Dar es Salaam just before sunrise to search out the story. Garrett had decided to focus on only two countries, mostly because she was working on an extremely tight budget, typical for NPR correspondents. She wanted to investigate Tanzania, which was struggling to face up to the fact that it was in the throes of the epidemic, and Zimbabwe, which was still rooted in denial of any crisis. These were the two faces of Africa in the first decade of the AIDS epidemic.

Garrett knew the name of only one Bukoba resident: Dr. Jayo Kidenya, the first physician to diagnose AIDS in Tanzania. He was the head doctor at the local hospital, but mostly he was known as "the healer." There was no phone service, so she could not call ahead to set up an interview. Garrett arrived on Tanzania's independence day, and to find the doctor a small group of Bukobans took her to his home.

Unannounced, this white American woman with notepad in hand walked into Kidenya's house. The doctor was amazed that someone had come all the way from America to ask him questions about AIDS in Tanzania. The "healer" had patients from all over the region. But he had no supplies to treat them. The only drug in his clinic was aspirin. Kidenya believed only one thing would alleviate their plight: getting outside help. The only way that would be done was by getting the word out, which Garrett attempted to do in a four-part series that ran between August 14 and 26, 1986.

Garrett visited Kidenya's crowded hospital where babies and mothers listlessly waited for death. The NPR audience could hear infants' cries of agony. Of course, Garrett's audience couldn't see the hand of a dying and emaciated woman that Garrett held. She seemed to have centuries of pain written into her eyes, yet the woman was thirty, close to Garrett's age.

The correspondent attended Muslim services, where she saw young men withering from the disease. She stopped in at the local disco. Two years ago, she was told, it was packed almost every night. Men and women would meet on the dance floor, go out the back door and make love in the bushes, then return to look for other partners. Now the place was nearly empty except for a few men, dancing alone. "The bartender says business is down," Garrett reported. "Girls stay away now. Twenty-eight-year-old Henry hovers nearby, listening with interest. He says the boys are afraid of the girls now, and the girls are afraid of the boys. Henry doesn't date anymore. He intends to remain a bachelor until a cure for AIDS is found."

In a society in which masculinity is defined by the number of children a man has, in which men often have two or three female lovers, and in which some describe "impotence" as being able to perform sexually *only* four times a day, infection is still spreading rapidly. AIDS researchers believe "the level of heterosexual activity in the region may approach those seen among homosexual San Franciscans before the AIDS epidemic," Garrett reported.

Sexual promiscuity among young city dwellers was not the way AIDS first came to Tanzania. It was suspected that the far-flung epidemic could be tied to the war between Tanzania and its central east Africa neighbor, Uganda, begun with Idi Amin's invasion in 1978.

The horrendous conflict required soldiers to exchange blood in transfusions on the battlefield, and to crowd into small towns. The sexual **227**
contact between soldiers and natives, along with the sharing of even a
small amount of contaminated blood, could have caused a more or
less dormant disease to explode.

Nearly ten years later, little was being done to stop the spread.
"Right now the clinics are so impoverished that they use the same
needles over and over again," reported Garrett. "And nobody in this
part of Tanzania has the equipment or chemicals to test blood. So nobody knows who is infected. Dr. Kidenya assumes the local blood supply is contaminated."

"It pains me to handle AIDS patients," said Kidenya. "No matter
what I give, I know it's not helping the patient[s] . . . . They suffer so
much pain. At times I would like that the disease kill quicker."

Tanzania's crisis was replicated in Zimbabwe, but made worse by
rampant government denial that there was any epidemic at all. Garrett
saw the sick and dying, estimated the cost of caring for these people,
and understood the despair that the health workers were silently
facing. In Africa, AIDS is but the latest unsolvable problem, alongside
drought and hunger and political turmoil.

Garrett was savvy about government manipulations. She started
her career covering the swine flu fiasco in the United States in 1976,
and it provided a hands-on education in how badly government, even
with the best of intentions, can screw up in health emergencies. Along
with a cynicism uncommon among science reporters, Garrett brought
a highly personal involvement in the AIDS story to NPR's coverage.
She constantly walked the line between "professional" disinterested-
ness and emotional, overwhelming angst.

The Politics of the Flu

The story of a young man's death and the spread of a virus that for
fifty years had confined itself to pigs made an interesting case study
for students of disease in 1976. For Laurie Garrett, at the time a Ph.D.
candidate in immunology at the University of California, Berkeley,
the unraveling political story was even more fascinating.

Earlier that year, Congress approved a measure to encourage drug
companies to develop a vaccine. And by the fall Washington had a

national inoculation program. The plight of President Gerald Ford was clearly a major reason for the quick response. Reeling from his role as pardoner in the Watergate debacle, he was desperate for a media event in which he could appear decisive and, more important, honorable.

Garrett understood more than the electoral pressures the Ford administration was under. She knew there was little evidence that swine flu was threatening to get out of control. The perception was no secret among trained immunologists. Some of her professors at Berkeley, as well as some of the other most renowned professionals in the field, in private admitted the immunization program could be worse than simply a waste of time and money. Because the vaccine legislation relaxed drug companies' liability, and almost guaranteed that the vaccines' purity would suffer, the inoculation effort could cause unpredictable health problems. But few of these scientists were willing to put their government grants on the line to make the point publicly. Finally, Garrett decided to uncover the story herself.

She had been working part-time at radio station KPFA in Berkeley, one of the five outlets of the left-leaning Pacifica media company. There she covered the emerging biotechnology and toxic-waste crisis in a documentary series called "Science Stories." In 1976 she dropped out of school to devote herself to the swine flu issue.

Garrett had been drawn to other causes before. In the spring of 1970, when the United States invaded Cambodia, she left the University of California, Santa Cruz to work full-time for the antiwar movement. Only after her mother died of cancer that same spring did she promise herself to return and make a commitment to science. Now she was determined to reveal the debacle that was one of America's most coordinated efforts against a single disease. Idealistic and outraged, Garrett produced with her colleagues a swine flu series that had the hard edge of self-righteous youth. The twenty-seven-minute report, run January 20, 1977, was dedicated to "former President Gerald Ford, who served and protected the American public from a nonexistent disease at a cost of nearly half a billion dollars, and at least fifty lives."

"The swine flu vaccine program is mass murder," said one quoted source, an Australian doctor. The report pointed out that "two weeks after the initiation of the vaccination program, at least thirty-five people had died following inoculation with the swine flu vaccine. In addition, data were pouring in from doctors across the country who said their patients were suffering from the flu after they had been vaccinated."

Congress finally put a halt to the CDC vaccination program. True to Garrett's initial fears, the efforts produced far more harm than good. In 1977 two public policy analysts commissioned to review the program described it as "the epidemic that never was." Some of the vaccine also caused an outbreak of Guillain-Barré syndrome, a debilitating disease that often included severe paralysis. The damages resulting from these tragic consequences along with the huge expense of the program have cost the United States hundreds of millions.

Garrett's piece on swine flu did not shake the corridors of Washington's power establishments. KPFA in Berkeley is far from a national agenda-setter. Only after the deaths of those inoculated did major news sources like the *New York Times* come to the story, and only then did the official attitude toward the vaccination program begin to turn. Garrett's reporting, however, did not go unnoticed. That same year KPFA'a "Science Stories" won the prestigious Peabody Award for broadcasting.

Garrett did not fit the mold of science reporter. The beat was barely a decade old at most media outlets, which began covering science usually as a result of audience interest in the space program. Those journalists who got the NASA assignment were mostly science innocents, and their coverage tended to be full of the "gee whiz" excitement that NASA most wanted to generate, without much critical evaluation of programs or approaches.

Garrett brought to her reporting some basic cynicism, questioning government sources and the experts. She used that approach to cover the swine flu fiasco, in which she criticized the highly regarded Centers for Disease Control. It was Garrett's advanced training in science and her political involvement in the antiwar movement that gave her the confidence to be critical of the medical and scientific establishment. Increasing numbers of journalists at major media outlets would take this unconventional approach to science reporting.

The NPR Alternative

For some in Garrett's generation of journalists, National Public Radio was an attractive alternative to the commercial networks when Congress created the Public Broadcasting System in 1970. NPR's mission, as its congressional sponsors saw it, was to provide a media outlet free of advertising pressures. The programs it produced would air on public stations across the country, much as PBS's television division would work. From the start, it was an odd institution in the free-enterprise world of American journalism. Government backing similar to the British Broadcasting Corporation's public financing might help guarantee that high-quality news programming would always exist in the United States. But how "free" would the broadcasters be if they had to be concerned about their budget being slashed if they angered Congress or the president? NPR has had to wrestle with that issue all its life, and for the most part, it has maintained an impressive independence.

It pays a price for its noncommercial charter: money is always tough to come by. Annual salaries ranged from the teens to $70,000 for the network's biggest star, Susan Stamberg. At the three major networks—which sometimes lured NPR staffers—producers, reporters, and writers routinely made Stamberg's salary, and the stars drew seven-figure incomes.

NPR keeps its best talent in part because it offers journalists a rare opportunity in broadcasting. Its two major shows, "Morning Edition" and "All Things Considered," allow for longer segments and more in-depth reporting than almost any other broadcast medium. The opportunity to pursue issues more fully always has attracted young, idealistic journalists. And, of course, the poor pay has kept many of the more experienced talent from applying. The commercial-free aspect of NPR also usually helps prevent it from pulling punches for fear of losing revenue or currying favor to raise it. As a result, it is not quite so sensitive about offending middle-American sensibilities. That's one of the assets that attracted Garrett to NPR in 1980, and it is one reason the network could cover AIDS as it did in the early years.

Death in the Village

On July 3, 1981, Garrett did a story on the high incidence of cancer in homosexuals. The lead came from the CDC report on forty-one cases of Kaposi's sarcoma in New York and California. Since the news came from a federal agency, someone in NPR's Washington headquarters would be the obvious choice to cover it. But Garrett thought the story should be told from the West Coast: the cases were first reported by a Los Angeles doctor, and some of the strongest reactions were likely to come from the highly vocal and visible gay community in San Francisco, where NPR's West Coast bureau was located.

Along with the CDC facts, Garrett reported that "eight gay men have died this year" from the disease. But, she added, "The gay community shouldn't be overly alarmed." The focus of the piece was typical Garrett: she did not prepare her story with the white, middle-class, college-educated heterosexual in mind, NPR's "average" listener. She talked directly to the group involved, in this instance gay men. After all, she had gay friends in San Francisco who needed this information. It was a brief, technical introduction to the crisis. It was also the lengthiest piece any broadcast outlet had done to date. NPR rarely set the agenda for national news. It rarely influenced the *Washington Post* or *Newsweek* or the networks. Often, NPR's broadcast sounded like a condensed version of the *New York Times*. Some correspondents even claimed that they had trouble getting ideas past editors if the stories had not already appeared in the *New York Times*. Because of the initiative of those covering AIDS at NPR, the radio network handled reporting the epidemic much differently.

Garrett's New York counterpart, NPR's Ira Flatow, had neither connections to nor an understanding of that city's gays. However, he was fascinated by the burgeoning disease. He heard the Garrett report and read the sparse news items appearing in the medical journals. He even followed up with his own piece on December 10, 1981: "Homosexual Men Prey to Fatal Disease." "This is the most baffling outbreak since Legionnaire's Disease," said Dr. Henry Majur of Cornell Medical College in this piece. Majur had first suspected a problem when he diagnosed two gay men with *Pneumocystis* pneumonia in 1979. Flatow reported that the number of cases had risen to 180.

None of the sources he contacted for the story seemed to have many answers, or even good questions. How did this disease work? Who beyond gays would be threatened by it? And how was the gay community going to handle this assault? The last query was the kind that most interested Flatow, who believed that at the heart of all science news is a great human interest story. He wasn't sure how he was going to tell that tale, until he met Larry Kramer, the gay playwright who had embarked on a campaign to warn homosexuals about the disease. Flatow was introduced to the impassioned author by Dr. Alvin Friedman-Kein, a New York University physician in the forefront of AIDS research. For the chance to spread the word about this disease, Kramer agreed to serve as Flatow's Virgil for a tour of the gay community.

The story took months to put together. On April 20, 1982, the "Gay Health Series" finally ran. The twenty-minute, two-part program reported the rapid rise in the cases of Kaposi's sarcoma and *Pneumocystis*. It gave a profile of the typical victim: "He is a thirty-five-year-old gay who lives in New York, San Francisco, or Los Angeles. . . . And he has had a total of 1,100 sex partners in his lifetime."

"Anal and oral sex" were two ways gays might be spreading the disease, said Flatow. Promiscuity, he reported, was probably a factor. Flatow ended his report in a disco, the most popular hunting grounds for gay New Yorkers. In the background could be heard a throbbing disco tune with the refrain "Loving you isn't worth the pain of losing you."

The mere mention of an issue related to gays sent commercial broadcasters scurrying from the story. NPR was not so circumspect. During the same period the "gay cancer" story was developing, the network had produced more than two hours of news programming dealing with gay issues, from fiction with homosexual themes to religion in gay communities. Likewise, language restrictions—real or perceived—at other networks and newspapers that forced journalists to devise confusing euphemisms such as "the exchange of bodily fluid" were much less formidable at NPR. Early on, Garrett and Flatow used terms like "anal and oral sex," at least on "All Things Considered." "Morning Edition" was a more formal program, but still less circumscribed than almost any other national broadcast medium.

Squeamishness with language at NPR was rare. One of the few instances occurred in 1985, when commentator Noah Adams asked Garrett to delete the term "full-blown" AIDS from a report. He considered the term too sexually suggestive.

Radio in general tended to be more explicit than television, and especially the networks, due mostly to the notion that TV, and not radio, was the common medium for America. However, during the mid-1980s the federal government began cracking down on what it considered "obscene programming" on some local radio stations. In Los Angeles, KPFK was cited for "indecent" programming by the Federal Communications Commission when it ran late at night a dramatization of a sexually explicit play dealing with the alienating aspects of AIDS. The irony was disturbing: the FCC under Chairman Mark Fowler was cracking down on the content of local broadcasting even while disregarding stations' public service responsibilities to provide news and other vital public affairs programming.

The quality of AIDS reporting by NPR was offset by its sparsity. During the first ten months of the epidemic, the network's coverage amounted to thirty-two minutes and thirty seconds of on-air reporting. That was more than any other broadcast medium up that point, of course, but it hardly suggested close scrutiny of the crisis. The brief record of reporting was in part an indication of a network severely strapped for finances. The Reagan administration's cutbacks in social programs forced NPR to slash staffing in many departments, including science. By mid-1982 the world of science was being covered by one reporter, Garrett, and her editor, Anne Gudenkauf. Flatow had become a free-lancer, and the network had let the other reporters go. For the next eight months, news of the epidemic disappeared from NPR.

Not until AIDS was discovered to be spreading beyond homosexuals did NPR report the story again. The turning point was a five-minute piece by Jay Balthazar, aired December 21, 1982, in which he said that the disease may be spread through blood transfusions: "AIDS is affecting more than gays, and more than just promiscuous gay men." Then came "AIDS Discovered in Children," on January 5, 1983. Garrett had been covering other science news, but now she came back to the story. She recognized that the issue was quickly becoming a much bigger news item. Those were the same factors that moved most journalists who wrote about the epidemic at the time to do so. Garrett had one other motivation: in 1983 a friend died of AIDS.

The AIDS Beat

In the three American cities most affected by AIDS, cities Garrett covered during the epidemic, the reaction of their respective gay communities had some influence on how the disease was reported. In New York, for instance, those gays like Larry Kramer who were calling for more coverage and more assistance sounded irrational. In Los Angeles they were inaudible. But in San Francisco they were both rational and audible. Also, the high proportion of gays in a city of only seven hundred thousand residents meant that San Francisco began to show wounds from the crisis early.

From NPR's San Francisco offices at Eighth and Folsom, the heart of the raunchy gay leather district, Garrett remembers watching the

234 parade of men dressed in tough-guy drag: tight-fitting jeans and levi jackets, chaps and leather coats, chains around a thigh worn like a macho bracelet. South of Market, as the area is known, was a nether world in the gay community. Mainstream gays generally circulated through the trendy shops, restaurants, and bars on Castro or Polk Streets. South of Market in 1981 was a nightly sexual marketplace, the streets full of men cruising, leering, and some having sex in the dark alleyways. By October of 1983, before Garrett and the rest of the NPR West Coast bureau moved to Los Angeles, there were only four or five desperate-looking characters on the street. Much of the regular crowd had drifted away, but Garrett knew that many had gotten AIDS.

Garrett's reporting was drawing praise from a broad range of her sources: she got the science right, and most often got the politics straight, too. Not everybody was content, however.

Back at NPR headquarters in Washington, D.C., news director Robert Siegel complained that he was seeing too many AIDS stories. And some listeners had been downright hostile to the coverage. "Why do you continue to cover a problem that perverts brought on themselves?" one letter-writer complained. NPR's AIDS reporting also may have exacerbated its already problematic relationship with the Reagan administration.

The Funding Scramble

In the early 1970s, members of the Nixon White House, livid over what they considered to be the liberal bias of the public television network, had gutted federal funding for it. The Reagan administration seemed to have the same agenda for NPR. The assault intensified after NPR covered the U.S. invasion of Grenada in 1983. The network interviewed some of the American students enrolled at the medical school there who said there really never was any reason for their being rescued. Some said that they did not feel frightened until the American soldiers arrived. A year later NPR soured relations with the White House even more with its coverage of the press conference held by Secretary of Health Margaret Heckler on April 23, 1984. It was a red-letter day for the politically embattled Heckler: she announced that the AIDS virus had been discovered, by National Cancer Institute scientist Robert Gallo.

Garrett was on vacation in Hawaii, so environmental reporter Daniel Zwerdling was given the story. Over the phone they discussed the news, and Garrett warned that it all sounded odd. She had recently talked to Dr. Luc Montagnier at France's Pasteur Institute. He claimed he had discovered the virus, too. The same day as the press conference, NPR reported that the French had come up with a similar discovery. Who had found the virus first? That question would reveal one of the most scandalous glory-grabs in modern science, with Heckler dismissing work that foreigners had done. (The French and Americans have since agreed to share credit for the finding, as well as profits from products developed from the discovery.)

This was a particularly tough time to be critical of the Reagan administration, as the president lobbied for sharp reductions in social programs. Between 1982 and 1985, the White House cut NPR's budget 50 percent. NPR used to receive about 80 percent of its funding from the Corporation for Public Broadcasting. In 1989 that source accounted for only a small fraction of the total funds for the network. Most of the money comes from the dues NPR charges the stations that use its services. And underwriters, for the most part large companies or agencies that want to generate goodwill, are becoming a much more important source of revenue.

Some people both in and out of NPR fear that turn of events has threatened the public radio network's independence. For example, when Daniel Zwerdling was first hired in 1981 to cover environmental issues, including activities at the Environmental Protection Agency, his salary was paid for with a grant from the EPA. That funding source was kept a secret, even from Zwerdling. No one claims that NPR's reporting has been biased toward a donor but the appearance of a potential conflict of interest is hard to deny.

Garrett also found herself in uncomfortable predicaments when trying to pull together the finances necessary to cover a major story, including her Africa reporting. She knew sub-Saharan Africa well. As a free-lancer in 1979 she had traveled to then-Rhodesia to cover the Commonwealth Meetings that set up the independent nation of Zimbabwe. She had been one of the first Americans to enter Mozambique after that country's bloody revolution. But NPR could not afford the expense to send her back to the continent. In those circumstances, the network attempts to hunt down funding sources such as philanthropies or major corporations. There were no takers for coverage of AIDS in Africa. Finally, in 1986 the Carnegie Foundation agreed to fund a reporting team to travel to Africa, but not to cover AIDS. The grant was to pay for reports on development issues there.

"Why Do Children Die in Africa?"—a series on child development and malnutrition—was one result of the five-week trip. It ran in early August of 1986 and won the Carnegie Foundation's World Hunger Award in 1987. But Garrett says AIDS was really the story she was intent on covering, which she also did with the Carnegie money.

Third World America

Garrett returned to the United States and to the science side of the AIDS story. A half dozen other NPR reporters were now covering the epidemic from the social and political angles. Garrett did not cover those issues again until March of 1987, when she traveled to Newark, New Jersey.

At a gathering of medical scientists in Atlanta in February of 1987, Garrett had met the team of professionals that handle the onslaught of children with AIDS in Newark. The United Children's Hospital Program was run by Dr. James Oleske, nationally known for treating children with AIDS. (He had long since discarded his "household-contact" theory of transmission.) The facility handles more than one hundred pediatric AIDS cases, the largest number of any hospital in America.

Oleske and his assistant, Nurse Mary Boland, worked with a home-care nurse who taught poor black and Hispanic women how to care for their children with AIDS. There was also a social worker who co-ordinated badly needed services for poor patients and their families. They had a fascinating story to tell, thought Garrett, a kind of front-line battle that was increasingly defining the disease, which was now being seen in the offspring of intravenous drug addicts and their sex partners. Garrett coaxed an invitation out of the staff at Children's Hospital.

The poverty and rampant disease she saw when she arrived in Newark were all too familiar to her; except for the intravenous drug abuse, the description of the besieged city sounded like Bukoba or parts of Zimbabwe. Gays make up a declining percentage of the total AIDS cases in America, and heterosexual blacks and Hispanics in the poorest areas of the nation constitute a rising percentage. Newark, with large concentrations of poor minorities, is the kind of community in which AIDS increasingly is centered.

That was the rationale Garrett gave her editor when she tried to sell the idea that spring. Stories had been done before on AIDS and children, on i.v. drug users, even on the disease affecting the urban minority poor. But no journalist had focused on how all three of these factors would be devastating some of America's cities. Newark was the grim future in the AIDS epidemic. It had the highest number of drug-related AIDS cases per capita of any city in the United States. Public health officials believed that probably all of Newark's needle users had been infected. And a full 5 percent of the entire Newark population was suspected of having HIV: an infection rate equal to that in some areas of Central Africa.

After she got Editor Anne Gudenkauf's approval, Garrett spent two and a half weeks in Newark. What she found at Children's Hospital, on the streets, and in the homes of people struggling to care for AIDS victims ran in a seven-part series between May 7 and May 29, 1987.

To do the reporting, she spent time in places where people said they had not seen a white person visit for over twenty years. She found herself in neighborhoods where young teens toted machine guns. People were living in apartments that had been condemned years earlier. No one ever made them leave, and someone was still coming around to collect the rent.

She began her report on the streets of Newark, where an estimated 50 percent of the prostitutes were infected with the AIDS virus. Many of them were intravenous drug users, which was how they got infected in the first place.

"Across the street from Newark's Lincoln Park is a Catholic grammar school," Garrett reported, with the playful screeches of children in the background. "Only a hundred yards away [a] prostitute . . . is with a customer in a parked car. She's also shooting heroin. After a time she gets out of the car and walks the streets again. . . . She's one of those women who say they know about AIDS, practice safe sex, yet risk sharing heroin needles every day. 'It scares you to death,'" says the prostitute.

Public health officials are worried, too, Garrett reported. "With the majority of clients being married men, these prostitutes might be the bridge that takes AIDS to the general heterosexual population."

The key to stopping the spread of AIDS in Newark is to impede the use of i.v. drugs, which seems all but impossible there. She found out why by talking to junkies like Robert.

When Robert talks about heroin or AIDS, it almost sounds like bragging. "I'm dually addicted. I'm an alcoholic. And I have a terrible problem. I'm afraid to death of AIDS. I love drugs. I like taking pills, I like taking hits. And I'm gay." Robert is a walking contradiction. At one moment he brags he's been celibate since he's heard of AIDS, a few minutes later he introduces his gay lover. Robert says he doesn't touch heroin any longer, then smiles and points out where his connection is and ambles off to buy more heroin.

The chances are less than one out of ten that [any of these people] will show up at the methadone clinic. "All junkies say they're cleaning up," says Howard, a former addict who now counsels others to stay off drugs. "All junkies say that life is going to change real soon. And these days all junkies say they've taken the AIDS test and passed with flying colors. Almost all of them are lying to themselves."

Those same junkies continue to infect their spouses and their unborn children. Rosalia was one of those children. "In Children's Hospital in Newark there is one particularly pretty four-year-old," Garrett reported in another segment in the series. A small voice could be heard chattering in the background. "She is tiny for her age, has big sad eyes and long, shiny black hair. . . . For two years, Rosalia has been fighting for her life, battling the AIDS virus. For the last two weeks, something has been wrong with her gastrointestinal system. Dr. Jim Oleske hasn't been able to figure out what it is." Outside the hospital room, the doctor whispers that Rosalia's mother tries to come to the hospital every day, but it isn't easy because the mother is dying too.

"Later Rosalia's mother, Sylvia, arrives. Her frail four-and-half-foot tall body moves slowly, her lungs are wracked with tuberculosis, her body is full of infections that are taking advantage of her weakened state. Sylvia says she doesn't care if we use her real name, or her daughter's. She says her situation is so bad that the stigma of AIDS no longer haunts her." Sylvia says she got AIDS from her husband, a drug addict who died in 1986. Now she and Rosalia have it, too, and her other daughter, seven-year-old Sylvia, has AIDS-Related Complex. Despite her illnesses, she has a feisty edge to her. "Do you feel any anger towards him?" Garrett asks tentatively. The reply: "Yes, I do. A lot. He asked forgiveness before he died, but I didn't care. I asked him to stop using drugs, but he always ignored me. . . . It hurts that I'm sick, but it hurts more that she [Rosalia] is sick. I try not to have anger, but I have it, it's there."

"What would you say to other people who use drugs?"

"Think about their families."

"Sylvia says there are days when it all seems so bad she feels washed over by waves of depression and can't get out of bed. But then she remembers Rosalia still needs her. 'As long as she's there, I want to keep fighting for my life. As long as she's there. After that, I don't know what's going to happen.'"

Garrett, audibly choking back the tears, asks, "Is there anything that you can turn to . . . that gives you strength?"

"God," Sylvia shoots back, still strong and defiant.

The Newark series followed Ira Flatow's rule of finding the human element behind the science story. It also echoed Garrett's Africa reporting. Combatting AIDS in Third World America meant more than fighting disease. It would require dealing with poverty, with prostitution, drug abuse, and the social welfare system.

The high-tension reporting, done in the battle zone of Newark, New Jersey, took its toll on Garrett. When she arrived back in California she herself fell seriously ill.

Getting Involved

Garrett had faced death before she began covering AIDS. Her mother's death, of course, had an affect on her. But she also lost her brother, who died of epilepsy, and several friends died of disease or in bizarre accidents. As a reporter covering medical stories, she found her experience with those tragedies helped her better cope with the dying. And she understood when some of her interviewees needed to grieve, needed to make sense of their loss.

But when does the reporter's empathy begin to interfere with the story? Knowing gay men who had the disease or who died from AIDS helped her understand the importance of the epidemic. Being forced to face the pain of individuals like Sylvia breaks down the vaunted

barrier between subject and reporter. That, in large part, is why her
Newark reporting was Garrett's most compelling.

However, did her getting audibly choked up telling Sylvia's tale
make that story better? Or did she step over the line that separates
reporting from participating? The emotional moment easily could
have been edited out. The AIDS story has made the line of objectivity
much harder to draw. The stoicism of a science reporter would seem
out of place in the face of a withering mother and child. That does not
mean objectivity is a useless part of the process. In early 1986 a friend
of Garrett's went to France's Pasteur Institute, just as Rock Hudson
had, to be treated with the latest drug, HPA-23. She withdrew from
covering the drug trial there, knowing she could never distance herself enough to report that story objectively.

Objectivity need not be emotionless, or without compassion. Good
journalism is not bloodless. It is intelligent and provocative and human. Garrett grasped that lesson increasingly as she covered AIDS.
NPR's listeners benefited from that transition, gaining a personal insight into how the disease was affecting individuals.

Garrett's coverage of AIDS was not faultless. She usually kept a
check on her own political leanings, but when she erred in being un-
critical, it was on the side of traditional liberals. Her coverage of San
Francisco's bathhouse controversy in 1984 provided an example. She
too quickly accepted the owners' claim that safe sex was the order of
the day in their establishments, thus embracing the word of those ostensibly fighting for their sexual rights. It was a tack many both in and
out of the media took throughout the 1980s.

Most important, though, Garrett kept her anger in check. Much
like the swine flu debacle, federal policy on AIDS frustrated Garrett.
In this case, it was a matter of the government not doing enough.
Garrett had clearly learned a few lessons since the days of satirizing
President Ford's vaccine program, including how to let the story tell
itself in all its tragic dimensions. Her increased expertise and ability to
find the human side of science news undoubtedly bolstered NPR's
reputation. While radio audiences decline nationwide, the network is
gaining in listeners. Pulled back from the brink of collapse in the
mid-1980s, NPR has since increased its audience by 25 percent, to ten
million listeners nationwide.

Whether NPR has become any more of an agenda-setter is debat-
able. The network is still short on scoops, and its news roundups often
seem familiar to readers of the *New York Times*. Garrett, who did

produce cutting-edge journalism while at NPR, has since left to report for *Newsday* on Long Island, New York.

NPR's struggle to maintain editorial independence from sponsors and the government continues. In 1987, some critics called for the Corporation for Public Broadcasting to do a content analysis of NPR's news to determine if there were a political bias. President Doug Bennett successfully fought off the idea. He had some new ammunition. Reagan appointee Admiral James D. Watkins, head of the Presidential Commission on the HIV Epidemic, sent NPR a ringing endorsement: "NPR is singularly responsible for dispelling much misinformation and fear and building a national base of knowledge about the epidemic."

Garrett, a child of the sixties weaned on the lies of Vietnam and educated by a public health hoax, now finds herself applauded by the same kind of people she lampooned only a little more than a decade ago. As with any good journalist, that fact makes her more than a little nervous.

Chapter 12
The second
wave

Max Robinson, the first black anchor on network television, was sitting for an interview with the *Washington Post* in the late spring of 1988, when the question of his lengthy illness came up. Was it AIDS? "I'm just not going to get into the subject of what I have," Robinson said. For months the rumors had been circulating throughout the Northeast media establishment, and in Chicago, from where the poised and professional broadcaster had last coanchored ABC's "World News Tonight." Ironically, one of the last stories he broadcast was on AIDS hysteria. He left the network months later, in early 1984.

Robinson's refusal to confirm or deny the whispers did not make them go away. He had an infectious disease and he almost died in December of 1987: that was as much as he would admit. Once the most influential black in American journalism, the forty-nine-year-old now was cloistered in his lakefront apartment.

Seven years since the epidemic first made news, the mainstream media establishment was giving occasional AIDS-related stories big play, though coverage of the epidemic overall was decreasing. The Robinson feature ran on the cover of the *Post*'s well-respected "Style" section. In the minority press, however, Robinson's illness was routinely disregarded, even though he had become a TV personality on the "Essence" shows, the black magazine-format program shown mostly on cable.

In the early 1980s, the mainstream media made AIDS a well-kept secret. Now the minority press was underplaying almost every aspect of the disease that was increasingly claiming the lives of blacks and Hispanics. And both the mainstream and minority media were ignoring the biggest threat to the larger population: the spread of the disease to heterosexual minorities.

Protecting Them from the News

"We have a family newspaper here," said William Egyir, managing editor of the New York *Amsterdam News*, the granddaddy of the black media. It was the spring of 1988 when Egyir made his defense of the newspaper's poor AIDS coverage. The statement echoed the attitude in the mainstream press a half decade earlier. The rationale was still dangerously faulty. Of the nearly 76,000 cases of AIDS diagnosed in the United States by late 1988, one in four were black, three in 20 were Hispanic. That meant blacks and Hispanics were being infected at more than twice the rate of whites in the United States. Increasingly, those coming down with the disease were not gay and middle-class. They were junkies from the barrio and the ghetto. In New York, the infection rate for drug addicts was estimated at about 60 percent in 1988. In Newark, New Jersey, authorities pegged it closer to 100 percent.

"These people don't read the paper," said Egyir. For the most part, he was right: addicts do not read any newspapers, as a rule.

In 1988, it already may have been too late to reach the junkies in New York and Newark. But it was not too late to warn their sex partners who did not use drugs. If addicts weren't reading the *Amsterdam News* or other minority-community newspapers, many of their partners were. Unfortunately, the newspapers largely turned their backs on these people, too.

The Voice of Harlem

When it was founded in 1909, the weekly *Amsterdam News* targeted itself toward the residents of the nation's most astute black community: Harlem. The paper built a reputation for covering every side of race politics, from the 1940s desegregation of the hometown Dodgers to the civil rights marches of the 1960s. In its most influential days during the mid- and late 1960s, it had a circulation of almost ninety thousand and was considered black America's paper of record.

The *Amsterdam News* necessarily became its own agenda-setter, because the issues it considered most pressing were often overlooked entirely by the mainstream press. The paper is much more likely to feature the latest jousting between Jesse Jackson and Mayor Ed Koch than news about Soviet-American arms negotiations or even a strike by New York Rapid Transit workers. "Few movers use the *Amsterdam News* as their sole news source," according to one black journalist. As its circulation slid, to thirty-five thousand in the 1980s, the *Amsterdam News* became less influential in the black community. The paper also was hit with competition from both within and without its own community. New York papers like the *Caribbean News,* for example, focused on immigrant populations and expanded coverage to cut into the *News*'s territory. And the city's growing black middle class, much of which no longer called Harlem home, reached more and more for what were formerly considered the "white" papers.

The *Amsterdam News* continued to focus on its traditional audience, that community-minded, middle-class, and politically interested black—the kind of reader who was also likely to patronize the restaurant or shop that advertises in the newspaper. Thus coverage at the *News* was determined by the same criterion that the mainstream media used: try to guess what that target audience wants to read.

AIDS Coverage at the *Amsterdam News*

For editors like Egyir, it was clear early on in the AIDS epidemic that his readers would not be interested in what the mainstream media defined as a disease mostly affecting gays. "That's not a part of the community that the black media covers," said Gil Gerald, director of the National AIDS Network, a public education project. Not until 1987 would the paper begin to give any attention to the plague that had taken hold in Harlem. Yet its coverage was about the best the minority press in New York City offered. During a twelve-month period ending in mid-1988, the *Amsterdam News* published about twice as many AIDS-related stories as the *Caribbean News,* and nearly as many articles as the two major Spanish-language daily papers, *El Diario-La Prensa* and *Noticias del Mundo.* Still, in that year-long period, the *Amsterdam News* ran only fifty articles on the epidemic.

Many of those articles were no more than three-inch notices of AIDS information meetings, for example. And there were opinion pieces from politicians like Harlem Representative Charles Rangel and public health officials, describing the epidemic and what it meant for the black community. But the most dramatic articles were those written by community members lashing out at "the white media." For instance, on a June 6, 1987, in "Putting the AIDS Blame on 'Black Mames,'" an unidentified writer complained about, and labeled as racist, recent articles in newspapers like the *New York Times* that cited the danger of transmission between black women and men. "Now that the AIDS disease is developing into an international health catastrophe they would put the blame between the sheets of 'Black Mames.' . . . What's most maddening is the deafening silence of our influential community in the face of this calculated media mud onslaught which continues to besmear our image."

As in its heyday, when the faithful read it in part to track the civil rights struggle, the *Amsterdam News*'s strength was its political sensibility. And as in the 1960s, it found itself playing the role of guardian to a community too often under siege. As a result, the tone of its AIDS news was often defensive. The coverage was also weak. When it described how the disease was transmitted, the most important information for its readers, the prose was often so subtle as to be misleading: "While white homosexuals contract AIDS from 'action' between themselves, the majority of Blacks and Hispanics get it as IVDU," the paper reported on April 4, 1987. Neither "action" (presumably anal and possibly oral sex) nor IVDU (intravenous drug use) were explained.

There were also repeated articles attacking basic, common-sense methods of prevention such as condom use. "Don't Give Convicts Condoms" read a headline on May 2, 1987, supporting City Councilman Enoch Williams's attempt to shut down the practice in New York City's jails.

Some of the newspaper's most ambitious reporting on the epidemic was done to track down conspiracy theories about the disease, such as the idea that AIDS is a product of a CIA experiment run afoul in the Congo. Other black media have printed the claims of Steve Cokely, who was an aide to Chicago's acting mayor, Eugene Sawyer. In 1988 Cokely charged that doctors, most of them Jewish, were responsible for the spread of AIDS by injecting the disease into blacks. He no longer works for the city of Chicago.

What Uncle Sam Didn't Do, Part II

Distrust of the federal government obviously underlay much of the coverage of the epidemic at the *Amsterdam News*. The minority media cannot be entirely blamed for taking this tack. The mainstream media also overlooked the fact that the crisis was affecting minorities disproportionately, and to a large extent still does. The image of the

AIDS victim that appears on the TV screen, for example, is almost always white and is much more likely to be that of a middle-class person than someone who is poor. The CDC has done little to promote the real picture of this epidemic until very recently.

As early as 1983, the CDC had such a clear understanding of how AIDS was spreading that the agency broke down the victims into racial groups: "57 percent of those [AIDS cases] reported have been white, 26 percent black, 14 percent Hispanic and 3 percent other or unknown," the CDC's *Morbidity and Mortality Weekly Report* declared on September 9 of that year. Even then it was obvious the disease was accelerating among minorities. Blacks, for example, were being hit far harder proportionately than whites. It was obvious that AIDS was not going to be contained exclusively in the gay population.

However, not until three years after that initial racial-group breakdown did the CDC get around to featuring the problem in the MMWR. Finally, in the issue of October 24, 1986, the CDC warned public health officials that "until an effective therapy or vaccine is available, prevention of [HIV] infection depends on education and behavioral modification of persons at increased risk," including minorities.

CDC officials could not explain why they had waited to publish the information. Perhaps it was because Dr. James Curran, Dr. Harold Jaffe, and other CDC officials were much better connected to gays than to the communities of blacks and Hispanics in the inner city, having worked with homosexual organizations on other diseases like hepatitis B. Some familiar with the agency also said that doctors there were afraid of stumbling into the same political mess as when early in the epidemic they labeled Haitians a high-risk group for the disease. The CDC was attacked as racist by black and Haitian groups both in the United States and abroad for that move.

Nonetheless, "the government should have reached out to the black press," said Gerald of the National AIDS Network. In the early years, that vehicle for public health information was almost completely ignored. In the fall of 1987, the Department of Health and Human Services commissioned the National Black Entertainment Network to produce a one-hour documentary. Called "AIDS in the Black Community," it was a straightforward introduction to how the disease was making headway mostly among heterosexual minorities.

Since then, the U.S. Public Health Service has generated ad campaigns directed specifically at blacks and Hispanics.

AIDS Coverage in the Other Black Media

As in all other media, the most important spur to the black media to cover the epidemic was personal involvement in the crisis. Some journalists at the black publications mourned the loss of friends who had died of AIDS, and certain "celebrity" obituaries shook the entire black community. Willi Smith's death was one of those.

The thirty-nine-year-old fashion designer, whose Williwear creations had grown into a multimillion-dollar business during the mid-1980s, was diagnosed with the disease. He died April 17, 1987. His death was covered by much of the black media and helped bring home the fact that the epidemic was touching black lives. As with Rock Hudson, the fact that Smith was gay would be largely overlooked.

However, there was one black medium that did not shy away from the epidemic, in any of its forms. From January 1984, the gossipy *Jet* magazine had been covering the disease as closely as *Newsweek* and *Time,* and far more closely than its counterpart, *People.* By 1985 the glossy weekly was running regular stories, from how the disease was spreading to how to prevent it. Its mainstay, of course, was the inside scoop on the black elite: "Richard Pryor denies having AIDS," one 1986 article began.

With a circulation of some 835,000, *Jet's* influence in the black community is substantial. Unfortunately, its sister publication, *Ebony,* with more than 1.7 million subscribers monthly, largely overlooked the crisis. Both magazines are published by the conservative Johnson family, which has long sought to put the best light on the black community. "The 100 Most Influential Black Americans," an *Ebony* article, is typical of the features run in the magazine.

Rock Who?

In the Hispanic community, there was no equivalent to the Rock Hudson death. Unlike the black media, Spanish-language print journalists and broadcasters tend to use Associated Press or United Press International news services. However, even as these resources began exploding with AIDS information after Rock Hudson's diagnosis in 1985, "Hispanics saw [the epidemic] as a Hollywood story," said Josefina Vidal, health editor of *La Opinion*. "It wasn't news that was affecting us."

The daily newspaper, based in Los Angeles, had run some news items on AIDS, beginning in February of 1985. But the same inhibitions keeping the story untold in the black and mainstream media also kept a lid on coverage in the Hispanic media. The Spanish-speaking community in the United States, though it comes from very different cultures ranging from South and Central America to the Caribbean, is generally considered conservative and very family-oriented. "Sex isn't a topic discussed much in the home," said Emilio Nicolas, Jr., general manager of WXTV, a popular Hispanic station in New York. If homosexuality is ignored by the black media, it is denied by many Hispanic journalists. José Sanz, a producer of a Spanish-language series on the disease, said the multi-part program did not use the word "homosexual" until a gay male being interviewed uttered the term himself.

Not until 1986 did progressive media like *La Opinion* produce original articles on AIDS. By that time, said Vidal, "the statistics were clear about the danger the disease posed for the Hispanic community." In fact, anyone closely covering either the Hispanic or black communities should have recognized much earlier that the epidemic was spreading fast among their ranks.

From late 1986 on, the figures on those coming down with the disease showed that AIDS was claiming two and three times as many victims, proportionately, among those two minority groups than among whites. Not all of the minority victims were junkies and gays. In Los Angeles, intravenous drug users were spreading the disease to their spouses, children, and lovers, though at a much slower rate than in such big cities as New York, Newark, and Chicago. The difference, according to experts, was that in sprawling Los Angeles, the distances that separated pockets of drug addicts kept those users from spreading the disease more rapidly among themselves. In addition, the dangerous habit of passing needles from one user to the next in a shooting gallery was much less common on the West Coast than in the East.

Hispanics on both coasts, however, shared special problems in trying to tackle the disease. For instance, in attempting to get the word out about AIDS, communicating it in simple terms could be extremely confusing when dealing with Hispanic immigrants from five or more countries—Mexico, Cuba, Puerto Rico, El Salvador, Nicaragua, etc.— each familiar only with their very distinctive dialect.

Telling Sonia's Story

Despite the difficulties, there were some impressive information campaigns kicked off in Hispanic print and broadcast media.

At *La Opinion* Josefina Vidal and other editors pulled together a special supplement, "SIDA: Epidemia sin fronteras" (AIDS: Epidemic without Boundaries), that ran in July 1987. The twenty-page tabloid was included in the eighty-five thousand copies of *La Opinion*. Since most of the paper's readers are conservative Catholics, Vidal focused on families to gain the attention and sympathy of this group.

There was Sonia, a young immigrant mother of two. She had been infected with the AIDS virus by her drug-using boyfriend. Worse still, she was pregnant, and the doctors told her that she might have infected her child. "I cried and beat my head with my hands. This couldn't be happening to my baby," she said. "[The doctor] recommended that I have an abortion, but I didn't have the heart for that and I told him I wanted to have my baby." Sonia did have her baby, and he was infected with the disease.

Even the gay men *La Opinion* reported on, such as thirty-two-year-old Sergio Rebolledo, were described in a family context. "[He] is a religious man, who goes to church to pray often, as his grandmother taught him. For him, God is a compassionate being, not someone that 'judges and punishes.'" His parents and sister still live in his native Mexico City, and they all know about his illness. "My mother is very worried, but when she comes to see me she feels much better," he said.

La Opinion followed up its first supplement with a second one in October 1988, "Juntos contra el SIDA" (Together against AIDS).

Perhaps because Vidal, who oversaw these special sections, was careful to couch these gripping stories in terms her audience could relate to—family, church, home—there was little negative response from the community. In fact, there were demands from throughout Los Angeles and even in San Francisco for reprints of the special sections. They eventually were distributed in clinics as well as at the San Francisco and L.A. AIDS projects.

Another significant effort was a documentary on AIDS in the Hispanic community, spearheaded by broadcaster Emilio Nicolas while at the Hispanic station in San Francisco, KDTV. And Univision, the Hispanic network with some 450 affiliates, in 1987 featured a series of AIDS shows on its "America," a more entertainment-oriented, Spanish-language version of "60 Minutes." Not surprisingly, these productions looked like their English-language counterparts: Although they avoided many of the foolish errors the networks and print media committed in the early years, the programs often focused on children even though adults make up the majority of those actually getting the disease.

Little Celeste was one such subject. The ten-year-old girl was described as the longest-living survivor of AIDS, and "among the youngest, and most innocent victims," on the "America" show of April 28, 1987. She had been infected in the womb, and her mother, father, and younger brother all had since died of the disease. The story of Celeste's horror was told mostly through her grandmother, Toy Santiago. Reaction to the piece was strong and quick. Thousands of phone calls poured into the network's affiliates across the country, some viewers offering compliments, a few complaints, and many wanting more information.

The event indicated the power of the televised word, perhaps especially in the Hispanic community. Many Latinos, even those who are completely bilingual, prefer to watch TV in their mother tongue. Although well-educated Hispanics traditionally have preferred English-language TV, even some of them are switching over to Univision and its competitor network, Telemundo Group, as their programming becomes more sophisticated. One of the strongest stations, KMEX in Los Angeles, part of the Univision network, often pulls in larger audiences than many of the English-language stations, even though it is stuck on the outback of local TV's channel 31.

Theirs versus Ours

U.S. mainstream media have ignored minorities as both a source of and an audience for news. With efforts like Univision's "America" segments on AIDS, it's even easier for editors at daily newspapers and TV producers to dismiss their responsibility to inform *all* Americans about pressing health issues like AIDS. The minornority media tend to set their own agenda and, particularly in the black press, to ignore major events other media have deemed important. As a result, some frustrated editors at metropolitan dailies have decided that minority readers' concerns are so different from their own that they can't possibly produce a paper that appeals at the same time to white surburbanites, black city dwellers, and Hispanics in the barrio.

That notion is wrong, according to the findings of an exhaustive study undertaken by the American Society of Newspaper Editors in 1986. To produce a paper that blacks will read, editors need no more to "mirror" that community—as the *Amsterdam News* claims to do, but fails resoundingly—than they need to understand Hibernian rituals to get the Irish to subscribe. Whether a person—white, black, Hispanic—regularly reads the newspaper depends on whether he or she has the habit. Helping to shape such practices early on, through schools, for instance, is more important to the future of newspaper readership than targeting minority groups for coverage.

But mainstream newspapers do a miserable job of attracting black and Hispanic readers. Despite feeble attempts by some dailies to capitalize on this untapped market, newspaper management has changed only slightly since the Kerner Commission report of 1968 excoriated the white media establishment for its racist practices. Print journalism is doing little to halt the move, especially by minority audiences, to television as the single source for news.

That has alarming implications for an American population that is increasingly minority-dominated. For the first time in the history of modern California, a majority of the state's public school students are black, Hispanic, or Asian—not white. When those children become adults, they very likely won't have the newspaper reading habit and will rely on TV news.

Does it matter that most Americans get their news exclusively from the television? Coverage of the AIDS epidemic shows just how much. TV news will continue to discount minority communities, even as crises like AIDS affect blacks and Hispanics more, and present fairly complex issues like disease prevention in dangerously simplistic terms, when it airs them at all.

Who will speak for the group now being devastated by AIDS: drug-using, poor, disenfranchised blacks and Hispanics? Who will tell their

story? Who will air their concerns?

"Personal Threat" Rule

Journalists are still led by the rule that has consistently determined how AIDS would be covered: the closer the threat of the disease seemed to move toward those setting the agenda, the bigger the story became. That was true in the spring of 1983, when data from a study of pediatric AIDS cases were wrongly interpreted to suggest the disease could be spread through routine, household contact. In the summer of 1985, when the diagnosis of virile "Every Man" Rock Hudson was made public, the press once again wrote itself into a frenzy. And in the spring of 1987, when the AIDS agenda turned to discussions of who should be tested, and how can "we" protect ourselves from "them," media interest boomed again. Since then, fears have largely been quelled, and so has the coverage. The media are slow to learn their lessons, but when they do they generally commit them to memory. So it has been with the fact that AIDS is not a threat to the average white, heterosexual, middle-class person. Even a flamboyant study like the March 1988 report by Dr. William Masters and Virginia Johnson, claiming that everyone was at risk of catching the disease, perhaps even from toilet seats, did not draw the firestorm of reaction they had hoped for.

As the media grasped that reality, coverage dropped off precipitously. Public health officials like Surgeon General C. Everett Koop feared that turn of events. Now that the epidemic has moved into its second wave, overwhelming Third World America, widely accessible information should be more important than ever in the fight against AIDS. But except for features done by the *New York Times,* the *Washington Post,* the *Philadelphia Inquirer,* and a handful of other outlets, the media are not responding. In some cities, more has been written about the purported transmission of AIDS by mosquitoes, which was proved impossible, than about the very evident spread of the disease from intravenous drug-using father to wife to child. The disease is shaping communities and cities, and yet the implications of this crisis are being disregarded.

There is also a pattern of missing out on even more obvious news opportunities to educate minorities about the disease. Max Robinson, for example, probably the most recognized black journalist in America, died in late 1988, without ever publicly acknowledging his illness. The following day, a close friend announced that Robinson had died of AIDS, and that the former network anchor had wanted his demise to serve as a means of informing others about the disease. He could and should have used his life more effectively for the same purpose.

Conclusion
Mortal lessons
for the media,
and America

Imagine a deadly disease that sweeps a population more quickly than AIDS —perhaps one that is passed through the air, making it easy to transmit and hard to stop. Then consider what would happen if it attacked a voiceless, powerless community: poor blacks and Hispanics, for instance. Or street people. Health officials are aware of the epidemic. As are doctors who work at the local public hospital, the facility where the city's indigent end up for basic medical care. Because the clinics and the wards are littered with these cases, and are taxing an already overburdened health-care system, some city officials are all too cognizant of the epidemic, too.

Being a disease of the poor, it has not touched the life of the city's newspaper editor, or even the beat reporter. No one at any of the local TV or radio stations knows a victim of the disease. It is just one more horror in the long list of unspeakable and unthinkable tragedies that the underclass must endure. Nothing is written about it; no one is so alarmed to prompt a reporter to be assigned to cover the issue. It is, in fact, not considered "news." For most people, the epidemic never happened, even though it rages on in the streets and the hospital wards of the city.

In America's Third World, as in other poverty-stricken parts of the globe, this scenario is all too real. Indeed, AIDS is just one of the many epidemics ravaging the population. Tuberculosis, that airborne, easily contracted malady of the poor, is rampant on the streets of New York and Los Angeles. Chancroid syphilis and a host of other sexually transmitted diseases are plaguing Newark, New Jersey and the Bronx. People are suffering and dying in unprecedented numbers from diseases that were supposedly conquered decades ago. Yet no one is writing about these most preventable tragedies. The editor, reporter, producer—in both the mainstream and minority media—who have yet to be touched by these diseases, will feel their effects nonetheless as the city's services buckle, as infections thought to be confined to the Third World creep ever closer to their world. Most shocking about this business-as-usual attitude is that it demonstrates the American media have learned so little from the AIDS epidemic.

Dr. Snow, Revisited

In the 1970s, public health officials like the Centers for Disease Control's Dr. James Mason and Dr. William Foege realized that government's role in future health crises would be less that of dismembering the water pump—Dr. John Snow's decisive action in curbing London's cholera epidemic—than teaching people how to avoid the infectious source in the first place. Now that so much more is known about how to prevent disease, the government should be in the business of preventive education. In the AIDS epidemic, that would have meant providing early on some basic information about how to avoid infection to those at highest risk, including blacks and Hispanics.

But because the government was so inept at getting out the word about AIDS prevention, health officials like Surgeon General C. Everett Koop have called on the *media* to fill in the gaps. American journalists, when they choose to, generally do a good job of "informing" the public about an issue that has somehow made it on the national agenda. For instance, by 1988 almost every teen polled in a broad survey had heard of AIDS, and knew that it could be sexually transmitted. But only a slim minority of those who were sexually active used condoms, one of the easiest ways to prevent exposure to the virus.

It is not the job of the journalists to act as public health experts, continuously encouraging behavioral change to stem threats like AIDS. It is their responsibility to cover the news in a sophisticated, unblushing manner. That does not mean every major disease or event warrants the assignment of a reporter to focus on that particular subject on a full-time basis. In 1988, newspapers across the country boasted about installing an "AIDS reporter," usually a science or medical writer who specialized in the epidemic. That kind of emphasis produces exaggerated coverage. When can readers expect to see the appointment of a "heart reporter," since heart disease claims far more American lives than AIDS? The networks and local stations certainly would improve with some increased specialization, but not to that extent.

Instead, journalists have to begin expanding their scope. News, the events that affect our lives, happens not just in the mainstream communities or those pockets of cities on which newspapers and broadcast outlets focus their coverage. News happens in gay and black and Hispanic ghettos.

Major metropolitan newspapers have reached out to cover outlying communities in a more in-depth fashion, but they also must cover other communities within their cities. For decades, of course, long-established newspapers have been disappearing. Rising costs, contracting advertising dollars, and shrinking profits have all conspired against the American print tradition. In the next generation, many more newspapers will die for lack of circulation. We have already quietly passed into the next information era, in which TV is the dominant news source. For that reason, TV must broaden its news boundaries, as well.

The new networking between local stations could improve reporting, from science and health to the economy and even politics. By simply coordinating national "units"—groups of reporters, producers, and camera operators located at different stations to cover these topics on a consistent basis—the broadcaster could cut down on costs while substantially boosting expertise. For example, a Boston or Los Angeles station could be home to a unit reporting on health issues; a Houston or Dallas station could be headquarters for a team covering energy issues.

There are scores of other ideas to help the media do their job better. TV, radio, and print outlets should be using straightforward language as a matter of course, rather than masking terms like "semen," "ejaculation," "penis," "vagina," and "intercourse" with phrases such as "exchange of bodily fluids." Just what constitutes the traditional beat also has to be reexamined. In a time when the homeless are a growing and visible part of the city, for instance, the media should be covering them. The health and science reporters should no longer wait to be told what is news from the weekly technical journals that land on their desks. By going on rounds with doctors at the local indigent hospital, by visiting labs at the nearest medical research institute, they would be in a much better position to understand just what is news, and what is doctor-hype.

Implementing these kinds of changes will require a spirit of innovation and commitment, the kind of sensibility Art Kern and Jim **257** Bunn at KPIX, former NPR correspondent Laurie Garrett, NBC's Robert Bazell, and the *New York Times*'s Max Frankel have tried to bring to the profession.

There is a role for the audience, too. Persistency on the part of an informed reader or viewer can pay off. Playwright Larry Kramer is proof of that: his frontal assaults on the *Times* left him angry and frustrated, and yet he touched the lives of dozens of reporters at the networks and at media outlets across America, and helped to shape AIDS coverage in significant ways. Since Kramer first fought to get the major media interested in covering "gay cancer," grassroots groups' influence on how the disease is portrayed has surged. In the fall of 1988, a protest organization the playwright founded, ACT UP, agitated to change the plot line of a TV drama, "Midnight Caller," in which a bisexual man knowingly continues to spread the AIDS virus. The group complained that, much like the Fabian Bridges story, the script distorted how the disease was actually being spread: not by sociopathic gays, but by people who did not know they were infected. ACT UP succeeded, and the story line was changed.

As Kramer did so successfully, complain by phone, write letters, demand meetings, talk to friends. It is the most basic way to spread the word, and to get newspeople interested in the real news. Those connections have always been important and will become more so in an increasingly complex world.

Touched by the Future

As the globe's geopolitical dimensions shrink, those groups that used to be considered "fringe" play increasingly larger roles. AIDS should make naturally insular Americans aware that there is more to the world than they had imagined. In fact, this disease that journalists have once again become convinced won't be affecting them or their readers, is making its way into the ranks of the nation's teens. Americans ages thirteen to twenty-one are spreading the AIDS virus through heterosexual contact at twice the rate of adults. That's another story the media are missing, and a tragedy the government, despite Surgeon General C. Everett Koop's call for sex education in schools, is doing very little to control. This latest surge in the epidemic—the third wave—crossing social and economic boundaries, could prove to be the deadliest of all.

From Africa's jungles to Europe's cities, from prostitutes to the wives of middle-class businessmen, from the veins of junkies to the bodies of our children, we are all more intimately connected than we may care to admit. That's the most important lesson we can all learn from this plague, and a lesson that should prompt us to act.

Timeline of the Plague
A medical, political,
and media history of AIDS

1969: A teenager in St. Louis, Missouri, dies after a bout of an inexplicable infection. Only a decade and a half later is his illness diagnosed as AIDS.

1976: Dr. Grethe Rask, a Danish surgeon working in Zaire, is stricken by *Pneumocystis carinii* pneumonia and dies shortly after. This extremely rare malady arises only in patients suffering from a more severe infectious disease.

1979: Two young gay men in New York are diagnosed with Kaposi's sarcoma, a rare skin disease that usually is found only in elderly Italian and Jewish men and in Africans.

Fall 1980: Pneumocystis pneumonia begins appearing in Copenhagen.

November 1980: Dr. Michael Gottlieb at UCLA sees his first case of *Pneumocystis* pneumonia in a young gay man.
  Ronald Reagan is elected the fortieth president of the United States.

February 1981: New York University's Dr. Alvin Friedman-Kien sees two patients with Kaposi's sarcoma who are young gay men. Researching past cases in New York state, he discovers six other cases of KS in young, otherwise healthy, unmarried men since 1979. San Francisco physician Marcus Conant confirms cases of KS in the Bay Area, as well.

May 18, 1981: Following up a tip from a reader, *New York Native* writer Dr. Lawrence Mass publishes a piece on "an exotic new disease" appearing in the city's gay community.

Late May 1981: Dr. Gottlieb notifies the Los Angeles County Department of Public Health and the Centers for Disease Control (CDC) of five cases of *Pneumocystis* pneumonia among young men in Los Angeles.

The CDC forms a task force to study the disease. Dr. James Curran heads it up.

June 5, 1981: Gottlieb and Dr. Joel Weisman, a Los Angeles physician, describe their cases in the *Morbidity and Mortality Weekly Report* (*MMWR*).

The Associated Press files a story on the report, and the *Los Angeles Times* and *San Francisco Chronicle* publish small stories, the first coverage in the mainstream press.

July 3, 1981: The CDC's *MMWR* announces that forty-one gay men in New York and California have been diagnosed as suffering from Kaposi's sarcoma and/or *Pneumocystis* pneumonia.

The *New York Times*'s Dr. Lawrence Altman covers the report.

July 7, 1981: Cable News Network airs a story on Kaposi's sarcoma, the first time the disease is mentioned on TV.

July 27, 1981: New York Native runs "Cancer in the Gay Community," written by Dr. Mass. It offers the most comprehensive look at the disease in the nonmedical media to date and is used as the centerpiece of the New York gay community's early education campaign.

December 1981: Two hundred cases of either Kaposi's sarcoma, *Pneumocystis,* or a combination of both—dubbed by some "Gay Related Infectious Disease"—are reported by the CDC. The federal government describes it as "an epidemic of immunosuppression."

December 10, 1981: The *New England Journal of Medicine* publishes three articles and an editorial on the new epidemic.

Late December 1981: Dr. James Curran appears on "Good Morning, America," the first such show featuring an expert on the epidemic. It runs forty five seconds.

April 1982: The Reagan administration's budget proposal seeks to reduce funding to the National Institutes of Health and to keep CDC funding stable. No money is given to fight the epidemic.

May 31, 1982: The *Los Angeles Times* is the first of the mainstream media to run a front-page story on the disease: "Started with Gays—Mysterious Fever Now an Epidemic."

June 16, 1982: NBC reports that "the lifestyle of some male homosexuals has triggered an epidemic," thus airing the first story about the disease to appear on the network evening news.

June 18, 1982: The CDC reports that intravenous drug users are contracting Kaposi's sarcoma and other opportunistic infections.

July 9, 1982: The CDC cites the rising number of cases of the disease among Haitians.

July 13, 1982: The first international symposium on the epidemic is held, at New York's Mt. Sinai Medical Center. Since February, cases have been reported at the rate of 1.5 per day, and in the past six weeks that rate has jumped to 2.5 per day.

July 15, 1982: Dr. James Curran releases the latest statistics on the disease: of the 413 cases reported, 155 have died; 85 percent of the victims are under the age of forty-five and the median age is thirty-five.

July 16, 1982: The CDC reports the first cases of the disease among hemophiliacs, supporting the theory that it may be transmitted through sex or *blood.*

The CDC, which had labeled the epidemic "Acquired Community Immune Deficiency," now clips the title to "AIDS."

August 19, 1982: Assistant Secretary of Health Edward Brandt states that the federal government plans to step up activities to combat AIDS, "a little-understood syndrome afflicting increasing numbers of people in the United States."

Six hundred Americans have been diagnosed with the disease.

September 27, 1982: Following several lengthy features in the local press on the AIDS epidemic in San Francisco, the city's supervisors approve $450,000 for the local clinic and other services, the first specific appropriations made by any government.

October 1, 1982: Cyanide is discovered in Tylenol capsules distributed in the Chicago area. Many of the major metropolitan dailies give the story front-page treatment, and the network nightly news devotes the first part of the newscast to it. The *New York Times* is on top of the news, with a story every day for the rest of the month.

December 12, 1982: The *New York Native* runs a piece titled "We know who we are," written by two AIDS sufferers and calling for gays to reconsider the community's propensity for promiscuous sex.

December 17, 1982: The CDC publishes a report on AIDS in infants, which draws more coverage than any previous news on the epidemic.

December 26, 1982: Pushed by San Francisco Representative Phil Burton, Congress appropriates $2.6 million for CDC's AIDS effort.

January 4, 1983: CDC's Dr. Donald Francis holds a meeting with the blood bank industry to talk about the need for more precautions in dispensing blood. The gathering is ignored by the media.

January 7, 1983: MMWR documents AIDS cases among female partners of male AIDS carriers and details the spread of AIDS in prison.

Early 1983: The number of AIDS cases passes the one-thousand mark, which results in a rash of news stories, many pegged to the fear that AIDS might be spread to those heterosexuals who do not use intravenous drugs.

March 3, 1983: The U.S. Public Health Service releases guidelines for blood donations and issues some sparse recommendations for "safe sex."

March 7, 1983: The *New York Native* runs "1,112 and Counting," a shrill indictment by playwright Larry Kramer of the federal government and Mayor Koch's administration for their failure to act quickly and effectively to stem the epidemic.

March 23, 1983: The *San Francisco Chronicle* publishes "Startling Finding on 'Gay Disease,'" announcing that one out of every 350 gay men in San Francisco is believed to be suffering from AIDS.

April 11, 1983: Newsweek features AIDS as its cover story in an expansive feature, "Epidemic."

April 12, 1983: Dr. Donald Francis, the man in charge of laboratory research efforts on AIDS at the CDC, pens a memo pleading for increased funding for the project. The document contradicts the "official" word from the bureaucracy, that AIDS research is being funded appropriately.

April 23, 1983: The spread of AIDS in the United States is linked by researchers to Africa for the first time. The *Philadelphia Inquirer,* National Public Radio, and the *New York Native* do small stories.

May 6, 1983: Journal of the American Medical Association publishes a study by Dr. James Oleske that suggests AIDS can be transmitted by "routine household contact." NIH's Dr. Anthony Fauci, in an editorial in the same issue, seems to give credence to the casual-contact claim. United Press International and Associated Press run with the story, as do most major media outlets including the networks. Lost in the surge of coverage is Fauci's follow-up, in which he refutes the casual-contact theory.

May 18, 1983: After a week of contradictory testimony from government officials, the House Appropriations Committee approves $12 million in new funds for the National Institutes of Health and the Centers for Disease Control to fight the epidemic.

Columnist Patrick Buchanan publishes a vitriolic diatribe about the "Gay Plague," citing the epidemic as the wrath of God.

May 20, 1983: Science runs an article from France's Pasteur Institute in which researchers there claim to have found the cause of AIDS, an agent called "lymphadenopathy-associated virus," or LAV, because it was first isolated in a lymph node of a patient.

May 25, 1983: Assistant Secretary of Health Edward Brandt labels the epidemic the nation's "No. 1 health priority." The announcement makes it on page one of the *New York Times,* the first time the paper gives AIDS front-page treatment.

Late July 1983: San Francisco General opens an AIDS ward, the first of its kind in the country.

264

August 30, 1983: CBS "Evening News" reports a recall of blood-product factor VIII because of possible contamination. But the network incorrectly identifies the product and causes a panic among hemophiliac-users of factor VIII.

September 15, 1983: The House Appropriations Committee approves $41 million for the AIDS budget. Seven U.S. senators sign a statement asking for increased funding for the Public Health Emergency Fund.

September 1983: A *Village Voice* ad features Larry Kramer's "2,339 and Counting," another angry protest against the inadequate response to the AIDS epidemic, which has claimed nearly 2,500 lives.

November 22, 1983: The World Health Organization holds its first meeting on the international implications of the AIDS epidemic.

December 6, 1983: A House report documents the poor response to the crisis by the federal government. The *New York Times, Los Angeles Times* cover it in small stories.

March 28, 1984: The San Francisco Bathhouse Debate—between gays, public officials, and bathhouse owners around the issue of closing the sex facilities—kicks off, with a front-page story by the *San Francisco Chronicle.*

April 9, 1984: The *New York Native* makes mention of the French discovery of LAV, buried in the back of the issue, making it the first American nonmedical publication to run the news.

April 23, 1984: Secretary of Health Heckler quickly pulls together a press conference to announce that the AIDS virus has been discovered by American researcher Dr. Robert Gallo and named HTLV-III (for Human T-Lymphotropic Virus). She claims there will be a test for the virus in six months and a vaccine in two years. Only a handful of media organizations, including National Public Radio, question Heckler's expectations.

September 1984: CDC reports eighty cases of transfusion AIDS. The disease also has been found to infect the brain and to mutate. There are six thousand reported cases of the disease.

October 11, 1984: Congressional hearings take to task the Health and Human Services Department for not passing on budget requests from AIDS researchers.

November 1984: News of HPA-23, a drug that seems to halt the AIDS virus in the body, is tested at France's Pasteur Institute.

Janaury 30, 1985: Eight thousand cases of AIDS are reported.

February 4, 1985: The Reagan administration recommends cutting the AIDS budget from $96 million to $86 million.

February 8, 1985: It's revealed in news stories by major media outlets that Dr. Robert Gallo, who took credit for discovering the virus in the United States, may have used information from the Pasteur Institute without acknowledging that source.

February 12, 1985: PBS airs a "Nova" special on AIDS, the first comprehensive look at the disease in the broadcast medium.

February 21, 1985: Congressional hearings are held on the Office of Technology Assessment's scathing "Review of the Public Health Service's Response to AIDS." The dismal report card on the government's handling of the epidemic gets little coverage.

March 7, 1985: The first AIDS antibody test is released.

March 30, 1985: Some nine thousand AIDS cases have been reported since the start of the epidemic.

April 14, 1985: The International AIDS conference is sponsored by the Health and Human Service Department and the World Health Organization. Dr. Curran announces that some five hundred thousand to one million people in the United States have been infected with the virus. Dr. Donald Francis calls for wider, voluntary testing.

July 1985: Life's "Now No One Is Safe from AIDS" cover story blows the threat of the disease out of proportion, but also helps to make it a heterosexual concern.

July 23, 1985: Rock Hudson has AIDS, the United Press International reports.

July 24, 1985: Hudson's infection focuses unprecedented media attention on the disease. The political consequences of this new interest: the Reagan administration had intended to cut the AIDS budget by $10 million and now decides to boost it by more than $100 million.

July 30, 1985: Twelve thousand cases of AIDS have been reported.

Late 1985: The Pasteur Institute files a lawsuit against Dr. Gallo, asking for a share of the royalties on the AIDS antibody test that is being developed from the discovery of the virus.

September 1985: Indiana teen Ryan White, a hemophiliac suffering from AIDS, is refused entry to school.
   The military begins testing for the AIDS virus among its personnel.

September 17, 1985: President Reagan, at a press conference, announces that he can understand why parents do not want their children "in school with these kids" who have "AIDS." It was the first time he publicly uttered the word.

October 2, 1985: Rock Hudson dies. His illness and death are the single most significant factors affecting public awareness and concern about the disease to date.

December 15, 1985: Under attack from conservatives for her high profile role with regard to AIDS, and criticized by liberals for her inept handling of the crisis, Secretary of Health Margaret Heckler resigns from the Reagan Administration.

February 18, 1986: Harvard researchers find that the AIDS virus is present in the saliva of those carrying the virus.

June 4, 1986: The Public Health Service holds a meeting of its top AIDS experts at the Coolfont Conference Center in West Virginia. Out of the confab comes the forecast that in five years, some 270,000 people in the United States will have been diagnosed with AIDS, and 179,000 will have died. What's needed, the eighty-five experts say, is massive public education, better federal coordination, and an AIDS commission.

The prediction of the future toll of the epidemic gets major coverage.

June 23, 1986: U.S. Justice Department allows employers to fire AIDS carriers.

August 2, 1986: McCarthy Hearings attorney Roy Cohn dies of AIDS.

September 3, 1986: Bill Cox, the *Honolulu Star-Bulletin*'s managing editor, reveals in a piece on the newspaper's Op-Ed page that he has AIDS and is leaving his job. He calls for greater understanding and acceptance of people with AIDS. The story is run by major media outlets throughout the United States.

October 15, 1986: The prestigious Institute of Medicine of the National Academy of Sciences releases a report calling the administration's response to AIDS "woefully inadequate." It suggests that $2 billion, or more than four times the current expenditure, would be a more appropriate annual budget to battle the epidemic.

October 23, 1986: Surgeon General Dr. C. Everett Koop releases his "Report on Acquired Immune Deficiency," a straightforward public health statement on the kind of broad-based education needed to stem the epidemic.

The report generates a flood of publicity, largely because Koop, a conservative pediatrician, calls for AIDS education "at the earliest grade possible."

November 4, 1986: A California initiative that, if implemented, could have resulted in the quarantining of and widespread discrimination against AIDS patients is defeated by voters by a margin of two to one. It was introduced by followers of political extremist Lyndon LaRouche. The defeat is followed by other attempts at similar measures.

Late 1986: The two nomenclatures for the AIDS virus, the French LAV and the American HTLV-III, are merged into HIV: Human Immunodeficiency Virus. It is the first step in settling the Franco-American conflict.

January 1987: The federal government proposes mandatory HIV testing for prisoners and immigrants and calls for wider voluntary testing.

March 1987: Formation of the President's Commission on the Human Immunodeficiency Virus Epidemic is announced by the Reagan administration.

March 31, 1987: With Jonas Salk serving as intermediary, the French and Americans sign a settlement of the battle over discovery of HIV, agreeing to share credit and the patent.

A drug called AZT is reported to halt the spread of the virus within the body.

May 7, 1987: Representative Stewart McKinney dies of AIDS. The *Washington Post* and the *Los Angeles Herald Examiner* are the only two major metropolitan dailies to mention that he was allegedly gay. The other media left the impression that McKinney could have gotten AIDS only through a blood transfusion.

June 1987: President Reagan opens the Third International AIDS Conference in Washington, D.C. with a speech calling for wider testing.

Summer 1987: The *New York Times* allows the use of "gay" as an adjective in describing homosexuals.

October 7, 1987: The top leadership of the President's HIV Commission resigns, citing a lack of direction and mandate from the government.

October 11, 1987: The March on Washington for gay rights and increased AIDS funding draws five hundred thousand participants. The major media give it extensive coverage.

December 18, 1987: Scientists report that dementia, the loss of mental capacity that has been associated with the latter stages of AIDS, is found to occur in individuals who do not have the full-blown disease but simply have the virus.

March 13, 1988: Seventy-five percent of those infected with the AIDS virus will get the disease or have AIDS-related conditions in six years, according to researchers at the University of California, San Francisco.

May 4, 1988: The U.S. Public Health Service distributes an AIDS awareness guide to every household in America as part of a stepped-up effort to inform the nation about the disease.

June 2, 1988: The president's Commission on the Human Immunodeficiency Virus Epidemic finishes its final report, recommending dramatic increases in funding to fight AIDS and broad antidiscrimination legislation to protect those with the disease. The proposal is largely ignored by the Reagan administration.

June 13, 1988: The CDC reports that a new AIDS case is reported every fourteen minutes.

September 24, 1988: The World Health Organization reports that 111,000 cases of AIDS have been documented worldwide. Authorities at WHO place the actual number of cases of the disease, including unreported incidents, at 250,000.

October 11, 1988: AIDS protesters, demanding a quicker approval process for drug treatments, shut down the Food and Drug Administration.

October 24, 1988: FDA Commissioner Frank Young calls for researchers to help speed the approval process for AIDS drugs.

October 28, 1988: President Reagan signs a bill making October—that is, the month that was just ending—AIDS awareness month.

November 6, 1988: CDC study reveals that 3 of every 1,000 college students are infected with HIV.

November 8, 1988: George Bush is elected forty-first president of the United States, with a platform of building a "kinder, gentler nation."

December 3, 1988: San Francisco blood bank is successfully sued for negligently providing blood tainted with HIV to a patient who went on to develop AIDS.

December 20, 1988: Max Robinson, former ABC news anchor and once the most prominent black journalist in America, dies of AIDS.

January 1989: National Academy of Sciences calls on the new Bush administration to lead the international fight against AIDS.

April 4, 1989: A Dutch AIDS educator, who also has the disease, is jailed by U.S. Immigration and Naturalization Service when he refuses to return to Holland after being prohibited from entering the United States. The case begins a process designed to change the law.

Early fall 1989: The number of AIDS cases in the United States exceeds 100,000.

Notes

My research assistant, Robin Nagle, and I began this project by reviewing the huge amount of newspaper and magazine articles and TV clips that had been produced on the subject of AIDS since early 1981. (Specific citations to this material usually can be found in the text and generally are not included below.) After gaining an in-depth understanding of how the epidemic was covered, we asked the question, "Why was it reported this way?" That required interviews with the people who produced the stories, as well as with their editors, producers, publishers, fellow journalists. Even seven years into the crisis, it was often difficult to separate what individual reporters thought was fact from what was fiction. To help us in that regard, we conducted extensive interviews with those involved in the stories, including scientists, politicians, and people with AIDS. What follows is a partial list of the interviewees, including the dates on which they were interviewed. Not all of those named are quoted or characterized in the book. And not all of those quoted are named: a score of journalists and scientists requested anonymity for a variety of reasons including fear of reprisal from superiors. This book is also informed by hundreds of other interviews conducted for articles that I wrote since 1982. Those sources are not cited. The interviews indicated below ran from forty-five minutes to as long as eight hours, and almost all were conducted in person. Occasionally, sessions lasted more than one day, and sometimes follow-up interviews were done over the phone.

Besides these sources, I used official reports, government documents, polls, and memos. I make reference to those in these notes, as well.

Any descriptions used, such as how the Centers for Disease Control appeared, were developed from first-hand impressions. Details about how people felt or reacted were almost always drawn from their own words. In other cases, the descriptions are attributed to particular sources. This book is not intended to be a novelistic interpretation of the incidents, but rather a journalist's careful approximation of what transpired.

Introduction: When Does Death Become News?

The remark about Libyan leader Moamar Gadhafi and AIDS, allegedly told by President Ronald Reagan and Secretary of State George Shultz, was reported on October 3, 1986, in the *San Francisco Chronicle,* under the headline "S.F. Anger over 'Jokes' at White House."

The Public Health Service's national ads were produced by Ogilvy and Mather and released in October 1987.

A helpful graph plotting the rise and fall of AIDS media coverage has been prepared by Don Berreth, the Centers for Disease Control's public information director, using the NEXIS data base of ninety magazines and newspapers.

The book that most informed my early thinking about this project is *Plagues and Peoples,* by William H. McNeill (New York: Anchor Books, 1976). McNeil's extremely readable and insightful look at how disease helped give shape to human society offered a good base upon which to build.

Two works of fiction were particularly useful in adding to my understanding of how epidemics influence human thought and action: Daniel Defoe's *A Journal of the Plague Year* (New York: New American Library, 1960) and Albert Camus's *The Plague* (New York: Vintage Books, 1972), in both of which journalists play significant roles. Defoe, of course, was considered a premier journalist of his time, and one of Camus's major characters is a correspondent.

Chapter 1: Whispers in the Whirlwind

Interviews: Dr. James Curran, head of the AIDS Task Force at the Centers for Disease Control (9/28/87 and 5/18/88); Dr. Donald Francis, former director of lab research for CDC's AIDS Task Force (11/17/87); Don Berreth, director of CDC's office of public affairs (4/21/88); Dr. Harold Jaffe, CDC epidemiologist (1/17/87 and 4/20/88); William Check, science writer and coauthor, with Anne Giudici Fettner, of *The Truth about AIDS* (4/20/88); John Bennett, former deputy director of Center for Infectious Disease (4/21/88); Dr. William Foege, former director of CDC (4/21/88); Betty Hooper, information officer at CDC

(4/25/88); Charles Henderson, editor of the CDC *AIDS Weekly* (4/14/88 and 4/22/88); Dr. James Mason, director of the CDC (4/26/88); R. Anne Thomas, director of public information for the National Institutes of Health (4/19/88); Dr. James Goedert, early AIDS researcher at National Cancer Institute (4/19/88); Dr. Bob Biggar, epidemiologist at NCI (4/19/88); Dr. Sandra Panem, author of *The AIDS Bureaucracy* (4/12/88); Dr. Bruce Voeller, director of the Los Angeles-based Mariposa Foundation (9/6/88); Dr. David Sencer, former director of the CDC (4/12/88). (Representative Henry Waxman [D-Los Angeles] and his aide, Tim Westmoreland, refused to reply to repeated requests for interviews. Representative Phil Burton [D-San Francisco] died of heart failure and his aide, Bill Kraus, of AIDS in the mid-1980s.)

The book by Dr. William H. Masters, Virginia E. Johnson, and Dr. Robert C. Kolodny, *Crisis: Heterosexual Behavior in the Age of AIDS*, was published in the spring of 1988 by Grove Press.

The Miami TV series on AIDS and syphilis was produced by WSVN. Titled "Deadly Error?" the show ran March 10 and 11, 1988.

Much of the initial work to determine which stories were reported in which media was done by using NEXIS, the computer data base. Many of the files of individual newspapers, magazines, Associated Press, and the networks were also thoroughly researched.

Details of the swine flu epidemic were gathered from a number of sources, including journalists who covered the crisis. Probably the best history of how the government's program went awry is retold in *The Epidemic That Never Was*, by Richard Neustadt and Harvey Fineberg (New York: Random House, 1983).

Dozens of government manuals were helpful in making sense of the U.S. health agencies, and two useful books were Stephen Strickland's *Politics, Science and Dread Disease: A Short History of the United States' Medical Research Policy* (Cambridge: Harvard University Press, 1972) and Sandra Panem's *The AIDS Bureaucracy* (Cambridge: Harvard University Press, 1988).

The Coolfont Report was named after the Coolfont Conference Center in Berkeley Springs, West Virginia, where the Public Health Service convened its meeting 4–6 June 1986. Along with projecting the AIDS caseload and level of infection, the report sets forth a series of goals to deal with the epidemic. Copies of the document can be obtained from the U.S. Public Health Service.

Government programs to fight sexually transmitted diseases are put into context in Allan M. Brandt's *No Magic Bullet: A Social History of Venereal Disease in the United States since 1880* (New York: Oxford University Press, 1987).

Chapter 2: Taking It Personally

Interviews: Charles Ortleb, editor and publisher of the *New York Native* (9/22/87, 10/2/87, 1/29/88, 2/26/88); Larry Kramer, playwright and AIDS activist (10/15/87 and 5/13/88); Dr. Lawrence Mass, former *Native* writer (9/25/87 and 10/2/87); Dr. James D'Eramo, science writer (4/8/88); Anne Giudici Fettner, science writer, coauthor, with William Check, of *The Truth about AIDS* (11/6/87); Dr. Jane Teas, researcher (9/23/87); Michael Helquist, writer for the *Advocate* (9/21/87); Dr. Dan William, New York physician (11/8/87); Laurie Berman, public information director, Gay Mens Health Crisis (3/28/88); Barney Frank, Massachusetts congressman (2/18/88); Kevin Kraus, assignment editor at WSVN-TV in Miami (5/5/88); Nicholas Ragish, reporter for the Montreal *Gazette* (5/6/88); Dr. Stephen Caiazza, New York physician (4/12/88); Dr. Peter Duesberg, researcher at University of California, Berkeley (4/5/88); Richard Goldstein, *Village Voice* editor and columnist (10/19/87); Loretta McLaughlin, *Boston Globe* medical reporter (11/12/87); Kay Longhope, *Boston Globe* general assignment reporter (11/12/87).

The CIA plot was reported by *Newsday* (Long Island, New York) in 1971.

One of the most readable studies of gays' political power in San Francisco can be found in Frances Fitzgerald's *Cities on a Hill* (New York: Simon and Schuster, 1986).

A history of the syphilis experiments conducted by the government on blacks can be found in *Bad Blood: The Tuskegee Experiment,* by James Jones (New York: Free Press, 1981).

Hannah Arendt's many volumes on totalitarianism and genocide include *Eichmann in Jerusalem: A Report on the Banality of Evil* (New York: Penguin, 1977).

Science magazine was the first technical publication to write about the findings of Dr. Luc Montagnier's laboratory. The article "Isolation of T-Lymphotropic Retrovirus from a Patient at Risk for Acquired

Immune Deficiency Syndrome (AIDS)" appeared in the June 3, 1983, issue.

Cindy Patton's book on the epidemic is titled *Sex and Germs: The Politics of AIDS* (Boston: South End Press, 1985).

A discussion of the connection between AIDS and syphilis can be found in *AIDS and Syphilis: The Hidden Link,* by Harris L. Coulter (Berkeley: North Atlantic Books, 1987).

Chapter 3: Frustration on the Wire

Interviews: Bill Ahearn, Associated Press managing editor (4/25/88); Warren Leary, former AP science writer (4/18/88); Paul Raeburn, AP science editor (4/25/88); Julie Dunlap, AP enterprise editor (4/25/88); Lee Mitgang, AP education editor (4/25/88); Chris Sullivan, AP assistant enterprise editor (4/25/88); Jan Ziegler, former science editor, United Press International (4/18/88); Chris Smith, UPI public relations (4/18/88);Desmond Maberley, former executive editor of Reuters North America (5/16/88); B. D. Colen, science editor, *Newsday* (Long Island, New York) (5/16/88); Don Drake, science writer, *Philadelphia Inquirer* (5/8/88).

The description of the decline of United Press International was gleaned from interviews with wire service reporters and executives as well as a review of news clips on UPI that appeared in trade publications such as *Editor and Publisher.*

The trend toward increased health consciousness and an interest in science and medicine news in the United States has been documented by a number of media surveys produced by firms such as Frank Magid Associates, Marion, Iowa.

Chapter 4: Sex, Death, and Good Old Gray

Interviews: A. M. Rosenthal, former executive editor of the *New York Times* (4/4/88); Max Frankel, *Times* executive editor (4/26/88); Dr.

276 Lawrence Altman, *Times* medical reporter (4/5/88); Richard Flast, *Times* science editor (3/29/88); Peter Millones, former *Times* metropolitan editor (3/7/88); David Jones, former *Times* national editor (3/9/88); Erik Eckholm, *Times* deputy science editor (3/22/88); Allan M. Siegal, *Times* assistant managing editor in charge of copy desk (4/26/88); Dudley Clendinen, *Times* reporter in Boston (3/22/88); Jane Gross, *Times* reporter (3/9/88); Michael Norman, former *Times* reporter (3/11/88); Phil Boffey, *Times* health policy writer (2/18/88); John Nordheimer, former *Times* Miami bureau chief (3/22/88); Glenn Collins, *Times* features writer (3/3/88); Wallace Turner, former *Times* reporter in San Francisco (3/28/88); Katherine Bishop, *Times* reporter in San Francisco (3/28/88); Virginia Apuzzo, New York gay activist (3/4/88); Ellis Cose, biographer (3/6/88); Dr. Alvin Friedman-Kien (4/8/88); Dorothy Nelkin, professor in Cornell University's Science, Technology and Society program (9/21/87).

A number of books on the *New York Times* were consulted before interviewing *Times* staff. Two of the most helpful were *The Kingdom and the Power* by Gay Talese (New York: Bantam Books, 1970) and *The Powers That Be* by David Halberstam (New York: Dell, 1979).

A rudimentary discussion of the coverage of AIDS compared to other health crises can be found in *The Virtuous Journalist,* by Stephen Klaidman and Tom Beauchamp (New York: Oxford University Press, 1987).

Figures on the size of New York City's gay population vary widely, from six hundred thousand to one million.

The first front-page article to appear in the mainstream media ran in the *Los Angeles Times* May 31, 1982, titled "Started with Gays: Mysterious Fever Now an Epidemic," by Harry Nelson.

The quote attributed to A. M. Rosenthal about the *Times*'s critics appeared in "Friends at the Top of the Times," *Newsweek*, page 125, November 22, 1982.

Several sources at the *Times*, who insisted on anonymity for fear of reprisals, mentioned Rosenthal's slighting references to gays.

Larry Kramer's play, *The Normal Heart,* opened April 21, 1985, at the Public Theater in New York City. It was first produced by Joseph Papp, for the New York Shakespeare Festival. The book was published in New York by New American Library, 1985.

Internal memos were provided by several sources, including Allan M. Siegal and Max Frankel.

Chapter 5: A Killer on the Cover

Interviews: Vincent Coppola, former *Newsweek* writer (4/13/88, 4/21/88); Rick Smith, *Newsweek* editor-in-chief (5/25/88); Jean Seligmann, *Newsweek* general editor (4/4/88); Mary Hager, *Newsweek* reporter, Washington D.C. (2/17/88); Meredith White, former *Newsweek* editor (4/13/88); Matt Clark, *Newsweek* senior writer (4/14/88); Terence Monmaney, *Newsweek* general editor (4/4/88); Marianna Gosnell, *Newsweek* writer (4/4/88); Peter Goldman, *Newsweek* special projects reporter (4/7/88); Dominique Browning, *Newsweek* senior editor (4/7/88); James Baker, *Newsweek* assistant editor (4/7/88); Abigail Trafford, former *U.S. News and World Report* science editor (2/17/88); Steve Findlay, former *U.S. News* reporter (2/17/88); Joseph Cary, *U.S. News* reporter (2/17/88); Avery Comerow, *U.S. News* assistant managing editor (2/18/88); Erica Goode, *U.S. News* reporter (2/18/88); Dick Thompson, *Time* correspondent (2/19/88); Claudia Wallis, *Time* senior editor (4/27/88).

The memos that are excerpted were provided by Vincent Coppola.

Circulation data for *Newsweek, Time,* and *U.S. News and World Report* are audited figures from late 1988, from Publishers Information Bureau.

The first lengthy feature done on AIDS by the *New York Times,* "Homosexuals Confronting a Time of Change," appeared June 16, 1983; the first by Associated Press, "Hemophiliacs, Homosexuals Forced to Make Difficult Choices," was sent across the wire on June 27, 1983. *Newsweek* ran its first major feature, "Epidemic," on AIDS April 18, 1983.

Chapter 6: Controlling What We Know

Interviews: Dr. Michael Gottlieb, former UCLA researcher (7/26/88); Dr. George Lundberg, editor, *Journal of the American Medical Associa-*

tion (5/19/88); Bruce Dan, *JAMA* senior editor (5/18/88); Dr. Donald Francis, former director of CDC's office of public affairs (4/21/88); Dr. Mathilde Krim, president of the American Medical Foundation for AIDS Research (5/11/88); Ben Patrusky, science writer and programs director for the Council for the Advancement of Science Writing (5/20/88); Dr. Uwe Reinhardt, Princeton University health economist (5/11/88); Dr. Robin Fox, the *Lancet* deputy editor (5/16/88 and 5/23/88); Martin Kenney, author of *Biotechnology: The University-Industrial Complex* (5/24/88).

The number of references to the *New England Journal of Medicine* in the mainstream media was found by using the DIALOG data base, which includes scores of newspaper and magazine abstracts. The time period used was January 1984 to April 1988. While the *Journal* was cited 500 times, JAMA was referenced 263 times and the *Lancet* 217.

An interesting discussion of the influence the individual journals have on other technical publications can be found in "Which Medical Journals Have the Greatest Impact," by Eugene Garfield, Ph.D. in *Annals of Internal Medicine,* August 1986. Dr. Garfield runs the Institute for Scientific Information in Philadelphia.

Franz Inglefinger was editor of the *New England Journal of Medicine* from 1961 to 1967. Arnold Relman became the editor in 1977.

Martin Kenney's book, *Biotechnology: The University-Industrial Complex* (New Haven: Yale University Press, 1986), offers an overview of the increasing connections, and conflicts of interest, between these two powerful spheres of influence.

Statistics on Cambridge BioScience were found in *Standard & Poor's,* Standard & Poor's Corp., New York.

Circulation data for the *Journal of the American Medical Association,* the *New England Journal of Medicine* and the *Lancet* are figures from early 1988.

The number of publications dealing with the AIDS epidemic in the United States is an estimate by the CDC *AIDS Weekly* editor, Charles Henderson, in the spring of 1988. He monitors hundreds of publications on a weekly and monthly basis.

The relationship between science and the media is discussed interestingly in *Science in the Street,* edited by M. J. Rossant (New York: Twentieth Century Fund, 1984).

Chapter 7: The Unphotogenic Epidemic

Interviews: George Strait, ABC correspondent (4/18/88); Sally Holms, ABC senior producer (4/26/88); Dr. Tim Johnson, ABC medical correspondent (5/22/88); Bill Lord, former executive producer of ABC's "World News Tonight" (4/28/88); Joe Lovett, producer on ABC's "20/20" (4/29/88); Ted Koppel, anchor of ABC's "Nightline" (5/24/88); Tom Bettag, CBS "Evening News" executive producer (5/6/88); Ernest Leiser, former CBS "Evening News" executive producer (5/23/88); Robert Bazell, NBC correspondent (5/19/88); Bill Skane, CBS medical/science producer (5/25/88); John Bianchi, NBC public relations (5/26/88); Reese Schonfeld, former Cable News Network president (3/29/88); Ted Turner, CNN president (4/25/88); Dan Rutz, CNN medical reporter and producer (4/20/88); Bailey Barish, medical producer (4/22/89); Bud Modersbach, Cutter Laboratories counsel (1/27/89).

The chapter on national TV focuses on the evening news shows because they are the clearest agenda-setting programs in the medium.

Clips from ABC, NBC, and CBS were obtained from the Vanderbilt University film archives. Clips from CNN were viewed on the network's premises or copied from its files.

The annual Roper TV poll, "America's Watching: Public Attitudes toward Television," is published by the Television Information Committee of Group W Television, Westinghouse Broadcasting Company, New York.

The audience for the evening news shows in late 1988 was thirteen million according to an estimate by A. C. Nielsen Media Research, New York.

The figure for the number of hemophiliacs in the United States, approximately twenty thousand, is provided by the National Center for Health Statistics.

The dangerously misleading story by CBS's Terry Drinkwater, and announced by Dan Rather, involved confusing different brands of the blood-clotting drug factor VIII. CBS claimed the potentially contaminated product was produced by Cutter Laboratories. The bottle that Drinkwater held up to the camera, in fact, was Cutter Lab's product. But the tainted-blood warning was actually coming from the American Red Cross, which had reason to believe that its own brand of factor VIII, made by Baxter Laboratories from American Red Cross plasma, was contaminated. The clarification, that Cutter Lab's factor VIII "is not the subject of a recall," served not so much to clarify as to confound further.

The "New Right's" conviction that Dan Rather is rabidly liberal is exemplified best by the 1987 movement to buy up CBS stock in order to make changes in the network, including firing the evening news anchor.

Data on the decline in the percentage of prime-time viewing audience claimed by the networks were provided by A. C. Nielsen Media Research, New York, and Saatchi & Saatchi, New York. Also useful in understanding viewing patterns is a comparison of A. C. Nielsen ratings from the various TV media. Using a one-week period in October of 1988 compared with the same week in 1987, it was found that the networks' overall ratings had dropped 4 percent. At the same time, the programs found on the basic package offered by any given cable company increased their ratings by some 38 percent, while the independent stations were boosted almost 8 percent. PBS viewership fell more than 7 percent in that period.

Also useful in understanding the change in viewing patterns of the American public was a survey done by CBS, which showed a sharp decline in ratings even for the networks' most popular nonnews shows, including "The Cosby Show" and "Moonlighting," which lost 12 percent and 25 percent of their audience, respectively, from 1987 to 1988.

The study on portrayal of people with AIDS by the Center for Media and Public Affairs appeared in "The Media Monitor," December 1987. The Center is located in Washington, D.C.

The quote by William Paley is taken from David Halberstam's *The Powers that Be* (New York: Dell, 1979).

President Reagan's first recorded, public utterance of the word "AIDS" was on September 17, 1985. At a press conference on children with the disease, he offered his empathy for parents who did not want their youngsters "in school with kids with AIDS."

The estimate that AIDS reporting in the print medium increased by 270 percent was established by using the NEXIS data base.

Michael C. Caruso of the University of South Alabama produced a helpful introduction to the video history of the epidemic, called "AIDS: A Medical History," 1987. His adviser, Dr. William A. Gardner, Jr., of the university's medical school, also provided assistance in understanding the link between science and the media.

Chapter 8: Chronicler of the Castro

Interviews: Randy Shilts, *San Francisco Chronicle* reporter (11/23/87 and 12/21/87); David Perlman, *San Francisco Chronicle* science editor (11/17/87); Bill German, *Chronicle* executive editor (11/17/87); John Jacobs, *San Francisco Examiner* reporter (11/18/88); Bob Ross, *Bay Area Reporter* publisher (11/19/88); Dr. Marcus Conant, founder of Kaposi's Sarcoma Clinic at UCSF (10/2/87 and 11/17/87); Holly Smith, former director of press relations for the San Francisco AIDS Foundation (11/18/87); Dr. Paul Volberding, San Francisco General AIDS Clinic director (11/20/87 and 11/25/87); Pat Franks, Institute for Health Policy Studies, UCSF (10/2/87 and 11/19/87); Dr. Tom Coates, psychologist and researcher, UCSF (11/20/87); Dr. Selma Dritz, epidemiologist, San Francisco (11/20/87).

The scientific study that provided the grain of truth for the "Patient Zero" stories was done by Drs. D. M. Auerback, W. W. Darrow, H. W. Jaffe, and J. W. Curran. "Cluster of Cases of the Acquired Immune Deficiency Syndrome; Patients Linked by Sexual Contact" was published in the *American Journal of Medicine*, no. 76, 1984. The theory presented in that paper places Canadian airline steward Gaetan Dugas at the center of a vortex of AIDS. The idea is based on the premise that the time from contact with the virus to the appearance of symptoms of the disease was about eleven months. In fact, the period from infection to showing signs of AIDS is generally believed to be from eight to ten years, according to A. R. Moss, et al. Their study, "Risk Factors for AIDS and HIV Seropositivity in Homosexual Men," was presented in *American Journal of Epidemiology*, no. 125, 1987. In a letter to the *New York Times*, December 8, 1988, Moss called on Shilts to "repudiate the 'patient zero' story. . . . It is a good idea to have as few myths floating around as possible."

A very readable history of the *San Francisco Chronicle* was written by Richard Rapaport and appeared in *San Francisco* magazine, November and December of 1987.

The story of Harvey Milk was developed through interviews with some of his acquaintances as well as by reading Shilts's compelling biography of the politician and San Francisco in the 1970s in *The Mayor of Castro Street: The Life and Times of Harvey Milk* (New York: St. Martin's Press, 1982).

Scores of articles have been written about the brutal murder of Harvey Milk and Mayor George Moscone. Exact details of that day are disputed from account to account. The description used here attempts to avoid the major areas of controversies to offer the clearest facts.

At other newspapers like the *Boston Globe*, gay reporters were allowed to cover stories in the homosexual community. But only at the *Chronicle* were individual reporters assigned to cover gays consistently.

Comparative statistics on AIDS spending among the states were available through the Institute for Health Policy Studies, University of California, San Francisco.

And the Band Played On: Politics, People and the AIDS Epidemic was published by St. Martin's Press in 1987.

The impressive change in gays' sexual behavior and attitudes in San Francisco has been documented in a number of studies by social scientists Leon McKusick, William Horstman, Thomas Coates, and Ken Charles. One such study is "Changes in Sexual Behavior with the Advent of the AIDS Epidemic" (November 17, 1987) by Thomas J. Coates, et al., University of California, San Francisco (unpublished).

A similar study on New York's gay population was done by Dr. John L. Martin, formerly of Columbia University. "The Impact of AIDS on Gay Male Sexual Behavior Patterns in New York City" appeared in the *American Journal of Public Health,* April 1987.

A series of reports done for the San Francisco AIDS Foundation, "Designing an Effective AIDS Risk Reduction Program for San Francisco," by Research and Decisions Corporation, describes some of the steps taken in the gay community to decrease dramatically high-risk sexual behavior and to reduce sharply the cases of sexually transmitted diseases among homosexuals.

Chapter 9: A Plague in the Villages

Interviews: Jeff Kerber, former *Mesquite News* reporter (5/10/88); Dave Barton, *Mesquite News* publisher (5/10/88); William Wayburn, Dallas Gay Alliance president (5/11/88); Dennis Vercher, *Dallas Voice* reporter (5/10/88); William Nelson, Dallas Gay Alliance (5/10/88); John Wiles, *Kokomo Tribune* managing editor (5/17/88 and 5/25/88); Sherry Jacobson, *Dallas Morning News* reporter (5/9/88); Christopher MacNeil, *Kokomo Tribune* reporter (4/29/88, 5/4/88 and 11/21/88); Arden Draeger, *Kokomo Tribune* publisher and general manager (5/5/88); Bill Skutt, *Tampa Tribune* editor (5/16/88); Bettinita Harris, former *Tampa Tribune* reporter (5/16/88); Diane Egner, *Tampa Tribune* reporter (5/12/88); John Edmonson, former *The DeSoto County Times* editor (5/10/88 and 5/11/88); Tim Adamson, *Arcadian* editor (5/11/88, 5/13/88 and 5/23/88).

Clips from the small-town newspapers were provided by the *Arcadian, The DeSoto County Times, Kokomo Tribune, Mesquite News.*

David L. Kirp's book on schoolchildren and AIDS, *Learning by Heart: AIDS and Schoolchildren in America's Communities* (New Brunswick: Rutgers University Press, 1989), served as invaluable background material in researching Kokomo, Indiana.

Also useful was Deni Elliott's unpublished report on the *Dallas Morning News*'s coverage of the Dr. Robert John Huse case, called "The Scarlet Letter: A Case Study of Public Disclosure and HIV Positivity," Rockefeller Fellowship, Dartmouth College, 1988.

Chapter 10: The AIDS Channel

Interviews: Jim Bunn, KPIX-TV reporter (10/5/87 and 11/2/88); Nancy Saslow, former KPIX-TV producer (11/18/87); Bruno Cohen, former KPIX-TV news director (11/18/87); Art Kern, former KPIX-TV general manager (11/16/87); Hank Plant, KPIX-TV reporter (11/18/87); Caroline Wean, KPIX-TV general manager (11/19/87); Gloria Rojas, former WABC-TV reporter (11/23/88); Nancy Mate,

WCCO-TV public affairs director (11/24/88); Don Hewitt, CBS "60 Minutes" producer (11/22/88).

Videotape records of local stations' programming were provided by the outlets themselves. KPIX-TV was especially helpful in consolidating material.

Ratings and other data for local markets were gathered from individual stations as well as from "The Broadcasting/Cablecasting Yearbook, 1988," produced by Broadcasting Magazine, New York.

Figures on the rise in the number of cable viewers were provided by Frank Magid Associates, Marion, Iowa.

The KGO promotion for its 11:00 p.m. news story "Male genital organ found on the railroad track" was provided by CBS "60 minutes," which aired a segment on San Francisco TV in March 1974.

Chapter 11: Third World Correspondent

Interviews: Laurie Garrett, former National Public Radio science correspondent (8/17/87, 9/28/87 and 11/24/87); Ira Flatow, former NPR reporter (11/22/88); Anne Gudenkauf, NPR science editor (2/18/88); Robert Seigel, former NPR news director, "All Things Considered" anchor (2/17/88); Doug Bennett, NPR president (2/19/87); Dan Zwerdling, NPR environmental reporter (2/18/88); Scott Patton, *Washington Post* reporter (11/22/88); Debbie Rizzi, United Children's Hospital press spokesperson (3/8/88).

All tapes were provided by National Public Radio in Washington, D.C. except "The Opening of the Flu Season," which was supplied by Pacifica Radio Archives, Venice, California.

An analysis of the swine flu fiasco can be found in "A Review of Selected Federal Vaccine and Immunization Policies," Office of Technology Assessment, U.S. Congress, September 1979.

Details of the spread of AIDS in Africa, as reported by Garrett, also appeared in (Long Island, New York) *Newsday*, December 26–28, 1988. It is in that reporting that Garrett describes the new AIDS scourge in Africa, viral variations on HIV. A virus known as HIV-2, believed to be somewhat less dangerous than HIV-1, has been documented in parts of Central Africa. U.S. scientists also have found evidence of a third and fourth strain on the continent.

"Third World America," for purposes of this book, is defined as those communities in the United States that either have been bypassed by or remain resistant to economic development and that have many of the health and social problems as undeveloped foreign nations. The South Bronx, parts of Los Angeles's South Central, pockets of Newark, New Jersey fall into that category.

Admiral James D. Watkins's letter of commendation to NPR was received by the network on February 10, 1988, and was addressed to Douglas Bennett, president, National Public Radio.

Chapter 12: The Second Wave

Interviews: Emma Carrasco, Univision director of communications (4/15/88); Jeff Rivers, Institute for Journalism Education, University of California, Berkeley (5/12/88); William Egyir, *Amsterdam News* managing editor (5/13/88); Lynn Nument, *Ebony* senior editor (5/18/88); Gil Gerald, National AIDS Network (5/19/88); Theresa Swain, senior editor, *Black Enterprise* (5/22/88); Josefina Vidal, *La Opinion* (5/24/88 and 10/24/88); José Sanz, "America" producer (5/18/88); Emilio Nicolas, Jr., WXTV general manager (5/25/88); Dr. Rudolph Jackson, professor of pediatrics, Moorhouse School of Medicine (5/25/88); Alberto Aguilar, KALI (L.A.) radio (5/25/88); Dr. Michael Wilkes, formerly of the Columbia University School of Public Health (5/18/88).

One of the few interviews Max Robinson granted in the year before he died was with *Washington Post* reporter Carla Hill. It appeared May 26, 1988.

Minority media coverage was investigated by conducting extensive research into individual, and representative, newspapers, magazines, and broadcast outlets. Following is a partial list of those publications: New York *Amsterdam News, Jet, Essence, Ebony, Black Enterprise, La Opinion* (Los Angeles), Univision, *El Diario* (New York), Black Entertainment Television.

The boom in Spanish-language TV is probably best represented by Univision, owned by Hallmark. The programming network as of late 1988 had 450 affiliates. Most of those stations are low-power outlets with small audiences, but Univision also serves ten large stations, including WXTV in New York and KMEX-TV in Los Angeles.

Hallmark's competition, Reliance, acquired five major Spanish-language stations in the late 1980s, including WNJU-TV in New York, KVEA-TV in Los Angeles, and WSCV-TV in Miami. It has also started a rival network called Telemundo Group, which has eighteen affiliates.

Data on minority readership can be found in "Minorities and Newspapers: A Summary of Readership Research," American Society of Newspaper Editors, April 1986.

The Kerner Commission's "Report on Civil Disorders," completed in 1968, included a groundbreaking section on the media (Chapter 15), which discussed how mainstream journalism kept blacks out of its ranks. The report informed this book and should be required reading for newspaper, TV, and radio managers throughout the United States.

A review of minority AIDS reporting in New York was done by Dr. Michael Wilkes, Columbia University's School of Public Health, in May 1988.

Dr. Michael Wilkes also provided information, most of it still unpublished, on the success of educational efforts aimed at intravenous drug users in the city of New York.

Another study that offered an overview of campaigns to educate intravenous drug users about the dangers of AIDS, and to help them implement behavioral changes, is "AIDS and Heroin: Strategies for Control," by Mark A. R. Kleiman and Richard A. Mockler, prepared for The Urban Institute, Washington, D.C., 1988.

Conclusion: Mortal Lessons for the Media, and America

The tuberculosis outbreak has been documented by both the Los Angeles and New York health departments. (In New York City, for ex-

ample, the number of TB cases leaped 17 percent in the year period
ending in mid-1988.) There are some small efforts under way to confront the problem: New York's health commissioner, Dr. Stephen C.
Joseph, called for establishing a shelter for homeless people infected
with tuberculosis. But such work has largely gone unnoticed by the
media.

A study of ways in which the media might better cover the epidemic was presented by J. Ronald Milavsky at the Communications
Industry Forum on What Media Can Do to Alleviate the AIDS Problem, sponsored by the Communications Study Program of the University of California, Santa Barbara in February 1988. I found the
most useful part of this report to be its description of public opinion
polls done on AIDS issues in the latter part of the 1980s.

Another helpful report was "The Effects of Mass Media Information and Education Campaigns to Promote Public Health: A Review
of Research," by Horst Stipp, Ph.D., and Rosalyn Weinman, Ph.D.,
both of NBC (1988).

The study of teens at risk for HIV infection is titled "Teens and
AIDS: Opportunities for Prevention," prepared by Kay Johnson in
December 1988 for the Children's Defense Fund, Washington, D.C.

Index